D1603206

The History of the British Film 1929–1939

**Films of Comment and Persuasion
of the 1930s**

The History of the British Film 1896–1906 (with Roger Manvell)
The History of the British Film 1906–1914
The History of the British Film 1914–1918
The History of the British Film 1918–1929
The History of the British Film 1929–1939 :
  Documentary and Educational Films of the 1930s

The History of the British Film 1929-1939

Films of Comment and Persuasion of the 1930s

by
RACHAEL LOW

London
GEORGE ALLEN & UNWIN
Distributed in the United States by R. R. Bowker Company, New York

First published in 1979

GEORGE ALLEN & UNWIN LTD
40 Museum Street, London WC1A 1LU

© George Allen & Unwin (Publishers) Ltd, 1979

British Library Cataloguing in Publication Data

Low, Rachael
  History of the British film.
  1929–1939: Films of comment and persuasion of the 1930s
  1. Moving-pictures – Great Britain – History
  I. Title
  791.43′0941   PN1993.5.G7   78-41296
                                 74-162852

  ISBN 0-04-791037-2

Distributed in the United States by
R. R. Bowker Company

Typeset in 11 on 12 point Baskerville by Trade Linotype, Birmingham and printed in Great Britain
by Cox & Wyman Ltd, London, Fakenham and Reading

Acknowledgements

I would like to express my gratitude first to the Calouste Gulbenkian Foundation, which by a Research Fellowship at Lucy Cavendish College, Cambridge, made the initial research for this and two other books on the British Film in the 1930s possible; and secondly to the British Film Institute, which has made annual grants towards the expenses of research since then. Lastly my thanks to the National Film Archive, and to Jeremy Boulton in particular, for endless patience in digging out innumerable small films for me to see, cannot be overstated. I would also like to thank Brenda Davies, Thorold Dickinson and Paul Rotha for their advice and encouragement down the years, and to add a word of tribute to the late Ernest Lindgren, who kindled my early interest in the subject and continued to help and advise me until his untimely death.

RACHAEL LOW

Contents

Illustrations

It is difficult to give any but a sketchy idea of a film when movement, editing and sound are not present. All these illustrations are frames of film, not photographs taken under special conditions by a stills cameraman. Their quality is therefore not that of the "art shot", but they are relevant to the text and give some slight indication of what the films looked like. I would like to acknowledge the assistance of the National Film Archive Stills Department in securing them, and of British Movietone for the first four.

The History of the British Film 1929–1939

**Films of Comment and Persuasion
of the 1930s**

1

Introduction

It has been argued elsewhere (*Documentary and Educational Films of the 1930s* by Rachael Low) that films other than the studio-made story became increasingly important during the thirties, and that a preliminary survey of the uses to which they were being put shows tremendous variety and vitality. The medium's value as a form of communication was emerging fast. Attempts to form a rigid classification of the films are not very helpful, since the categories overlapped both in intention and in use. A rough and ready grouping is possible, however, in order to survey the field. Such a survey can hardly hope to be comprehensive. The enormous number of films we can account for – many short but not all, many factual but not all, many non-theatrical but also many commercial – are still only a fraction of those actually made. But from them we can make some sort of order and draw some conclusions, preparing the way for further study.

In the companion volume to the present book it is maintained that the classroom film made comparatively little progress in this country but that the documentary movement, which was also broadly didactic in aim, played an important part in British cinema. It developed into two broad streams, the serious lecture film of social significance and the dramatic documentary. Both of them gradually lost the neutrality of the purely instructive and took on a more persuasive function. Within the latter, especially, were the seeds of both the wartime documentary drama and the eventual blurring of the line between the fact and fiction which had previously been taken so much for granted.

But many other films were also being made outside the feature studios at this time besides those intended to instruct. To help us thread our way through them we may distinguish very broadly between those intended to persuade and those intended merely to pass on their makers' observations of the world around them. We avoid a category "to entertain" since it is clear that any film, whether it wishes to teach, persuade or simply comment, must in some sense entertain if it is to hold the attention. It is better to regard them simply as films of comment, or personal statement.

The frankly persuasive film seeking to affect its audience by making it think or do some particular thing included commercial persuasion in the advertisement film, social or moral persuasion in the religious film and the many and varied "good cause" films promoting minority views on social matters, as well as the political progaganda films whose social pleading was connected with recognised political groups. Films of observation, on the other hand, sought to call attention, to convey some special interest, experience or reflection, but without instructional or doctrinal aims. They ranged from commercial newsreels and interest films to the work of an unclassifiable band of amateurs and professionals trying to record and express something of interest to themselves. All, of course, tended to be used as educational films in these early days when the teaching film, narrowly defined, was still very hard to find. Most, also, were operating under difficulties. News films were confined within limits set by a form of self-censorship yielding to official and unofficial pressures both actual and anticipated. All the other films, both long and short but especially the latter, in so far as they needed economic viability and therefore a commercial audience, were affected by the quota legislation of 1929. The documentary and educational film movements, also, were greatly impeded by this legislation, the Cinematograph Films Act of 1929.

The Act had been intended to protect British film production. It required all films which were to be shown at commercial cinemas to be registered with the Board of Trade, and obliged renters and exhibitors to include a small percentage of British footage in the films they respectively distributed and showed. No distinction was made between long and short films, and most firms fulfilled all or most of their quota obligation with long feature films. But some films were exempt from the need to be registered and these categories, as laid down in the Act, add up to a very rough attempt to group together factual or actuality films. They included firstly films consisting wholly or mainly of news and current events, a provision which let the newsreel companies avoid the time-consuming procedure of registration, as they did that of formal censorship. But it also included those consisting wholly or mainly of natural scenery, of industrial or manufacturing processes, or of commercial advertisement; those wholly or mainly for educational purposes; and scientific and natural history films. As they were not registered these films could not help firms with their quota footage and to that extent were less attractive to rent or show. The makers of some of them, however, did seek registration, wishing to have their films shown in the cinemas. In such cases they were usually given a registration number not prefixed with "Br.", which meant eligible as British quota, but with "E", which was defined as "British, but not eligible for quota". Some of the results were strange. In the case of natural scenery, for example, foreign and Dominion travelogues circulated in great numbers but British firms and individuals found their offerings labelled with an E, and with very little chance of distribution unless, as was discovered by some very smart operators, they concentrated "wholly or mainly" not so much on scenery as on buildings or people. However cheap or boring they were, and some were very cheap and boring indeed, in this way they could be sure of distribution. Indeed, they were a popular way for big American distributors to offset some of their imports.

Examining the Board of Trade numbers given to the many shorts offered for theatrical showing during this decade, one is forced to the conclusion that when a known member of the commercial shorts industry, and there were comparatively few of them, submitted his films they were dubbed Br. without difficulty; but that anyone else – whether documentary film maker, professional cameraman working independently or complete outsider –

had little chance of quota status. If the film could not be classed as mainly or wholly natural scenery or commercial advertisement (the latter, in particular, was stretched to cover most sponsored films) it could usually be forced into the categories of industrial or manufacturing processes, science or natural history or, if all else failed, into that most elastic of all classes, educational.

It took a little time for this to become clear. In the first few years of the sound film some studios experimented with the new techniques by filming many short musical or comic turns. Series of elementary film recordings of popular vaudeville acts, sketches and short playlets appeared, and these also formed items in the magazine films made by some of the large companies. After the first few years these turns were more likely to be used in feature films held together by some thin thread of narrative, usually a show business story. Hardly a vaudeville or radio act or a dance band in this country can have been omitted from the many films of this kind made between 1934 and 1939. Producers shuffled the turns like a pack of cards. However, it was to certain feature studios that this pilgrimage of vaudeville performers went and their work is outside our scope for the moment. Nevertheless during the first few years their work inflated the number of quota short films.

During the quota's first year of operation, however, a series of scenics by British Screen Classics and a series of short films on Empire regions and products made by British Instructional Films were already allocated E registrations. Yet the first two Empire Marketing Board films, *Drifters* and *One Family*, were given Br. registrations. Moreover, even *Michael Faraday*, registered in 1931 by the electrical firm British Thompson-Houston, was Br. although it was both sponsored and, as a historical film, educational. But from now until the new quota Act of 1938 almost all films not made by a small fraternity of interest film makers were E. There were some exceptions and anomalies, amongst both the documentary films and others. John Grierson made a major effort to break into theatrical exhibition with his "Imperial Six" in 1933 and two more batches in July and November 1934, but all were given an E, and after this he decided to concentrate on the non-theatrical market. This was greatly facilitated by the growing use of substandard film, that is to say film of a narrower gauge than the normal 35 mm. width of the commercial film. The effect of the system of registration was severe not only on the documentary movement but also on Gaumont-British Instructional. Economic viability for their school films was intended to be secured by making more entertaining versions for cinema distribution, but this was largely denied them by an E registration. After *Drifters*, Grierson's rather similar *Granton Trawler* was E. It seems that by then the Board of Trade had clarified its aims.

Thus, although *Song of Ceylon* was Br., *Windmill in Barbados* was E. If Marion Grierson's *Heart of an Empire* was Br., why was her *Key to Scotland* E? And however glad we are that Rotha's *Today we Live* was Br., on the grounds no doubt that it was mainly about people, we must also regret that *Nightmail*, presumably dismissed as an industrial process, was E. There were other oddities. Harry B. Parkinson, who was an established maker of cheap shorts in the twenties, got Br. for *How to Play Tennis* although G-B I never received it for any of their sports films, which included tennis instruction films. *Black Diamonds* and *Men Against Death*, two seriously intended documentary dramas made by outsiders, one of them a coal miner, got E and as a result failed to make enough money for their shoestring producers to continue. But Norman Lee, a commercial jack of all trades, got Br. for his *City of Shadows*, a film which made great play of its "documentary" nature. Stranger still, among pure expedition films *Kamet Conquered* was Br. but *Northern Lights* was E. And, oddest of all, Gaumont's early *Round Africa with Cobham* in 1929 was Br. whilst by 1932 the policy had crystallised and their *With Cobham to Kivu* was E.

The number of registered shorts from all sources for the three years ending 31 March 1931 was 829, 1,065, and 1,058. Of this the British percentage by length was highest in the first two years, 18·1 per cent and 16·9 per cent respectively, but fell abruptly to 5 per cent in the third. This sudden drop reflects to a great extent the disappearance of the isolated cabaret turn, but also the hardening attitude to shorts from any source but the narrowly commercial. The total number of shorts from all sources fell to 663 in 1936. The British footage was low for most of that time, actually falling to 4·5 per cent and 4·9 per cent in the years ending March 1932 and 1933. It rose a little thereafter to 6·8 per cent and 8·2 per cent and even to 12·8 per cent in 1936. The reason for this was apparently the emergence of the few shorts producers who knew how to put the very minimum of effort and·, expenditure into a film and yet exploit the regulations to secure quota registration. Strings of shots of buildings, even of pictures of buildings, were "travel pictures" which brought disrepute to the genre but provided renters and exhibitors with British footage for next to nothing. The winners in this deplorable game were the kings of the shorts field. The losers were many individualists and independents who felt they had something original to con- tribute and although certain renting companies like L.M.B., Kinograph and Denning performed a valuable service in handling some of their output, with the handicap of an E they had little hope of wide showing and the returns necessary to continue in business.

New quota legislation was due in 1938. In the middle of 1936 various groups with an interest in production, including the Association of Cine Technicians, the Federation of British Industries Film ·Group and Associated Realist Films Producers, began to agitate for a separate quota to be included in it. The T.U.C. also proposed that a minimum cost of 5/– a foot for shorts should be introduced. When the official Moyne Report came out in November 1936 it proposed separate quotas for long and short films, the shorts quota to be 15 per cent for renters and 10 per cent for exhibitors. Needless to say both the exhibitors' and the renters' associations vehemently opposed a shorts quota of any sort. However, the White Paper came out in August 1937 with a proposal for a shorts quota rising over the next ten years from 10 per cent to 20 per cent for renters, and from 5 per cent to 15 per cent for exhibitors, although without a cost test. Grierson, and Bruce Woolfe on behalf of the British Substandard Cinematograph Association, complained that this quota was too small. And when the Act finally came into effect in 1938 it established a shorts quota for renters rising from 15 per cent to 25 per cent, and for exhibitors from 12½ per cent to 22½ per cent.

The immediate effect was impressive. The total number of short films registered in the year ending 31 March 1939, the first year of the new Act, rose again to about a thousand, and of this the British footage was as high as 27·3 per cent compared with the renters' quota obligation of 15 per cent. The actual number of British short films was 275. Part of this was a backlog of films made earlier and now acceptable as quota, as well as a number of Gaumont-British Instructional items and productions such as the *Ace Cinemagazine* which had also not been eligible before. But it was noticeable that there was also a number of new firms specialising in commercial short films of a better quality than the earlier trade product. Also, and this was even more important, sponsored films and documentaries were now eligible for quota. Thus the work of the mainstream documentary was now in a position to compete for places in the supporting programmes. Strand's *Animal Kingdom* series registered in May 1938 were destined for the cinemas from the start, but the earliest true sponsored documentary from the Grierson school to get quota status under the new Act was Strand's *Watch and Ward in the Air* of 1937, which was registered for quota in June 1938. The G.P.O. films *North Sea*, *We Live in Two Worlds* and *Book Bargain* followed quickly in July. Harry Watt's *North Sea* was one which found particular favour with critics and public, breaking new ground in documentary as it did by dramatising a real incident, but had it not been for the new quota arrangements it would have been less advantageous to renters or exhibitors to handle such a film. Productions from the Progressive Film Institute, the new firms of Technique Films and British Foundation and others, as well as various T.I.D.A. and other mainstream documentary companies were also available now for quota and some were even distributed by the major American companies. Above all, the kind of independent who before had to be content with an E registration handled by one of the small distributors, could now reasonably hope for a better cinema booking.

However, the working of the new Act was not to be given a real trial, for war broke out and most of the film makers in question, as well as those from the feature studios, were before long gathered into an official network making films for war propaganda and instruction. By the time the war was over the whole scene had changed. Bearing this in mind, let us take a look at some of the films being produced outside the feature studios during the years between the coming of the commercial sound film and the outbreak of war in 1939.

2

News Films

News films, or regular series on current events, included newsreels and *The March of Time*. The newsreel companies made a few isolated longer films, usually about sports events or royalty, which can be included here as they were the same in their basic approach. But the compilations of news material which dealt with other subjects, principally the issue of peace or war, were different in motive and treatment and usually made by different people, and are described elsewhere.

Newsreels were part of the commercial cinema, although a separate part of it, made by different companies and personnel from the feature films. These companies were subsidiaries of major feature film producers, and were expected to supply short secondary films as part of the entertainment package. Audiences had always welcomed a chance to see the people, places and events they read about in the newspapers. Films showed them in action, and were even better than the illustrated papers, made possible in the comparatively recent past by developments in photography and printing. Treatment so far had necessarily been superficial, speed and topicality being the virtues rather than the revelation of meaning, and the films themselves were part of the fun of going to the pictures. But, when the sound track came to the newsreel, its immediate effect was not so much to convey the sounds as well as the sight of the material, for in fact many subjects continued to be shot silent and fitted with music and a commentary afterwards, but to shift the interest from the visuals to their significance. In the early part of the decade, when a heavy sound van with all its gear travelled to a news event the main camera was linked by cable in order to shoot sound with picture, but the other cameras were silent, and much of the astounding thudding of horses' hooves, the remarkably sharp plonk of tennis balls, was dubbed in the studio. Later in the thirties synchronous recording was better and at the same time less conspicuous. But once you had the sound you had to say something. And although the earliest sound newsreels were often made in two versions, silent film with titles and sound film with commentary as well as titles, in the end the greatest change brought by the sound film was the fact that what was said became almost more important than what was shown. However unvisual the material, the voice of the commentator was free to say what he liked. Without wishing to, the newsreels found themselves filming topics rather than images, and being dragged reluctantly into the world of journalism. The news cameraman, incidentally, lived up to the popular idea of the adventurous and enterprising journalist with an image of newshound unscrupulousness, hard drinking and competitive cameraderie. And, although the visual content was no longer the most important thing, the cameramen themselves were skilled professionals and the technical standard very high. With the use of many cameras, the exact location of these in order to give the best coverage was important, and the photographic quality achieved under difficult conditions was frequently outstanding. It has often been said that the thirties and forties were the best days of the newsreel cameraman.

The market was monopolised throughout by five very stable companies. The old Topical Budget and British Filmcraft's British Screen News lingered on for a few years but never acquired sound. The first to introduce it was the British Movietone News company, a subsidiary of the American Fox Film Corporation which had developed sound film in the first place, and who set up a London branch of Fox-Movietone very early with half a dozen American cameramen. In July 1929 British Movietone News was registered as a £5,000 private company jointly by Fox and Lord Rothermere's Associated Newspapers interests, under the control of Esmond Harmsworth. The Managing Director was

W. J. Hutchinson and the company was run by Gerald Sanger, formerly with Associated Newspapers, who was editor until he became producer in April 1935. Sir Malcolm Campbell, the famous racing driver, became editor in 1935 and Sir Gordon Craig, previously of New Era, became general manager. Ivan Scott was made news editor. It is generally believed that the company had a close if unofficial connection with the Conservative Central Office, and certainly Sanger, Craig and Campbell were Conservative in politics and the extreme Toryism of the newspaper backer was well known. But it was stated at the time that they strove for impartiality,[1] and indeed it was this company which made three longer compilation films on political subjects described elsewhere, featuring such liberal speakers as Professor Joad and Vernon Bartlett. It seems likely that they were marginally more interested in politics than other newsreels without Fleet Street connections, and might have been willing to try a more thoughtful treatment of the news had it been possible within the limits set by two things. These were, first, the British Board of Film Censors' sanction hanging over them; and, second, the pusillanimity of the exhibitors themselves.

The Gaumont Sound News started in November 1929, although the company had covered the Derby in sound in June of that year with its home-grown system, British Acoustic. Gaumont's, one of the oldest companies in films, had of course been in the newsreel business for many years, and cautiously carried on with their silent edition, the Gaumont Graphic, for a time while establishing their sound Gaumont-British News. This began with a traditional town crier ringing his handbell and the loudly declaimed slogan "Presenting the World – *to* the World!" Based at the Lime Grove studio of the parent company, it was run by production manager H. W. Bishop with E. V. H. Emmett as editor and commentator and the lively Castleton Knight as producer. It went from strength to strength and by 1939 had a large staff of cameramen. Also Conservative in outlook, its tone was safely middle-class conformist with little outright political opinion.

The next of the five to get sound, after a fashion, was the small English firm British Pictorial Productions. William and Clifford Jeapes had also been in the "topicals" business from the early years and had registered this company, with its Empire News Bulletin, in the twenties. They started with sound-on-disc in June 1930 for British Talking News. They later became Universal News, but well into the thirties the film continued to be shot silent and dubbed afterwards. The company, with a tiny studio in Wardour Street, was run by C. R. Snape with commentator R. E. Jeffrey and cameraman Harold Jeapes, who had been in the industry since 1899. A small company, it was the poor relation of the other newsreels and later formed an association with General Film Distributors. According to the same writer in *Sight and Sound* in 1933 it was at that time more inclined towards comedy items than the others.[2]

In March 1931 another big American corporation, Paramount Pictures, having previously shot material here in order to send it home for the American newsreels, started a British edition with labs and studio at Acton and with up-to-date mobile recording vans. British Paramount News, wholly owned by the parent company, rapidly established itself under G. T. Cummins with its signature shot of a camera turning and the slogan "the eyes and the ears of the world". Later the same year the historic firm of Pathé, oldest of all although only fourth in size, turned their newsreel over to sound. The Pathé Sound Magazine had started production in June 1929 under the British Talking Pictures licence, their sound newsreel slightly later, with its early trademark, the Pathé cock, now able to crow loudly. Their small studio fifty feet square in Wardour Street – with four cameramen under production manager and general factotum Fred Watts, who had been with Pathé since 1914 – had a large output of magazine and cabaret items as well as the Pathé News, as it became. The magazine *Pathétone Weekly* was launched in March 1930 using R.C.A. sound.

All these newsreels had distribution outlets in the big cinema circuits except Paramount, which survived by competing with the others for a share of the very large number of independent cinemas. All had some sort of international organisation or at least arrangements for gathering film from other countries. They acquired well-known signature tunes and recognisable commentators, especially Gaumont-British and Movietone with the confident, educated voices of E. V. H. Emmett and Leslie Mitchell respectively. In so far as there was any difference in style between them it depended on the key figure of the editor, who decided what was to be included, and the equipment they had at their disposal, which marginally affected their coverage. But the unpopular rota system, widely imposed from the mid-thirties where permission to film was required, meant that only one cameraman was admitted and dupe negatives were supplied to the other companies, and this greatly reduced the possibility of competition.

The newsreel companies worked together to a considerable extent to avoid arousing antagonisms which might have led to demands for censorship. They maintained some similarity in style and content. Each produced two one-reel issues a week, which circulated through first-, second- and third-run bookings and so on down through the cinemas at descending rental prices. This time factor made it necessary to combine topical items with those of general interest which would not date too quickly. They usually included some half-dozen items each, covering more or less the same range of main subjects and in much the same way. Despite the coming of sound and the importance of the commentator, titles lingered on as chapter headings to introduce each new item. The commentators, in loud, clear, insistent voices, posh without being affected, leavening authority with a light touch of flippant banter and the weak puns supposedly loved by the British, became familiar but almost too alike to be personally identifiable to their enormous public. They told us what we were looking at rather than what it meant, and subtly moulded our attitudes by their very correct respect for established authority, their irreproachable sentiments at natural or man-made disasters, their hearty self-assurance, their bland confidence that all would yet be well. The importance of the editor, who chose what to cover, especially if he was also the commentator or what later audiences would call the presenter, should not be underestimated. But they were so aware of the delicacy of their position that they hesitated to show anything that was not already acceptable, or say anything that was not already almost universally agreed.

The need for a film library, international links and a very large distribution outlet made it more or less impossible for a beginner to break the monopoly of these five companies, and throughout the thirties the same ones, with virtually the same style of product, remained almost unchallenged. All the same, changes in the treatment of current events were on the way. Sanger returned from a visit to the U.S.A. early in 1935 full of the developments taking place over there. News was to be more "departmentalised" as it was in the newspapers, and greater stress laid on named commentators. Movietone, and in various ways the others, did modernise along these lines. Another American development, that of "dramatising" the news, was not expected to be popular over here, although in fact its chief exponent, *The March of Time*, was just about to sweep all before it. The single attempt to start a new and more individual newsreel failed. This was the National News, in 1937. Sound City (News) Ltd was registered in July 1937 with £5,000 capital and with Norman Loudon of Sound City Films and C. R. Snape from Universal News on the board. The commentator was to be the B.B.C. star Thomas Woodroofe, and there were to be weekly cartoons by Dennis Connolly and a "Behind the Headlines" item. The idea of getting a cartoon into production quickly enough for it to have any topicality was ambitious. But, not content with that, they were to have items in Dunning Colour. The lab. work, by George Humphries, was optimistically expected to be almost as quick as that for black and white film. However, technical disasters and the difficulty of securing outlets were too much for it. The first issue came out in October 1937 but the colour was bad and the animated sequence poor and it received nothing but condemnation. It was suspended and Lord Beaverbrook's son Peter Aitken, already on the board of Odeon Theatres and Sound City Distributors, became a director. But it was too late to save it, and although more issues were attempted the venture collapsed.

Beaverbrook, who had early wartime and post-war connections with films, made several attempts to get a foothold in the news film as his fellow newspaper magnate Rothermere had done. Not only did he at one time unsuccessfully try to get control of Universal News but in 1935 the British Trans-Lux News Theatres Company was formed with his associate Will Evans as chairman and his son Peter as a director. This company had an arrangement with Trans-Lux Movies Corporation of America, and its professed aim was to lease between 150 and 200 cinemas in this country. Newsreel theatres, small cinemas in busy non-residential areas of large towns, showed a mixed programme of about an hour in length made up of newsreels with interest, travel and cartoon or revue items. They increased in number for a while in the mid-thirties. In 1934 there were seven in London and three more about to open, and by late 1936 there were eighteen. But it seems likely that the demand for what was bound to be a stopping-off place rather than a main attraction, owing to the shortness of its programme, was overestimated and by 1938 there were signs that the expansion was over. In point of fact, the nature of their function had been somewhat misunderstood. Although they were called news theatres they were in fact an outlet for short films rather than for news films, and their existence did not show the greater interest in newsreels for which Beaverbrook had hoped. He thought they might lead to a more politically developed editorial treatment of news, but this did not occur. Later it seemed, for a short while before the war, that the arrival of television was going to give them a new function as the appropriate place for public rediffusion of major events. By the outbreak of war, however, the fact that television was moving into individual homes rather than into public exhibition was already becoming clear, bringing with it the seeds of the ultimate decline of the newsreel itself in the ordinary cinemas. The news theatre movement was already virtually dead, and the war put a stop to the development of television for the time being. Meanwhile the newsreel companies prospered. In autumn 1937 they formed a Newsreel Association of Great Britain and Ireland to protect their interests, under the secretaryship of Neville Kearney of the Federation of British Industries.

Since more or less the same subjects were covered by all the newsreels and in more or less the same form, competition showed itself in other ways. It lay, as it had always done, in speed and exclusives rather than in content or editorial viewpoint. From the earliest days companies had tried to be first to get unusual items into the theatres. Despite better transport it was actually more difficult and expensive now, with the commentary and music to add and with more complex editing and printing. During the thirties elaborate networks were set up to get film from all over the world into the cinemas as soon as possible, although even a week's delay or more was not unusual. According to *Kine Weekly* in 1936, to get films of the Abyssinian war on the screen in eight days was creditable.[3] It was Gaumont-British who proudly claimed to show after a mere three days the arrival of C. W. Scott and Campbell Black in Australia after the first London to Melbourne air race in October 1934. Bishop and Castleton Knight had a few frames of a shot transmitted as still pictures by means of the picture transmission beam service of Cable & Wireless Company, and put together in London with what was described as a modified animation technique by the repetition of frames, to make a short, jerky and rather dubious "shot". At £22 a frame, and still taking three days, it seemed hardly worth the trouble and the experiment does not seem to have been repeated.

Exclusive films of big sporting events had also, like speed, long been the cause of legendary exploits by the cameraman. The Pathé Super Sound Gazette of 27 March 1933 announced that Pathé "exclusively presents the only authentic and official pictures" of the Grand National, described by Captain G. H. Gilbey, "the Famous Racing Journalist of the *Daily* and *Sunday Express*", in a reel-long film for which they seem to have sent a staff of as many as twenty-six to Aintree. The promoters of big sporting events like cup finals, fights and races might sell exclusive film rights to one company, but they could rarely succeed entirely in keeping hidden cameras from being smuggled into the grounds, or distant lenses being directed from the air or merely from the other side of the fence, and the legal holders of filming rights took many desperate steps to protect their monopoly. The industry seemed to have an ambivalent attitude to all this, not knowing whether to be more proud of the enterprise of those who secured rights or of the piratical skill of those who thwarted them. So keen was the struggle, and so much did the profits tempt the promoters of sports events, that when negotiations broke down before the Cup Final of 1936 Wembley Stadium announced that they would produce the only F.A. Cup Final film themselves.

It was to be edited by H. A. Saunders and handled by a company, Featurettes, which had already successfully filmed the Petersen–Harvey fight on the same basis despite an attempt by the Exhibitors' Association to prevent its showing. The newsreel companies tried through the C.E.A. to get the cinemas to boycott the film, followed by their usual breaking-in tactics at the event itself, but in 1937, again, the Cup Final was filmed by Featurettes. In 1938 the newsreels accepted the inevitable, and pooled their resources for the match.

In view of the enormous amount of equipment which had to be brought to the scene of action, there was little attempt to compete with each other in the way of scoops, although now and then one might come their way. But they found that anything off the beaten track tended to land them in trouble. Early in 1933, for example, British Paramount had secured films of rioting in Paris which were rushed out of the country before the French were quick enough to prevent them, but according to Cummins they were delayed by diplomatic pressure for several days, just long enough to destroy their news value.[4] Later the same year it was a Paramount cameraman, again, who filmed the assassination of King Alexander of Yugoslavia in Marseilles. Shots of the assassin jumping on the running board of the car, the sabre blow, the assassin's body lying on the ground and the dying king in the car as it drove away must have sent the cameraman home feeling he had done pretty well. But although "the worst pictures were not used"[5] one M.P. complained that the pictures were "revolting"[6] and the Warwickshire County Council, notorious for its tender susceptibilities, used this instance to bring up the whole question of censorship. Another scoop which had unfortunate consequences of a different kind was Gaumont-British's film of G. A. McMahon drawing a gun on Edward VIII during a procession on Constitution Hill in July 1936. They enthusiastically advertised their film with a placard reading "Assassination Attempt" and the film contained a caption "Attempt on the King's life". McMahon's solicitors forced them to withdraw this as calculated to prejudice the trial and, when McMahon was later given a one-year prison sentence convicted only of "unlawfully producing near the person of the King a pistol, with intent to alarm his Majesty", he threatened to sue Gaumont-British for libel. Meanwhile Gaumont-British Distributors, along with a cinema manager and the proprietors and editors of the *Evening News* and *Daily Express*, were charged with contempt of court. Gaumont-British, who had distributed the film to 263 cinemas, was fined £50 and costs.[7]

Faced with such pressures and hazards it is not surprising that the newsreel companies played safe. From the beginning of the British Board of Film Censorship's existence it had been accepted that speed was so important to newsreels that they should not be required to submit their film to the censors, with all the delay that this might cause. This privilege was so important to them that, fearing to endanger it, they confined much of their coverage to safe, acceptable and familiar events, especially those arranged well in advance which enabled them to plan their operations. Regular sports events and the occasional fight or record-breaking attempt by car or plane, ceremonials of all sorts, disasters or at least their aftermath if time permitted their filming, spiced with interest or comedy items of general topicality, launchings, big celebrity weddings and suchlike were their stock in trade. Occasional shots of politicians, or of sensitive subjects like the wars in China, Abyssinia and Spain and the hunger marches of the unemployed in Britain, could not be avoided entirely. But they took their place with the other items; and the commentaries or sometimes a few platitudes from the politicians, were for the most part faultlessly neutral and bland. As September 1939 drew near, contemptuous, or often contemptuously humorous, references to Hitler and Mussolini became more frequent. But in this the newsreels were following public opinion, not leading it.

It is interesting, although no more is claimed for it than that, to examine the entire contents of one newsreel, British Movietone, during two random four-week periods, one in 1932 and one in 1937. It may be felt that the newsreels of these months are not necessarily typical, or at least that we do not know how typical they are. Certainly there is no way of knowing this short of an extensive analysis of all that is left to us of the five newsreels, that is to say whole issues of some, others broken into items, some on tape, some only as contents sheets and some as commentary

1 British Movietone in June 1932 shows "Prudential Building Becomes Fire Claim", on magenta stock.

2 British Movietone in June 1932 films the Viceroy in Peshawar; Lady Willingdon lurks tactfully in the background, almost hidden by her large parasol.

3 British Movietone in September 1937. An item about the Army is quickly followed by "Terpsichore – U.S. Kilted Chorines Trip Light Fantastic on Rolling Bubbles".

sheets. Nor is it possible, here, to make any but a sketchy reference to what the newspapers and radio were covering at the same time. However, a detailed description of at least a few of the films we are discussing may make them more real to the reader. Contents analysis, giving a statistical comparison of the number of items concerning various subjects, although an attempt to be objective, can be misleading. To say that an item shows Mussolini at Stresa gives no idea of how he is shown or what is said about him, and statistics built up on such a classification need to be rounded out by a detailed look at some, at least, of the films themselves.

British Movietone's eight issues numbered from 156 and 156A in the first week to 159 and 159A in the last date from June 1932. In the first issue the items consist of *Cruise on the S.S. Mauretania*, a few random snapshots with casual voices, mostly apparently post-synchronised, and no commentary; *Fatal Crash Mars Airmen's Congress*, with narrator and dramatic music as well as a long title, is about the death of two Hungarian fliers in Rome, and includes shots of the funeral and the wreck, all in a pink or mauve tint; a motor cycle scramble is in the thrills-and-spills category, with bright music and no commentary; *Khyber Pass Visited by Willingdons* shows the Viceroy of India at what the title calls "this far-flung outpost of Empire", and among the martial music and the inspections Lady Willingdon, from under her large-brimmed hat and huge sunshade, glances as she chats and says "Ooo, they've turned the cinema on us" and then, keeping calm and being very co-operative, asks "Are we to talk?"; long shots of a French luxury liner burning on her maiden voyage are apparently a scoop, and the narrator explains that the captain tried to bring her to shore before she sank, which gave Movietone time to film her. The second issue of the week has shots of the Carnera-Gains fight with music and titles as well as crowd sounds, punches and foot scuffles so loud that they seem to have been recorded separately and dubbed later, although the man in the ring announcing the fight seems to be in synch; the 1932 Derby, won by Tom Walls's horse, is shown at some length with the crowds arriving, the horses, the pearlies, the King and Queen, gypsies and stuntmen; then with a title and music the race is off; the audibility of thudding hooves and distinct crowd dialogue in some shots and not in others is very conspicuous, and there is a coda in which the finish is shown in slow motion.

The third issue includes Trooping the Colour, a "pageant that symbolises Britain and its ages-old loyalty and love for King and country"; again the sound is variable, and the item, less dramatic, has less shape and pace than the Derby. This issue includes "Topical Section of the Gala Performance", which shows Mussolini in the crowd watching 400 airmen in ceremonial and stunting flights over Rome, without commentary; Betty Nuthall and Fred Perry win at tennis against Helen Wills and S. B. Wood, introduced by a commentator; an item entitled *Women at Brooklands* introduces us to two ladies standing in their car surrounded by admiring or possibly curious people after winning a two-day event, and one of them says into the microphone "I'm awfully glad we won this race, I think we're the only women to have won a big race" (the subtitle is "Feminine Triumph"); and a final item shows King Carol of Roumania and his son Michael touring on a yacht, Movietone having apparently secured another scoop in being allowed these "intimate pictures". The fourth issue begins with the "little Royal lady" Princess Elizabeth at the Aldershot Tattoo, with music and guns but neither titles nor voice; a comedy item about the Sydney Bridge which consists entirely of the traffic being first speeded up and then reversed by the camera; *New German Cabinet Undertakes Big Task* takes the camera down the line of von Papen and his colleagues standing in a garden, shot mute except for a few words from von Papen; a general interest item with ceaseless commentary about nesting time on Lundy Island is followed by shots of the 500-miles race at Indianapolis which include the three crashes which took place, and the routine few words into the microphone from the winner, still at the wheel.

Next week we start with Gene Sarazen winning at golf at Sandwich, again with commentary followed by the winner's few choice words; neither titles nor voice are used for a few shots of events at the Royal Horse Show; taking off and formation flying at the annual Hendon air pageant are shown with martial music but no titles or narration; *De Valera in U.K. but Fails to Agree with the British Cabinet* shows him arriving at Euston Station, the narrator pointing out that he has not been in England since 1921 and also, with heavy significance, that he is not smiling; he is also seen at No. 10; heavyweight Sharkey is shown "preparing" to fight Max Schmeling in a joke item in which he plays various musical instruments. Later in the week an item about the Navy testing anti-submarine tactics has a commentary; Ramsay MacDonald and M. Herriot meeting before going to the Lausanne Conference at last shows us politicians addressing the microphone, but both are disappointing, with a few prepared clichés and no questions from an interviewer; MacDonald, for example, says "We have to create a peaceful world"; polar bears are shown without commentary but with natural sound and jokey music, as they try to get at fish which are frozen in blocks of ice at the New York Zoo; *Movietone reveals China's Mystic City* includes aerial views of Peking and the Great Wall, with travel-type commentary; and *Ascot* shows fashions, the royal drive down the course, and then titles and music before the races themselves.

The last week starts with *Express derailed near Stafford*, showing the wrecked train and people hurrying about, with a rather literary commentary; *Ellsworth Vines beaten at tennis at Queen's Club by H. Hopman* includes loud and clear sounds of the ball, clapping, and the umpire's voice; various events at the International Horse Show; a pink-mauve tinted sequence of the burning of the Prudential building, with no commentary but menacing music and natural sound, gives exceptionally good shots of the long ladders up the side of this high, ornate building, the burning roof, and shots from inside as firemen hack their way in through the tiles; Jack Petersen of Cardiff is shown as a British boxing hope, cropped and slicked down in the sunshine and beaming as he says a few modest words and demonstrates a little PT; *Viceroy Concludes Stay in Peshawar* shows the Willingdons again at a Government House garden party, and good sport Lady Willingdon, a gift to newsmen, hovers tactfully and terribly nonchalantly in the background with her parasol until the gentlemen move on. Finally, later in the week *President Auteuil at the Grand Steeplechase* is yet another racecourse item with jolly music, ladies in fashionable gowns, the murmur of crowds and the thud of hooves, overhead shots of the course and low angles at the corners to get a good view of the approaching horses, again with a part in slow motion, and again without commentary or titles; cross-bowmen display a mediaeval weapon in Italy; *Cardinal Lauri from the Pope comes to Ireland*; this is followed by an item about a nursery school at West Norwood in which the voice of the common man of which Grierson was later to speak so weightily was heard to some effect when a child, asked what she was doing, said in exasperation "I'm makin' a *puddin'* "; *Air Foes of the War Fraternise in Peace* relies heavily on the commentary for an item about two German air aces over here for the Hendon air pageant; and *Trooping of the Colour by the Marines past Admiral Sir Roger Keynes* shows the parade with distant band and no commentary.

If this seems dull to read, it is a great deal duller to watch, and it is difficult to feel immersed in the events of the day as one so easily does when perusing old newspapers. It will be seen that titles are still used a great deal. According to one veteran[8] many newsreels continued to be made in both sound and silent versions for several years, and these issues of Movietone could be seen mute without much loss. Politicians had hardly begun to have microphones thrust in front of them yet, but winning sportsmen could expect to be asked for a few words strictly of their own choosing. Cross-examination in front of the camera had not begun. Each issue was up to about 850 feet long and the items were fairly uniform in length although a few, for example the Ellsworth Vines tennis item, were considerably longer than others. Typically, each issue had one item showing people in the political news but without background explanation of the question involved, one or two sports items and institutionalised events like regular pageants, shows and races as well as fights, an occasional item about a "personage", disasters if there was time to film them, and every now and then a simple interest or funny item. With regard to the treatment of politics, it is worth noting that the Chinese item was included without reference to the fighting which had already broken out when Japan invaded Manchuria in 1931, and the de Valera item, although it hinted that he was here on a point of some disagreement, did not even go as far as the Pathé Super

Gazette 32/47 of 13 June 1932 in mentioning the Oath of Allegiance and the Land Annuities as the subject at issue. The possibility that a United Ireland, as a republic, might cancel the Land Annuities paid to Britain, scrap the Oath of Allegiance and leave the British Commonwealth would perhaps be known to newspaper readers but they would never have learnt it from this newsreel. Even more important, perhaps, is the way in which the background to the meeting of Ramsay MacDonald and M. Herriot is ignored. Having disarmed Germany, France and Britain could not agree about their own disarmament and were on their way to Lausanne to discuss this, and the possible cancellation of reparations and war debts. None of this was made clear.

By 1937 Movietone had been modernised after Sanger's visit to America, and its format was usually one major item with commentary by Leslie Mitchell, "Reports" with commentary by Ivan Scott, and sports items edited by Tommy Scales and commented on by Alan Howland. Issues 428 to 431A cover four weeks in August and September. The lead was no longer a simple flag as before but a sectional screen with various events in the sections, "Gerald Sanger" at the top and "edited by Sir Malcolm Campbell" at the bottom, the flag appearing briefly at the end of the titles. Although the overall length is the same there are far more items, many of them little more than snippets, and a greater number of curiosity or novelty items. Natural sound is taken more easily with less emphasis on it but there is much more commentary, with music in the background. Although titles are used to introduce each item, they no longer appear throughout as in silent films but simply as chapter headings. There is no more toning of stock. The mood of each item is set abruptly by the music, doleful music to a sad item giving way sharply to bright jolly music or whatever was appropriate as the new title appeared.

Issue 428 starts with a 98-foot item by Mitchell about the Far East, *Sino-Japanese crisis boils over into open fighting in Shanghai*, which shows some burning and barricades; the arrival of a few British, American and French forces is mentioned, and Mitchell says that we wait to see if "counsels of peace will avert the actual tragedy of war . . . or will the temper of the Japanese involve the other nations in an Oriental quarrel, the end of which no man can foretell?" "Reports" by Ivan Scott are 65 feet on a cross between a seaplane and a flying boat, 29 feet on a thick fog in Melbourne, 72 feet on Beating the Bound in Poole Harbour, and 97 feet in which Scott introduces the new Secretary for War, Leslie Hore-Belisha – "The Army has found a great advocate in Mr. Hore-Belisha, and Tommy Atkins a champion" – who gives some idea in a desk chat about his plans to alter service terms to encourage soldiers to stay on longer. This is followed by 88 feet (almost as long) on American chorus girls dancing on bubbles, and 97 feet (the same length) on a "churkey", a cross between a chicken and a turkey, humorously commented on by their favourite funny man Maurice Braddell. Sports by Scales and Howland ran to as much as 233 feet, and included soccer, athletics, pole vaulting, car racing and motor bikes, ending with a joke shot of a man so frightened by the motor bikes that his hat rose in the air and had to be held down.

In the next issue Mitchell's item was 124 feet about the dedication of a memorial to the 568 American soldiers who died on British soil during the 1914–18 war. Ivan Scott's "Reports" were 68 feet about the festivities held in celebration of Berlin's 700th birthday, 45 feet of a stunt driver, 89 feet about the Zoo in the heat wave, 52 feet called *In China Now* which carries right on from the heat-stricken polar bears to say "It's worse than frayed tempers in China, it's war", but repeats the hope that it will be no more than an Oriental quarrel. Manoeuvres in Italy are accompanied by the remark "Afterwards troops parade before the Duke of Aosta and Marshal da Bono, of Abyssinian fame", 54 feet. An item of 106 feet about gliders at Dunstable and the American Flying Fortresses is followed by a facetious item of 94 feet about Wakes Week at Blackpool. The sports section of 93 feet is about the trampoline, and about hunting in Melbourne.

The next week began with an item on fur coats, glamorous but lightly humorous in tone, with a commentary not by Mitchell as usual but by Beryl de Querto. Scott's "Reports" included Japan bringing up reinforcements, which he ventured to deplore, the Crystal Palace in flames again, roadmaking by dynamite on the steep rocky bank of the Hudson River, and elephants working

in Ceylon; Australian girls are shown practising shooting, and
then there is a follow-up item to the Hore-Belisha interview in
which funny-man Carl Bernard, in phoney Cockney accent, claims
the new military plans are "a bit of orl right", with stress on
success with the girls. The sports section includes Tommy Farr,
who was to fight Joe Louis, children in a boat pool, a trawler race
at Brixham and the Grasmere games. The second issue of the
week is less like a silly season edition. Ivan Scott comments on
New Atlantic Flight and Paris Air Race and his "Reports" include
items about the American Naval Reserve, an Indiana swimming
pool, a "crazy rodeo", a pony club for girls in Berkshire, Naval
training for girls, and George Eyston's new car; *At the Front in
China* takes an even more critical tone than the last issue. It
was apparently possible to criticise the Japanese, with their
annoying Oriental quarrel, before it was safe to be anti-fascist.
But he switched gladly back to *Southern Carnival* with a carnival
queen, lights and processions. Leslie Mitchell has a section called
Names and News. Here he comments on the Duke and Duchess
of Kent visiting the royal family of Yugoslavia, a foreign girl with
a long and unusual name who wins at tennis but in 34 feet is
simply asked to repeat her name three times, followed by the
would-be funny question "Are you *sure?*" *Mr. Chamberlain and
Mr. Eden* are seen in London but "There is no alarming significance in the meeting, but there *is* the Shanghai situation to
discuss", says Mitchell in this 27-foot item; 28 feet is also devoted
to *Il Duce*, coarser and in a more ornate uniform than five years
earlier, but according to Mitchell's ambiguous introduction "A
name to conjure with . . . to hear Il Duce on peace". The sports
section has soap-box racing in America, trotting also in America,
athletics in Paris and motor cycling in Germany.

The third week gives pride of place to Mitchell's report on
Robert Taylor's arrival in London. Scott's "Reports" include Sir
Samuel Hoare launching two lifeboats at Cromer, news about
irrigation in Kansas with glancing reference to the dust bowl,
the Lympne Air Rally, and Dobson winning a 200-mile race at
Donington Park at an average speed of 69·67 m.p.h. Sport has a
special report on the All Blacks versus Ireland, and the usual
miscellany of yacht racing in Long Island Sound, running, soccer,

cricket and boxing. In the second issue Scott gives 142 feet to Tommy Farr being beaten by Louis. "Reports", this time by Mitchell, have an item on the Navy at Alexandria which includes a funny commentary by Braddell, and 83 feet on congratulations to their own editor, Sir Malcolm Campbell, who had won the water speed record in Bluebird on Lake Maggiore on 1 September. Sir Malcolm, like other sportsmen, gives his graceful few words after winning, and the commentary lets rip with "Britain is justly proud of you Malcolm, of whom we can say in your absence 'No finer or more gallant gentleman exists' ".

The last week begins with 83 feet of Mitchell reporting on the wedding of tennis star Dorothy Round, 44 feet about piratical submarine attacks of unknown origin on British ships in the Mediterranean, 40 feet announcing the fall of Santander to Franco, in which the commentary limits itself to saying that fortunately the town has suffered little, but which does casually mention the Italian troops with Franco. The next short 22-foot item is of Japan's premier playing golf. A 69-foot item follows in which it is explained that whales are being found in Indian waters, 52 feet of the Imperial Airways flying boat *Caledonia* flying over Blackpool, 41 feet of trams being replaced by trolley-buses in Sydney, and a whole 100 feet of a faked Indian rope trick with funny commentary by Braddell. 96 feet are devoted to Howland's report of the TT International at Donington Park and no less than 100 feet to "ballroom eccentricities", including the Lindy Hop, on Broadway described by Lowell Thomas. The final issue has "Reports" by Mitchell which begin with 63 feet on Hore-Belisha ("He's doing great things for the Army") seeing a troopship off; 41 feet on *Madrid Today* with the irreproachably neutral comment that neither side wants to harm Madrid but in war destruction is inevitable; 43 feet of stunts with a plane landing on a car; 37 feet of *Twins by the Score* with a mass meeting of twins; and 60 feet in which *Wandering Reggie*, a little boy who has run away ten times, explains "why I run away to Wood Green, 'cos I like the police there. They give me pineapple and custard". As much as 80 feet is given to Enid Lowe on hat fashions, 93 feet on another help-the-army item, *The "Horse-into-Tank" idea almost makes H.A.C. Men Weep,* with another Cockney Tommy voice played by Carl Bernard. As usual the sports item is long, 205 feet of firemen playing ball, Wimbledon, and Tommy Farr, very game and dignified after being beaten by Joe Louis.

The diplomatic neutrality of Movietone's references to Franco and Italy is marked, Italian success in Abyssinia and the equally successful intervention in Spain having apparently been accepted. More remarkable, perhaps, is the way Movietone exercised caution beyond the call of duty at a period when the British Ambassador to China had been shot during the Japanese attack on Shanghai, and both the *New Statesman* on the left and *Morning Post* on the far right were worrying about the implications of the struggle in the East. Japan was beginning a new policy of systematic bombing of other Chinese towns, involving the killing of non-combatants. The Tory *Evening Standard* of 29 September had no difficulty in publishing a cartoon by their independent cartoonist David Low called *Mass Murder in China*. But British Movietone, apart from a couple of crochety references to the "Oriental quarrel", simply gave us 22 feet of the Japanese Prime Minister playing golf.

Five companies were issuing two films a week like these, so it is clear that film was being shot in large quantities. Not all of it appeared at the time, for much went into the growing stock libraries. By the same token, the weekly items on current events sometimes contained a proportion of film from the libraries masquerading as new film, especially in the case of unexpected events. The old companies Pathé and Gaumont-British, especially, had very rich archives. This mass of material was to be one of the sources for later compilation films of strongly political views but these were not, for the most part, made by the newsreel companies themselves. Virtually the only extended treatments, retrospectives or short feature-length spreads they could permit themselves were on the safe subjects of sport and royalty.

Pathé started the ball rolling with restrospectives in 1931, with a compilation film from their own archives to mark their 21st birthday in the news field. The long film of this type, not always a compilation, lent itself particularly to royal subjects. There was plenty of material, audiences liked them and they were non-controversial. Butcher's Film Service very early in 1932 had a three-reeler called *Our Farmer Prince* about the Prince of Wales, and Gaumont-British followed in late 1933 with a six-reel *The Prince of Wales*. The wedding in 1934 of Princess Marina to the Duke of Kent was covered extensively by the newsreels, for the romantic Princess's foreign chic struck a new note in the royal family and aroused a great deal of admiration. Preparations for the Silver Jubilee in 1935 to celebrate twenty-five years' reign by George V set feature companies as well as newsreel companies to thinking, and not only did B.I.P. turn out one of the longest and dullest feature films of its career, *Royal Cavalcade* – part compilation and part dramatic vignettes acted by an enormous cast – but Alexander Korda, also, planned one of his many unmade films, a *Reign of George V* which was to have been written by Winston Churchill and directed by Anthony Asquith. Gaumont-British Picture Corporation, drawing on their large archives, were able to put out a two-reel compilation in 1935 called *The King's Jubilee*, edited by Castleton Knight and narrated by Emmett, and Pathé had *Twenty-five Years a King*. This film of short feature length directed by Aveling Ginever owed a lot to the Pathé production manager Freddie Watts, and was said to have been compiled "with the collaboration of John Drinkwater and Sir Austen Chamberlain". The Jubilee itself was a field day for the newsreel companies, and in 1936, it is said, there were queues outside the newsreel cinemas in London on the day of George V's funeral. The year of the coronation of George VI and Queen Elizabeth, 1937, was full of promise and Pathé started early with *The House of Windsor*, in three reels, a compilation this time by Watts and with a commentary by the Liberal M.P. and broadcaster Commander Stephen King-Hall. At the same time Warner Brothers had an independent six-reel British film directed by John Stumar, a Hungarian-American cameraman over here at the time, and written by Drinkwater. This was *The King's People*, not entirely newsreel-based. The poet John Drinkwater, who also contributed to a number of feature films, presented this film in the form of a family album from Queen Victoria's Jubilee to the accession of George VI. *Kine Weekly* complained, however, that there was "a little too much Drinkwater" and although a useful second feature it had too much of the poet's "insistence on emphasising his own erudition and place in literature", an unfortunately cruel review as Drinkwater died unexpectedly, aged only fifty-four, the following week.[9]

One royal event upon which the companies agreed to observe a unanimous silence was the wedding of the Duke of Windsor to Mrs Simpson in 1937, a notable example of self-censorship not followed by the press. The Coronation, however, was the perfect occasion for the newsreel companies to extend themselves and they did so in collaboration. Permission was necessary for film to be taken in Westminster Abbey, and this was granted by the Archbishop of Canterbury on the eve of the Coronation. The five companies pooled their resources for filming in the Abbey, two cameramen being present on the wooden structure erected within it for newsmen. Parts of the B.B.C. commentary were made available for the sound-track but this led to some argument later as some of the actual ceremony as transmitted by radio was used, apparently without proper permission. The resulting film, the first to have been shot within the Abbey, although a little dark, is impressive. Owing to the long distances and low illumination, Kodak Super X, described as "a film stock of unbelievable sensitivity", was used. The Pathé cameraman used a Taylor-Hobson 56-inch focal length telephoto lens built on to a standard Vinten camera, and this could take a head and shoulders shot at 250 feet. Paramount used a Dallmeyer telephoto with the equivalent of a 40-inch focus. According to R. H. Cricks, most shots were successful. Highlights of the ceremony are shown and the cries of "Vivat", the fanfares, the Archbishop's voice and the King's replies, so new to the public, must have been very moving. The ladies-in-waiting, amidst all the traditional velvet, ermine and cloth of gold, still manage to look strangely mid-thirties. In addition to the film within Westminster Abbey, Movietone had one reel of Technicolor film of the Coronation procession outside, and Pathé one reel of the same thing in Dufaycolor, less bright and probably less successful than the other although held to be an improvement on their Dufaycolor footage of the Jubilee. All the cinemas, of course, wanted Coronation films as soon as possible. In order to make the most of limited printing capacity and meet this unusual demand the trade got together to produce short items or "flashes", which were available the day after the Coronation. Four days later one reel of the procession outside and one reel of the ceremony inside the Abbey, together with just over 1,000 feet of Technicolor from Movietone and 854 feet of Dufaycolor from Pathé, were put out. And a week later still, two five-reel versions were available from Pathé and Gaumont-British respectively. An unedited collection of Pathé Dufaycolor material shows the difficulties of filming with limited camera sites or focal depths, the camera turning on its axis a little but mostly filming in long shot the procession from Buckingham Palace, round the Memorial and beginning to recede up the Mall, and also outside Westminster Abbey. The colour is soft and pleasing, every carriage and coach and its occupants are seen and shots of the varied and picturesquely costumed troops from all over the Empire, then at its zenith, are visual signs of its vast extent.

There was, as it happens, a great deal of dissatisfaction from the exhibitors with the way the films were handled. The prices were high, regular customers of the companies were believed to have had priority and the flashes disappointed many audiences who had expected longer films, whilst their production delayed the appearance of the fuller versions. It is noted that Movietone made 502 copies of its Technicolor film, and as many as 1,826 black and white prints, in order to satisfy as quickly as possible a world public estimated at a record 100 million people.[10]

The single most outstanding royal film of Coronation year, however, was probably Paramount's *Crown and Glory*, which was trade shown in April and planned for showing as a second feature during Coronation week. Four reels, it was described as a documentary drama although, apart from some feature excerpts mixed with the news shots of the pre-1914 sequences, it was actuality material. Starting with the Proclamation of 1936, it traces the royal family and public events from 1895 to the Coronation by the same device of turning the pages of an album, and with considerable skill uses the trappings of royal ceremonial, the crown and orb, the fanfares and excellent news shots, to make an interesting film which was much admired and enjoyed, with its comforting message, "Britain and her Empire emerge strengthened and triumphant!" Beginning with the trams and carriages of 1895 it first brings us up to the war of 1914. Here, a long and horrifying sequence of a ship sinking, turning over and going down, with sailors running desperately all over it, jumping off, clinging and slipping and finally submerging as the hulk disappears, is presented as a German ship sinking at Jutland, although according to the best of authorities this is not what it was.[11] The war at sea is shown in the wham-wham style of repeated climaxes, followed by meetings at Versailles, scenes of the future Queen Elizabeth as a child and then her wedding to the Duke of York. The film continues with shots of Hitler, Lenin and Mussolini when young, the seizure of the Rhineland and the Abyssinian war, the *Queen Mary* winning the Atlantic Blue Riband to the tune of "Britons never, never, never shall be slaves!" on the sound-track, and shots of the little Princesses as they grew up. The General Strike of 1926 is mentioned, but in the hurrying tones of the commentator there is no time for explanation or reflection. Possibly realising that the King's subjects were somewhat conspicuous by their absence, Paramount introduced a few shots of a "little man", very respectable with moustache, glasses and bowler, making unexceptionable remarks meant to represent the views of the man in the street. George V's funeral is seen and the film adroitly slips over the abdication with no hint that a woman was involved at all, only saying with respect that "rather than upset the Constitution, Edward had renounced the throne". The film ends on the note of rearmament "as a bulwark of peace", and a shot of George VI accompanied by the speech "This sceptred isle, this other Eden" in its entirety.

As a historical résumé, of course, it was very inadequate but as a royal item it was better than most. Further royal extended news films appeared in 1938 when the new King and Queen visited Paris and Pathé brought out a whole reel in Dufaycolor in July, and in 1939 when they toured Canada and the United States Gaumont-British had 2,600 feet called *The Royal Tour*, with commentary by Emmett.

The habit of going to the pictures grew throughout the thirties, but because of the feature films and the outing, not because of the supporting programme, although the audience certainly expected this and felt cheated if it wasn't exactly as usual. The fact that every cinema, at every performance, included a newsreel meant that a small group of people played a significant part in determining not so much the general knowledge of world events, for this was treated so much more immediately, thoroughly and frequently in the daily press that the latter remained the prime source of information, but in its visualisation. The selection of items for visual presentation, however uninformative, in itself implied that the items were important. If anyone actually took the newsreels' balance seriously, a very strange picture of the world they must have had. But in fact cinemagoers understood very well that the newsreel was a sort of magazine, full of oddities and illustrations. Not until a month before the war, when under pressure from exhibitors against "unfair competition" the Newsreel Association banned the use of newsreels for 35 mm theatrical shows at the Savoy Hotel in London, full as it was of anxious patrons waiting to see pictures of the latest preparations for war, was it fully realised by politicians that the country relied on a handful of people, guided by their own commercial interests, for its film news. Questions were asked in the House of Commons and a Cinematograph News Film (Prevention of Abuses) Bill was introduced by an Independent M.P., Sir Ernest Graham-Little.[12]

Newsreels continued the process begun by universal education and mass circulation newspapers which altered the ordinary person's conception of the world. But their potential influence in teaching people about international and political affairs, at a time when there was no mass television and foreign travel was by no means widespread even among the middle classes, and unusual for the working classes, is evident. An attempt to quantify it has been made by Nicholas Pronay in several interesting papers.[13] In the first he uses Simon Rowson's contemporary figure of 18·5 million average weekly cinema attendances in 1934, and a figure of 21 million for 1941 estimated on a basis of Rowson's earlier figures and the Board of Trade statistics, and he concludes that by 1938–9 over half the population excluding the very young saw what was on the cinema screens each week. By working out the geographical concentration of cinemas and seat prices, he further demonstrates that the vast majority of this audience was working-class. In support of the importance of the newsreel in forming their political attitudes he compares this with figures quoted for the average circulation of daily newspapers in 1938–9 at 10·48 million, the Sunday papers at 13·59 million, and the number of radio licences at 8·95 million.[14] Even allowing for multiple use of both radio and newspapers, and the fact that some papers had a circulation bigger than the average, he considers that these figures indicate the greater influence of the newsreels. But these figures deserve a little qualification. Since it is known that a large number of people visited the cinema two or three times a week during the thirties, a figure of 21 million attendances does not, in fact, mean attendance by 21 million people. It is also important not to underestimate the widespread family ritual of listening to the news, which was broadcast several times a day. And, as for the newspapers with mass circulations far bigger than the average figures given, it should be remembered that they circulated among just that working class which was in the habit of going to the pictures, but that they were read daily, and contained an amount of background information and editorial guidance which makes the kind of political item we have seen in our Movietone samples, for example, seem weak.

Moreover, the newsreels were working under difficulty, and can be said to have exercised an influence only in a negative way. As we have seen, it was of overriding importance to them, as part of the entertainment industry, to get their films on the screens quickly. This meant not falling foul of the British Board of Film Censors or, even more difficult, of any pressure group which might try to arouse the Board or the government. Complaints came from all quarters. Certain instances where newsreels failed to escape interference are well known. British Movietone film of rioting in Bombay was subjected to three cuts at the suggestion of the India Office early in the period.[15] According to *Kine Weekly*, newsreel film of Hitler supporters which included complimentary references to Hitler was raised at the L.C.C. Entertainments Committee in March 1933, and so was a specially recorded British Paramount film of a spokesman of the British Union of Fascists, said to be "expressing the hope that a forceful seizure of power would take place in England such as had taken

place in Italy and Germany.[16] Herbert Morrison, leader of the
L.C.C. and a Labour Member of Parliament, said that he had
twice called the attention of the L.C.C. to this.[17] Later in the year
the General Secretary of the Transport Workers' Union, Ernest
Bevin, speaking at Bradford, criticised a newsreel of Lord Lloyd
and condemned "propaganda which is aimed against your own
class, and I appeal to you to show resentment against such
tactics".[18] In the same month an interview in which Lloyd George
said that the Great Powers had broken their word to Germany
by not disarming as agreed was quietly deleted from a newsreel
shown at Gaumont-British theatres.[19] We have already mentioned
the delay caused by diplomatic circles over film of the rioting in
Paris in August 1934. The assassination of the King of Yugoslavia
in October 1936 gave Warwickshire County Council, already
offended by films of air and liner disasters, the chance to demand
parliamentary action, and the Home Secretary felt obliged to
see the heads of the newsreel companies and issue a Home Office
circular warning them to exercise restraint on the subject of
violence and public events. At the time of the formation of the
first National Government British Movietone had thought to
include short talks with the political leaders, but public and
official displeasure at such propaganda dissuaded them. Pressures
on *The March of Time* once it had appeared were worse, as it
required a censor's certificate. In April 1936 its issue *Geneva*
dealt with the failure of the League of Nations to check the war
started in Abyssinia by Italy. The B.B.F.C. insisted on cuts despite
the fact, maintained by Viscount Cecil of Chelwood, that everything in it was common knowledge and freely discussed in the
papers. The result was a travesty of the original film.[20] It may be
remarked that this was the time when Rotha's short Peace Film
was with difficulty shepherded past the censor in favour of
collective security. Paramount and Universal film of air raids
from Shanghai in 1937 showing scenes of the Sino-Japanese war,
which seemed horrific to a public grown used to "ghastly carnage"
being safely romanticised in stories of the 1914–18 war, caused
much public outcry, with especially virtuous cries of outrage
from Jeffrey Bernerd of Gaumont-British, which had no film of
the incidents.[21] During 1937, also, official pressure seems to have

been behind the unusually high number of very loaded items about Hore-Belisha and how he was improving terms for the ordinary soldier. Arousing enthusiasm for rearmament was difficult when the aggressive behaviour of our potential enemy was being played down. But only 20,000 men were entering the army every year against the 30,000 leaving on the expiry of their terms of service. Hence the newsreels included a large number of items maintaining that life in the army was fun, and an answer to the problem of unemployment, items clearly prompted by official request.

Two of the best known instances of interference were those over Eden's resignation in February 1938, and the Munich crisis of September 1938. By now there was growing opposition to the Government's policy of appeasement of Hitler, and Paramount prepared an item in which the Labour M.P. Clement Attlee made some remarks about Eden's resignation, which the whole country knew from the newspapers was caused by his disagreement with this policy. According to *Kine Weekly*, "within a few hours of the delivery of this reel to the exhibitors urgent orders were issued that the item must be deleted".[22] The incident is significant, for the newsreels went much further in compliance with this sort of request than the press. Again, in the *Evening Standard* Low had a cartoon on 25 February called "Would you oblige me with a match, please!" showing Chamberlain innocently sitting on a chair with a bomb underneath it, musing on Eden's portrait; "Muzzler", Mussolini with Hitler's quiff and moustache, holds the fuse and asks for a match. Low has explained :

Eden's resignation from the Chamberlain Cabinet in dis-agreement with the policy of starting new talks with Mussolini after Italy's violation of the Non-Intervention agreement in Spain implied the determination of Chamberlain to continue his efforts to buy off the dictators. Eden was not alone in foreseeing that they would use concessions to strengthen their power for even greater demands. (The composite figure of Muzzler in place of individual portraits of Mussolini and Hitler was Low's contribution to appeasement after an official protest from Berlin against his caricatures of Hitler's person).[23]

Such protests, in fact, were frequent but were never taken to heart either by the *Evening Standard* or by Low himself, whose "contribution" on this occasion was simply a private joke, as he continued with the two usual caricatures of Hitler and Mussolini forthwith. Official and unofficial protests were certainly made by the dictatorships, which had already suppressed free speech in their own countries, but were ignored here not only by Beaverbrook and Low but by a growing number of politicians, journalists, broadcasters and others with an influence on public opinion. Jonathan Lewis cites Churchill, Eden and Vansittart along with Low as public men who raised their voices in warning.[24] But there were other well-known journalists, including A. J. Cummings, himself the father of a future cartoonist, as well as Wickham Steed, both of them soon to figure in a notorious case of backdoor film gagging, although able to express themselves freely in print. Many M.P.s, too, like Stephen King-Hall and Harold Nicholson, spoke and wrote openly against fascism.

For there was no formal press censorship structure in this country before the war and although official circles might "lean" on the press there was a strong tradition of free speech within legislative bounds set by Parliament concerning libel and other, possibly archaic but still alterable, rules. If you broke these rules you might pay the penalty, but there was no question of getting prior permission to print, the essence of censorship.

But the newsreels, also, were officially free of censors. Interference, and it may be assumed that there was far more of this than has yet been traced, was exercised unofficially. It could have been ignored, as some of the press ignored it, had it not been for the willing co-operation of the film industry itself. For the explanation of this one need look no further than the original *raison d'être* of the B.B.F.C., the prospect of individual exhibitors and small· circuits having to wage individual battles with licensing authorities all over the country when all they wanted to do was to entertain people, not to enlighten them.

The cinema manager was nearest to his public. He was sensitive to what they wanted, and the first to ask the newsreels to play safe. Public opinion, informed by a growing number of politicians and commentators but not by the newsreels, took a long time to move from their initial acquiescence in, even approval of, the existence of "strong leaders" in Italy and Germany to a late realisation that oppression and aggression were going to have to be met by force. Movietone interviewed Mussolini in 1930, a historic interview according to *Kine Weekly*, which referred to him as a great man and quoted him thus, less than five years before he attacked Abyssinia: " 'Italy', he says 'will never take the initiative in promoting war'."[25] The mood of pacifism and disarmament faded slowly. The British Fascist's interview of 1933 is significant. His expressed wish for a forceful seizure of power in Britain along Italian and German lines was met by muted protests from Labour leaders but no censorship pressure seems to have been exerted, nor does it seem to have offended the public to any extent. Yet to anyone who remembers the thirties the idea of the Communist Harry Pollitt, for example, expressing a similar wish for a forceful seizure of power and the establishment of a state resembling that of Soviet Russia in this country being allowed on a public screen, or tolerated by the audience, is inconceivable. It would seem that the newsreels gauged the public's indifference to fascism, or even sympathy with it, correctly at this stage. Germany's open rearmament in 1935 was marked by news film of the ageing Bernard Shaw, enjoying a good paradox as usual, assuring us that it was the best possible guarantee of peace. But as the thirties wore on the facts of the situation as conveyed by some of the press and the radio, especially after the Munich crisis of 1938, led to a substantial body of opinion that opposed appeasement. How big, is the subject of argument. But it was not until after the completed invasion of Czechoslovakia in March 1939 that the newsreel commentators really felt safe to criticise and jeer at the dictators. Where celebrity journalists led, celebrity newsreel men like Emmett, Campbell and Sanger could only follow.

The difference was that however choleric the Low cartoons might make the Tory reader of the *Evening Standard*, for example, if he decided to cancel his subscription to the paper with a letter signed "Disgusted", there were plenty of other papers for him to buy. Papers of all shades of opinion appeared, not all of them rich and prosperous, but at least not outlawed.

But the structure of the film industry, on the other hand, was still monolithic and despite the spread of film societies, amateur film making groups and a small number of specialised minority cinemas, it remained inconveniently true that the staple feature film so loved by the public was expensive to make and depended on a safe mass market for its profit. It was not for the newsreels, which simply filled up the programmes, to rock the boat and bring into question a trade censorship system which was working so well for them. Had Beaverbrook's idea of the earlier thirties come true, whereby the proliferation of news theatres had led to minority audiences with politically diverse opinions expressed by different newsreels, a new form of political film journalism might have appeared. But the public itself was not yet ready for any fragmentation of the ritual of going to the pictures.

A few instances of pressure are related again and again. There is the oft-quoted story told by Edgar Anstey about the time he was arrested for filming during an anti-appeasement demonstration in Downing Street, film later removed from the item of *The March of Time* for which it was shot because the B.B.F.C. regarded it as hostile to a "friendly power" – Germany. It was widely believed that this was done at the behest of the Foreign Office. But perhaps the most famous incident of all took place during the Munich crisis of September 1938. On the day of Chamberlain's second visit to Hitler, Paramount interviewed three critics of the policy of appeasement, the journalists Wickham Steed and A. J. Cummings and the taxi-driver writer then enjoying something of a vogue, Herbert Hodge. The item was deleted after the newsreel had been delivered to the cinemas, and the story went that the Foreign Office had persuaded the government to get the American Embassy, where the Ambassador Joe Kennedy had previously had big film interests, to put pressure on the American headquarters of Paramount Pictures and thence back to Paramount British News. The Liberal M.P. Geoffrey Mander, in general defence of freedom of expression and with a particular interest in the cinema, raised the matter in the House of Commons. The official attitude was that the film's appearance during Chamberlain's talks with Hitler at Bad Godesberg was unfortunate. The newsreel companies themselves made no protest, it seems, being only too ready to fall in with hints from above. It is not without interest, incidentally, that Pathé Gazette dated 2 September 1938 includes 100 feet showing Daladier in London, a Trafalgar Square demonstration against Hitler and pictures of Czech troops in training followed in exactly similar deadpan vein by 80 feet of beauty queens on the west coast and a wine festival in Italy. A demonstration somehow seems less significant when it is put on the same footing as a beauty competition, as the newsreel editors well knew. But then nothing very trenchant could be expected from Pathé, who had been getting their German and Italian footage from those countries' official sources of film propaganda for several years. When questioned later a Pathé veteran apparently saw nothing strange in the fact that what was generally believed to be Pathé's own "world-wide organisation" was, even in 1938, relying on German material supplied by Ufa and Italian material supplied by Luce.[26]

Yet the film industry, many of whose members were Jewish, had good reason to know and care what was going on in Germany. Jonathan Lewis speaks[27] of a Movietone item of April 1933 about the labelling and picketing of Jewish shops in Berlin as the last traceable item shown on the persecution of the Jews until the arrival of two hundred German Jewish child refugees in December 1938. But throughout 1933 the trade press was full of news of the German censorship, and control by Goebbels as Minister of Propaganda and Enlightenment. The article by Austrian director Joe May on the new insistence on "Aryan descent" after he had escaped from Germany,[28] and the flood of refugees from Europe which now began, made conditions in Europe only too familiar. Some Manchester cinema proprietors wanted to boycott German films in the middle of 1933 but such moves were not generally supported. It was accepted that films were entertainment, and that the trade should steer clear of politics.

So the British newsreels continued to treat the events which led to the Second World War with the same bland avuncular commentary as items on beauty queens and King George VI's annual boys' camp singsong of "Underneath the Spreading Chestnut Tree". In August 1937 Pathé showed, without alarm, the launching at Trieste of Italy's largest battleship "to extend Italy's sea power from the Mediterranean to the oceans of the world", followed without comment by a jolly little number: "In the heart of Manhattan's mountains of stone and steel there's a camp for city kids on top of a skyscraper . . . and everything in the garden's lovely." In September 1937 the Nazi Party Congress at Nuremburg gets 30 feet in Pathé Sound Gazette 37/72, an item supplied by Ufa itself. In the same month Pathé Super Sound Gazette 37/74 has 52 feet supplied by Selenophone on Austria with the commentary:

> Austria's Chancellor Kurt von Schuschnigg . . . looks as if he's out hunting . . . but it's merely his way of being comfortable while watching military manoeuvres – somewhere in the mountains. . . . Austria is a very small country between several giants . . . so a periodical display of her strength doesn't make many headlines . . . but gives her a feeling of security. Anyway with plenty of good food . . . the boys say it's like a holiday.

This all seems less fun when one remembers that seven months later Hitler's troops marched into Austria and took it over. By the end of September 1937, after Mussolini's visit to Hitler in Munich which ended in the creation of the Rome-Berlin Axis, Pathé Super Sound Gazette 37/78, using 190 feet of film supplied by Ufa, was falling over backwards to be fair:

> Around these two men and the system of government they represent has been more furiously aroused feeling than about almost any other subject in the world. Pathé Gazette takes no sides in the endless discussion . . . But we feel that the facts must be faced. Behind these two figures are over 100 million people . . . who regard them as saviours of their respective countries. . . . On the one hand Italy's Duce in fifteen years of power . . . has made his people believe that at home they are marching to a new prosperity . . . and abroad Italy is rebuilding the Roman Empire. On the other hand, Germany's Fuhrer in four years has completely reorganised the life of his adopted country . . . and has somehow or other brought about "the rebirth of his people".

Later in the year Pathé has 114 feet from Luce :

> *Fighters in a foreign Land*
> Italy Honours her Dead.
> In the great square before Rome's magnificent memorial to her
> war heroes Italy remembers . . . not only those who fell in the
> Great War . . . but those who have died in more recent
> times. . . . In the grim struggle that for more than a year has
> gone on in Spain . . . the vast crowd that stands to attention
> pays homage . . . not with solemn music but with the martial
> drum beats of modern Italy.

The intervention in the Spanish Civil War was politely accepted by
Pathé, although they did not mention here those who had died
in the attack on Abyssinia. In January 1938 Pathé Super Sound
Gazette 38/1 had 61 feet from Luce showing Italians helping to
rebuild a bridge in Spain, and during the next few months
Chamberlain was conducting talks with Italy. They were to pre-
serve the Mediterranean *status quo* by an arrangement under
which Mussolini undertook to remove Italian forces from Spain
and the British Government undertook to recommend the League
of Nations Council to recognise Italy's conquest of Abyssinia. Low
on 20 April drew Chamberlain as Pontius Pilate, washing his
hands in the Mediterranean, with the victorious Roman Mussolini
standing over him. It may not have been everybody's opinion of
events, and the *Evening Standard* probably received many angry
letters. But since local authorities all over the country did not
have irrelevant powers to interfere with the content of newspapers
under the fire regulations, as they could with films, the Beaverbrook press did not consider self-censorship necessary. Indeed,
they were well aware that the Low cartoons increased their
circulation with many non-Tory readers.

So the newsreels battled on, begged by timorous exhibitors not
to offend anybody, pushed about from time to time by officials,
trying to avoid the attentions of the British Board of Film Censors.
These gentlemen were, of course, anonymous. But in 1930 the
Vice-President and senior examiner C. H. Husey died in harness
at the age of eighty-one. Without generalising too unkindly, one

wonders how relevant to the problems of the approaching war were a set of attitudes and precedents worked out under the leadership of a man born in 1849?

Was the resulting treatment of serious matters trivial or not? The question would probably have caused amazement in the thirties. Neither the newsreel companies nor their parent firms even wished to present an independent informed opinion on serious matters. And although their brushes with authority may have been annoying, they were part of the entertainment industry and did exactly what they set out to do, which was to present a light magazine about current events similar to the more popular papers, and to avoid antagonising anyone who might possibly demand that newsreels should be passed by a censor before exhibition. Editorial comment or a balanced picture of world events were somebody else's business. Charles Grinley wrote in 1937[29] that current interest events had ossified into the familiar format because of the need to avoid censorship, and any meaningful development would only be possible in a different type of film. The nearest approach to a serious newspaper with more weight in the editorial, as we shall see, was *The March of Time*, and this was to have many censorship problems of its own. But as for the newsreels, intellectuals, middle class, lower class, what Pronay amazingly calls the "guilt-ridden cognoscenti" and all, went to the pictures for the feature film and simply sat through the news as part of their money's worth, knowing better than to expect any insight into politics from it.

Yet many years later Pronay, questioning whether the newsreels of the thirties were trivial and ignored the vital issues of the day, cites 112 political items out of a total of 778 Paramount items in 1933 as quantitative indication to the contrary.[30] Tony Aldgate, also, after careful and interesting analysis comes to a similar conclusion as to the coverage of serious matters "on a purely quantitative level at least".[31] But surely our own examination of British Movietone political items has shown that it is the qualitative level that counts. The coverage of important issues on a trivial level remains trivial, however often you do it. Everything we know about the newsreels, their overmastering need to keep out of the power of the B.B.F.C. – their unimportance in the

structure of the film industry, the contempt in which they were
held by renters and the touchiness of official circles – indicates
that they had no option but to treat serious matters, if they
mentioned them at all, in as brief and bland a manner as
possible. What we have been able to see of their actual presentation of political events suggests that they were limited in scope,
monotonous, timid and superficial in their selection of political
news items and, until the general change of mood shortly before
war actually broke out, any influence they may have had was
used to pretend that all was well.

The element of controversy, the presentation of both sides with
an air of objectivity, came from another source, and was one of
the most successful of all instances in which film was used by
people from outside the entertainment structure. A complete
contrast to the newsreels, this was a regular series of short films
on current events called *The March of Time*. It was founded in
America by Louis de Rochemont in 1934 and the first number,
which came out in U.S.A. in February 1935, included an item
on Britain. It began to be shown in this country in the autumn
of 1935. It was backed by Henry Luce's *Time-Life-Fortune*
publishing group. The weekly illustrated news magazine *Time*, now
nearly ten years old and with a circulation of half a million, had
pioneered a condensed, racy and far from bland style of journalism.
Louis's younger brother Richard de Rochemont came over to
England to take charge of European operations for *The March
of Time* and a British company was registered in August 1936,
with a capital of £5,000. The ubiquitous John Grierson seems
to have acted in a consultative capacity, and the documentary
director Harry Watt shot their first numbers in Britain. But
Grierson's other, more favoured, protégé, Edgar Anstey, who had
worked in New York as one of their foreign editors,[32] was
appointed as their British film director after he had finished work
on the two outstanding British documentaries *Housing Problems*
and *Enough to Eat*. His first two items were on malnutrition in
Britain as it affected recruits to the army, and the poor state of
the British coal industry.

This was news of a different kind, shown in the cinemas but
with financial and journalistic resources which the newsreels could

not match. A world-wide network, research facilities, a large staff, a library and years of experience in journalism were backed up by money. Advertised as a "new invention", *The March of Time* was a monthly two-reeler, at first covering up to half a dozen topics but gradually reducing this until finally each issue dealt with one subject only. The items dealt not so much with isolated events as with some topic of current importance, treated in depth like a feature article in a newspaper. The aim was to give an "inside story", and the editors went out of their way to seek controversial questions. Their international coverage was wide and, although they too, like the newsreels, had their lighter moments, on the whole whether at home or abroad they plunged into the areas where trouble was at its worst. Perhaps the most famous issues were *Geneva*, about the League and the international situation in No. 8 of the first year; *Rehearsal for War*, about American and European involvement in the Spanish Civil War in No. 6 of the third year; and *Inside Nazi Germany* in No. 12 of the same year, all of which had censorship troubles in this country.

It was a new technique, freely mixing news and library shots with frank reconstructions of events played either by the people concerned, re-enacting their own participation, or by actors. In addition there were speeches and interviews in which the interviewer figured only as a questioning voice, or at best perhaps the back of a head and shoulder. According to Harry Watt[33] what the company wanted was a large number of shots of and around the subject, which were cut by their key editorial staff in U.S.A. to illustrate a commentary also composed in the American headquarters. Put together as a quick-fire succession of short close- and mid-shots, with a loud, insistent, stirring commentary backed heavily by music and loaded with emotive words, the style gave a tremendous feeling of getting inside some subject of momentous importance. The journalistic tone was like that of *Time* itself, deliberately seeking social and political areas of disagreement. Jay Leyda pays tribute to skilled cutter Jack Bradford, and later to Lothar Wolff, an experienced editor trained in Europe.[34] Louis de Rochemont himself was a brilliant editor in the journalist's sense of the word.

As in the newsreels the burden lay on the commentary, and

visuals were cut as illustrations to this to a far greater extent than in the newsreels. Another point of difference was that they contained reconstruction which abandoned the pretence of actuality. Reconstruction had always been present in topical films, whether in the early faked news films or with the unacknowledged use of stock shots to build up a story not adequately covered by new filming. But not until now had it been openly said that truth is best served by using all the techniques possible to film. This was a businesslike acceptance of the fact that even factual film can only be an illusion of reality, since the very act of filming implies selection and also, in so far as the participants are aware that you are filming them, you alter the very situation you wish to record. The more compilation and reconstruction are used, of course, the more selection is involved and the more is a viewpoint implied. *The March of Time* was very careful to assume an air of neutrality. But the *Time* and *Life* interests did, as was well known, have a very definite political position. Anstey has defended *The March of Time* editorial viewpoint on the grounds that it was frequently liberal both on social issues and in international politics.[35] It may have been so. But this is not the same as saying the films were impartial, and to others the claimed neutrality has seemed more apparent than real. Leyda writes :

> The possibilities for distortion were unlimited and full advantage was often taken of this opportunity, to give the almost invariably conservative point of view an appearance of "objectivity".[36]

Graham Greene, also, described them as often politically partisan.[37] With a strong editorial approach determined in America whatever filmed material landed in the cutting room, the actual filming was the very opposite of true investigative journalism, and the vigorous lead given by the selection of material made sure that, whilst the appearance of showing both sides gave the maximum opportunity to stir things up, it was a canny and ambiguous "objectivity" which usually led to only one conclusion. The heavy commentary was perhaps too emphatic for British audiences to find truly persuasive.

The series was a sensational success, however. Even by May

1936, 800 cinemas in the U.K. were taking it, and by March the following year the figure had risen to 1,300. Although it was easy to laugh at the style and to parody it, with its marching music and final declamatory "TIME ! . . . MARCHES ON !" and the terrible falseness of the amateur actors, its contrast to the boredom of the newsreels was greatly appreciated, especially among the more thoughtful, whether they agreed with it or not. It was greeted as the first adult newsreel. Graham Greene admired it, as did John Grierson and the documentary film makers. The *Life and Letters Today* set who had inherited the mantle of *Close Up*, and who disliked the Grierson school of documentary intensely, joined them in praise of *The March of Time*. Robert Herring, writing in *Life and Letters* in the winter of 1935–6, contrasted it not so much with the newsreel as with our own documentary films and said that it made "our own use of living material seem silly".[38] And Alistair Cooke wrote in *Sight and Sound* that the G.P.O. films "suddenly appear as conscientious dramatisers of platitudes".[39]

In 1937 *The March of Time* in America received a Special Academy Award from the American Academy of Motion Picture Arts and Sciences "for its significance to motion pictures, and for having revolutionised one of the most important branches of the industry – the newsreel".[40] In fact its effect on newsreels was less noticeable than on documentary, upon which it did have an important influence.

There were several attempts to emulate it over here. The most important was a series called *Point of View*. This series was made by Spectator Short Films, formed about the beginning of 1938 under the chairmanship of advertising agency head Fleetwood C. Pritchard, with film man G. F. Noxon as managing director and George Noble as cameraman. The moving spirit, however, was Ivan Scott from British Movietone. They sought to distinguish their films from documentary, which they regarded as propaganda. By 1939 the board included J. S. Fairfax-Jones of Denning Films and the Everyman Cinema in Hampstead, and they had a small studio and two more cameramen. They had a genuine intention to present both sides of social and political questions affecting this country, and titles included *Should This*

Country Grow More Food?, *Should Our Transport be Unified?*, *Do People Prefer the Dole to Work?*; other topics were State-run hospitals, how many milkmen there should be, and voting. The first six issues came out in 1939,[41] but although the firm lingered on for a couple of years the war made it impossible to continue.

Paramount seems to have made an abortive attempt at a similar series produced at Olympic Kine Labs in 1938 and 1939, called *Inside Goods*. Frank A. Richardson, R. E. Jeffrey and Eric Barrow, the latter from the National Film Agency of Manchester, made a couple of films in a *Voice of Europe* series in 1939 which were handled by G.F.D., a company which was also interested in breaking into short documentary subjects at the time. In 1939, just at the outbreak of war, an outsider called British Fine Arts Pictures using a professional cameraman, T. A. Glover, began a *Passing Show* series, *The World in Our Time*, with three two-reelers, *Britain's Life Line*, *In Silent Service* and *The Colonial Question*, which received good reviews. And that durable commercial maker of interest and magazine films, Andrew Buchanan, also tried his hand. In an interview with Arthur Vesselo for the British Film Institute he announced a new series called *Close Up*, "to project the life of the nation fairly and squarely in all its aspects". He claimed that issues on the theatre and medicine in Britain were already prepared, but denied that it was to be a British *March of Time* as it would be all newly shot material and, most characteristically, non-political.[42] None of these units, however, could rival the enormous resources of the *March of Time* and besides, however good they might or might not have been, the outbreak of war made it a bad time to launch a commercial series.

The person who was perhaps most influenced by it, however, was John Grierson himself. This is discussed more fully in *Documentary and Educational Films of the 1930s*. Here it is sufficient to note that his imagination was captured by this new extension of the information film. Never an aesthete, he was not deterred by the fact that this powerful new tool was basically verbal journalism :

March of Time does what the other news records have failed to do. It gets behind the news, observes the factors of influence, and gives a perspective to events . . . the thought of a revitalised citizenship and of a democracy at long last in contact with itself.[43]

He was, in time, to have a similar series of his own in Canada. Meanwhile it was not without influence on the documentary film makers who followed him in this country, although possibly its direct influence has been somewhat overestimated. It is hard to imagine that the cool, meticulous films of Arthur Elton, Edgar Anstey, John Taylor and Basil Wright were influenced by the loud, emphatic, breathless style or tendentious spirit of the American films, which always required some journalistic angle, a scandal, an abuse or a recent headline to act as anchor. Dealing with topical issues, racily described as photo-reporting, *The March of Time* made a virtue of opening up controversy. The British films had social rather than topical significance and aimed to provoke thought rather than to coast in on a wave of argument. What were the other characteristics of *The March of Time*? Synchronised interviews predated it in this country, even the direct recording of non-celebrities, apart from newsreel items like our exasperated little puddin' maker, having been used in Elton's *Workers and Jobs* and the Anstey-Elton *Housing Problems* before the arrival of *The March of Time*. The use of newsreel film, and the re-enactment of newsworthy events, were two *March of Time* specialities not favoured by the British documentarists. The one important thing which was adopted by some of them and to some extent changed their direction was the use of commentary to bear much of the burden of the message, with visuals downgraded to illustrations. To a lesser extent the reconstruction of typical events and behaviour was also introduced. But the style, quiet and casual with an unseen observer, is markedly different from the staged appearance and fragmented structure of the American films. The latter, bursting into the cinema from outside, had all the advantages of financial backing and wide theatrical distribution, which made it a marked contrast to the documentary movement. But both were part of the same growing social awareness and a sharper and more self-conscious relating of film to the problems of the world around them, in which both played a changing and developing part.

Before we leave the question of news, the arrival of television and its challenge to the comfortable existing structure of theatrical near-monopoly should not be forgotten. The origins of television in this country were closely connected with the cinema, both in rivalry and in co-operation, and especially in regard to its potential for the transmission of news items. Rediffusion in news theatres was for a time widely believed to be one of its greatest possible applications, and its development during the thirties was assisted by two of the biggest exhibition circuits. In time, of course, the existence of television was to kill the cinema newsreel, but at this date it was still seen as an ally.

John Logie Baird, the British television inventor, gave his first demonstration to a group of scientists in 1926. His system was a mechanical one, and although the idea was already some fifty years old he was the first person to get it working effectively. In 1928 he invited members of the B.B.C. to a demonstration and, despite the secretiveness which was a marked feature of his character, he seems to have begun experimental transmissions in co-operation with the B.B.C. in 1929. The system was an alternation of sound and picture, and the first public show was a piano recital by Cyril Smith.[44] In August 1929 the Baird Television Development Company demonstrated a sound film of George Robey, and it seems clear that Baird himself was already thinking in terms of "tele-talkie" for rediffusion to cinemas.

By March 1930 the B.B.C. could transmit sound and picture at the same time, and they began a programme service. Baird commissioned the manufacture of 1,000 television sets with tiny screens, familiarly called "tin Lizzies". He broadcast from a studio in Long Acre, London, and according to Robert Herring, who owned one of the sets, from here he sent out regular shows and a weekly typewritten programme.[45] The first play was put out on 14 July 1930, and showed only one person at a time; a chequered board was moved across the picture at every cut so as to avoid blurring the picture. Baird also demonstrated the first run of television in a public place of entertainment at the Coliseum

Theatre, where people in the building were televised.[46] From 28 July to 9 August 1930 it was a regular part of the programme here, on a screen 3 by 6 feet square, and the first talking film to be televised in public was sent from Long Acre, a mile away, on 8 August. Two big circuits were already said to be interested in the system as a news medium, and the first daylight, or outside, broadcast was the Epsom races of 1931.[47]

In January 1931 the record company H.M.V. entered the field with demonstrations of another system at Imperial College and at the Physical and Optical Society Exhibition, televising films. Baird claimed that they were infringing his 1925 patents. But H.M.V. and Columbia, finding the market for records inactive, got together in 1931–2 and formed E.M.I., which linked up later with Marconi. The Marconi-E.M.I. Television Company was formed in May 1934. Their system used 120 lines as against Baird's 30, and instead of his mechanical system they used a cathode ray tube system, suggested as far back as 1911 by Campbell Swinton, which gave much clearer results.

In February 1932 Gaumont-British Picture Corporation stepped in and acquired most of Baird's £300,000 company. The line-up was beginning, and in future Baird's directors were to include Maurice Ostrer and Sydney Moseley. Broadcasting House was opened in May 1932 and the B.B.C. made their resources available to Baird, who repeatedly promised demonstrations of higher definition, lobbying against the other systems meanwhile and pointing out that his own was all British, and carefully maintaining his secrecy all the time. From August 1932 the B.B.C. gave weekly half-hour television broadcasts and Baird marketed a home television receiver with a 4 by 9 inch screen.

However, in September 1933 the B.B.C. announced the end of its exclusive agreement with Baird, and shares in his company dropped heavily. A. G. D. West from the B.B.C. was now in charge of technical and development work. They had home cathode-ray receivers with screens up to eight inches square, and were experimenting with transmission from the South Tower of the Crystal Palace, with a 30–40-mile radius. At the same time Baird was working on an eight by six foot large screen for theatres, and West was reported to have said that in his view home television would never seriously compete with the cinema. Many others also thought of television at this time mostly in relation to its installation in cinemas for newsreels and the simultaneous transmission of sports events.

In May 1934 the government set up the Television Committee of Inquiry, which consisted largely of B.B.C. and G.P.O. engineers, under the former Postmaster General, Lord Selsdon. This was to decide whether they should enter the field of television and, if so, which system to adopt and how to set up a public service for individual receivers.

The Selsdon Report was published early in 1935. It recommended that television should be made a B.B.C. monopoly, that definition and wavelength should be fixed but that the Baird and Marconi-E.M.I. systems of transmission should be used alternately. This was later arranged on alternate weeks, with two sets of equipment, the secrets of his system being jealously guarded by Baird himself. Both systems would be receivable on any type of receiver, and the Report contemplated a picture of 8 by 5 inches, the sets costing some £50–80. Programmes would be for three hours a day, and London would be able to receive them first. It was intended to have direct transmission from the studio, and also from sports events. The transmission of films was also contemplated, although there were still technical difficulties about this. The large screen issue was left open.

Shortly afterwards the Postmaster General announced that Alexandra Palace in London was to be the first television station. Reconstruction of the south-east wing was begun in November 1935. The Selsdon Committee had hoped for a picture of at least 240 lines, and E.M.I. actually planned one of 405 lines. Baird's little receiving sets were now obsolete, but he was kept in the system largely because his mechanical method had an efficient film scanner. He persisted in his secrecy and his optimistic forecasts. Alexandra Palace was ready by the autumn of 1936, when sets were for sale at the show at Radiolympia for about £100. The service was inaugurated in November 1936, transmitting with a radius of 20 miles. A two-reel film produced by Dallas Bower and Gerald Cock in 1936 called *Television Comes to London* and shot by two cameramen previously known chiefly for scenic films, Leslie Barbrook and James Carr, with commentary written by Cecil Lewis and delivered by Leslie Mitchell, shows how Alexandra Palace was converted and the service set up, ending with Adèle Dixon performing a rather brashly concocted song about television.

Two ladylike announcers were engaged, Elizabeth Cowell and Jasmine Bligh, and programmes at first were from 9 to 10.30 in the evening. The first producer was Cecil Madden, who produced plays under great difficulties as they had only one monitor and could not cut, but only mix, which took eight seconds to do.

According to Madden there were 300 sets in use in the country when transmissions began,[48] although *Kine Weekly*, a year later, possibly unwilling to face facts, put it at only 100.[49] One way or another, 1937 was a year of remarkable progress. The number of sets increased so much that it was estimated that there were some 2,000 of them by the end of the year,[50] a figure born out by Madden's estimate of 3,000 at the outbreak of war. The price of sets fell, and at the 1938 Radiolympia they were available at from £22 upwards from a dozen companies. The range within which broadcasts could be received also increased. *Kine Weekly* said in April 1939, with clear unfriendliness, that reception was still only possible in a 40-mile radius,[51] but this is certainly an underestimate. The first high definition outside broadcast, the Coronation in 1937, is said to have been received over 63 miles away, and in the summer of 1938 it was claimed that Bournemouth at 104 miles, Ipswich at 72 miles and Northampton at 66 miles were getting pictures. There were programmes now every afternoon except Sunday, as well as in the evening. By 1938 the B.B.C. were regularly doing outside broadcasts of such events as Wimbledon and the Boat Race from a mobile radio-transmission van.[52] Meanwhile, in February 1937, very soon after the beginning of the service, it was decided to settle for the Marconi-E.M.I. system exclusively. Baird had to vacate his part of the studio, although he was able to continue selling sets.

From the beginning there were two chief difficulties, the extension of the radius and the technical problems of incorporating the use of film into television. What *Kine Weekly* called extraneous shots,[53] in other words location shots, flashbacks and all the variety which made film structure so much more flexible than the theatre, required the incorporation of film. As for the range of reception, in May 1939 the G.P.O. was reported to be about to extend reception to the provinces. In the commercial cinema, the relation of film to television was full of problems from the start. Even during the preliminary discussions the film industry resented the fact that they were not asked for their views, and there were even signs of suspicion of the G.P.O. Film Unit's close official connections. As it turned out, strangely enough neither Grierson, Tallents nor the Unit showed any interest in television at this time, or even when the B.B.C. was able to televise newsreels and features. The film industry feared that feature films on television would compete with the cinema, and discussions between the Exhibitors' Association and the Renters' Society about how soon new films should be made available to the B.B.C. took place very early. A proposed new standard contract discussed in November 1935 had a clause forbidding the lending of a film until three months after its last booking. The C.E.A. and newsreel executives also held discussions in December 1935, as the B.B.C. was expected to use newsreels right away. They were to form their own film unit under Gerald Cock, Director of Television, and also to film news events and "can" them for viewing hours. At first there was co-operation from the newsreel companies but the exhibitors gradually became hostile to this. Then in March 1938 the B.B.C. announced the formation of a film unit under Barbrook. The slight uneasiness felt by the film trade at the beginning hardened as television became an established fact. In March 1938 the first feature film was televised.[54] The industry did not know which to worry about most, lending the B.B.C. films which would compete with the cinemas, or not lending them films, which might lead them to go into production themselves.

As 1938 wore on the renters' attitude stiffened and they opposed letting the B.B.C. show anything but old films. The issue finally crystallised in 1939, when the K.R.S. Report of April mentioned that it had refused to supply the B.B.C. with copies of current films. There was a brief flurry in May when it appeared that Cock had an understanding with Will Hays's organisation in

America enabling the B.B.C. to show American shorts and short features, and even had an agreement for supply from the major companies. There was an outcry in the trade and K.R.S. representations persuaded the American producers to reconsider the plan. At the same time both the C.E.A. and the K.R.S. proposed that the two newsreels who supplied the B.B.C. at that time should stop doing so. In the event, the outbreak of war put an end to all the arguments, for B.B.C. television immediately closed down.

On the whole there was considerable complacency about the possibility of television driving people out of the cinema. Many people were sure that the family outing, the personal visit to a theatre and the superior technical resources of the film would be decisive. At first, *Kine Weekly* wrote:

. . . a rational survey of its possibilities apparently proves that it no more concerns our business than the streamlining of trains, or a revolution in South America.[55]

And Richard Ford even wrote in *Sight and Sound* as late as 1939, when the sales of home sets were growing, that

. . . there is no ground for supposing that home television will have a continuously serious effect on cinema attendance.[56]

Much more interesting in contemporary eyes was the possibility of using television for large-screen diffusion in the cinemas themselves. Public rediffusion seemed to offer openings to the trade, particularly in the sphere of news and the newsreel theatre, and occupied their minds when the antics of the B.B.C. were merely a petty annoyance. Baird himself also seems to have thought this was the more important application of television.

There were two systems, Baird and Scophony, and experimental work early in the thirties was followed by keen competition from 1936 until the outbreak of war. Scophony Ltd was founded in 1930 by Solomon Sagall, a businessman of Russian origin, to perfect a large-screen picture which could be televised to cinemas. The lab work was by G. W. Walton. In June 1936 it was sufficiently advanced for the company to become public and the authorised capital to be increased from £140,000 to £300,000. The managing director was Sagall; the chairman was the investment banker Sir Maurice Bonham-Carter; and other directors included W. S. Verrells of the radio manufacturers E. K. Cole, Walton himself and, significantly, Oscar Deutsch of Odeon Theatres. In August 1936 they demonstrated a picture of about $4\frac{1}{2}$ feet,[57] and had hopes of getting a 12-foot picture[58] which would pick up B.B.C. broadcasts and televise news events and eventually films. Meanwhile Baird's company, acquired by Gaumont-British in 1932, demonstrated on a screen 8 by $6\frac{1}{2}$ feet at the Dominion Theatre in December 1936. Gaumont-British announced they would have three shows a day at the Dominion and later at other cinemas, and as they could not at that time get B.B.C. programmes they would televise from a temporary studio in the building. The two systems were radically different, the one using an optical-mechanical scanner and the other a purely electronic method, magnifying the image of a small cathode-ray tube.

In 1938 competition started in earnest. In June Baird and Gaumont-British had a successful private show of the Derby on an 8-foot screen at the Tatler News Theatre, Charing Cross Road, and announced that they were ready to market the system. At the same time Scophony showed the Derby to 600 people at the Kensington department store Derry and Toms, on a 6-foot screen, and announced that they were about to install the system at the Baker Street Monseigneur news theatre. Both used the B.B.C. transmission via Alexandra Palace. When Baird further announced in November that they would show the Lord Mayor's Show and the Armistice ceremony at the Tatler the thing seemed to be under way, but two problems began to emerge. One was the question of copyright and payment, since it was not possible to charge admission for commercial exploitation of public ceremonies; and the other was the realisation that filling a theatre was going to depend on the time of day. Big fights, taking place in the evening and open to the purchase of transmission rights, became the most successful subjects, indeed virtually the only ones, for this type of exploitation during the following year.

Early in 1939 the fourteen-round Boon-Danahar fight at Harringay Stadium in February was a great success on both systems. Baird and Gaumont-British secured the rights from the promoters and showed it to paying audiences at both the Marble Arch Pavilion and the Charing Cross Road Tatler News Theatre. Scophony, also getting it through the B.B.C. but showing it only to an invited audience, demonstrated it on an 8 by 6 foot screen at the Monseigneur news theatre. The audiences, consisting of fight fans, were satisfactory and according to R. H. Cricks both systems got good technical results. The future seemed bright.

Isidore Ostrer of Gaumont-British seemed convinced that television would eventually replace the second feature in cinemas. He was said to be going ahead with 15 by 25 foot screens in seventy or eighty London cinemas, at a cost of £1,000 each, but felt that the B.B.C.'s monopoly was an obstacle and wanted up to twelve more stations to be set up.[59] But while exhibitors were still looking at television with some favour the K.R.S., not unnaturally, was firmly against it. Moreover the copyright side of it posed real problems. Journalists, actors, boxers, musicians and others saw themselves being exploited, the B.B.C. was concerned, and radio and television manufacturers were not pleased at the turn things were taking. In April 1939 the Boat Race showed the difficulties involved in a government-subsidised service being exploited by private commercial firms, in an event which was not promoted for money, and not even on private property. The Football Association, long used to the squabbles over film rights, announced firmly that the Cup Final at Wembley on 29 April was to be televised but not rediffused.[60] The Baird system secured the Burman-Farr fight of 13 April for showing to an audience paying from 2s 6d to a guinea at the Marble Arch Pavilion and the Tatler, while this time Scophony, hoping to show it at the Marble Arch Monseigneur, found the promoter's price too high.

It is significant that on this occasion the Marble Arch Pavilion was not full. It seems reasonable to suppose that once they lost novelty value, and certainly as the number of home sets increased, these shows would have become less popular. The cost of installing a big screen was now put at between £1,250 and £2,000 and some doubts were beginning to be expressed. All the same E.M.I.

entered the field with a third system, with a 15-foot screen still in the experimental stage.[61] The Derby was shown in May on all three systems, as well as the Armstrong-Roderick fight and the Trooping of the Colour in June. True, there were signs that Baird was in financial trouble. But there was still considerable interest just before the war and Ostrer announced plans to equip at least fifty cinemas immediately. Deutsch, who was in favour of sponsored television, planned to put Scophony into some of the Odeons. Not only E.M.I. but also Philips were continuing to experiment. All this, however, was to stop abruptly when war broke out.

4 British Movietone introduces a sports section in 1937.

5 "I say, Amy, do you mind if I tell the chaps at school it was a man I went up with?" asks Amy Johnson's young passenger (*Dual Control*, 1932).

6 *Across the Sahara*, 1933.

3

Films of Travel and Exploration

Travel films, which observe places and people rather than events, range all the way from the short commercial travelogue seen in the cinemas to the film made during a scientific expedition or voyage of exploration. All, of course, could also be described as educational or interest films, and jungle pictures or the big polar and mountaineering films were *par excellence* the films which middle-class parents liked their children to see, although this preference was not always shared by the children.

The most basic, of course, was the simple scenic of part of the home country, usually chosen for picturesque qualities in the old Hepworth tradition. Simplest of all to make, they were a temptation to many a good cameraman for they could be tackled without financial backing, and the names of professional cameramen were associated with them from time to time, as well as local advertising and commercial production companies. Some were also made for promotion, especially of seaside resorts, either for the local authority itself or for the railway companies, who sponsored a large number of films at this time. Later the Travel and Industrial Development Association sponsored a similar type of film, some of them connected with the documentary movement and described in the companion to this volume. The National Trust for Places of Historic Interest or Natural Beauty, also, co-operated with International Productions in a series of travel or interest films called *The Nation's Heritage*, intended for theatrical distribution as well as non-theatrical. Some of these simple films were beautiful, even if the type did lend itself to clichés. They were greatly improved when a sound-track with music and commentary became possible, if these were used with subtlety. But it is the American James Fitzpatrick who is credited with the first use of a voice-over narration and the British cinemas were, in fact, full of foreign travel films, especially the American *Traveltalks* and *Magic Carpet* series. The most prolific English operator in the field was Horace Shepherd, who also dominated the crude interest film. Born in 1892 and educated at Birmingham University, he was originally a composer and musical director. By chance we find him in 1934, credited with an irritating and unsuitable background of ballet music trolling endlessly on, ignoring cutting and subject matter alike, in a film extolling the virtues of Blackpool called *England's Playground*. Shepherd discovered the secret of getting his films registered as quota. He formed his own company, most inappropriately called Inspiration Films, and for the next few years poured out one long series after another of routine shorts, all used as quota by big American companies : *Romance of England, Romantic England, Symphonies in Stone, Old Homesteads of England* and *Old English Taverns*, and *This England*. Rumour has it that he relied heavily on post cards of these scenes, yet these films were assured of a market by their Br. registration.

Films about other countries were even less often made by British film makers. Leslie Barbrook made one in 1934 called *Shqypnia*, a two-reeler registered by Zenifilms about life in Albania and its traditional folk music. This, however, over-lapped the interest or even documentary categories and was frequently used as an educational film. The cameramen S. R. Bonnett and V. Veevers shot material for a Gaumont-British series called *Secrets of India* in 1934 when they were in the East to film the Mount Everest flight. But the most successful British purveyor of foreign travel films was C. E. Hodges, whose many titles fill pages in the educational catalogues. He, like Visual Education, seems to have been a producer who edited acquired stock and the films, competently made, were clearly aimed at the educational market as well as the supporting slot in the cinemas. They were, however, marred by the unsuitable and hackneyed classical musical backing and the interminable commentary. Other professionals or semi-professionals occasionally put out a foreign travel film but on the whole there were very few, and they tended to rely on some special attraction. Carveth Wells's *Russia Today*, for example, a four-reeler of 1934 handled by Zenifilms, was apparently little more than a protracted travelogue of Moscow and through the Caucasus to Mount Ararat, but depended hopefully on what *Kine Weekly* described as "the attractiveness of the title to the intelligentsia".[1]

Travel films had suffered especially badly from the quota legislation of 1928, which had made no provision for the obligatory renting and showing of a proportion of British short films. Most English travel films were given an E registration by the Board of Trade, which meant that although British they did not qualify as quota footage. At the same time, strangely enough, many of the promotional short films sent here by the Dominion governments were given registration as British films available for quota. By 1935 the percentage of British shorts shown in the cinemas had fallen to about 4 per cent and there was a strong movement to get a shorts quota included in the new Act due in 1938. This was duly achieved and at the end of the period there was a noticeable increase in the production of shorts of all kinds, including travelogues and scenics. Kinograph was one firm which provided distribution to a number of individuals who made independent films that fell in this class. Towards the end of the decade colour was also beginning to be used in them. Rayant Wonderfilms, using Dufay, claimed that slow motion in colour was used for the first time in their 1938 film *St. Moritz*. World Window was formed in 1938 by Hans Nieter, the film director and editor who had made the political film *Thunder in the Air*, together with the Kellers and British feature cameraman Jack Cardiff. F. W. Keller had already made three short Technicolor films in Italy for United Artists in 1938, accompanied by music but no commentary and perhaps better described as impressions or exercises in the use of colour than as travel films.[2] World Window, a British company, made one-reel travel films in 1938 and 1939 for United Artists in Technicolor, which included *Jerusalem*, *Petra*, *River Thames*, *Arabian Bazaar* and *Ruins of Palmyra and Baalbek*.

However, it is no use looking to the normal cinema travelogue for anything interesting or original. Two films made with other than the usual commercial motives were *My Song Goes Forth* and *Across the Sahara*. The first was the work of the veteran Joseph Best, who had been working on the fringes of publicity, education and feature film production since 1906, and who was later to take the opportunity of the new quota arrangements in 1938 to dispose of his two-reelers *Historic Cities of India*, *Temple Cities of the East* and *Capital Cities of India*, all used for quota by Columbia. But much more interesting was his film about Africa. This, registered by Best himself in October 1936 as a five-reeler called *Africa Looks Up*, was later trade shown by Ambassador in March 1937 under the new title of *My Song Goes Forth*.[3]

This strange film seems to have started life as a job lot of old, not very good, footage about South Africa which showed the disparity between the life of the white and black populations, whether it had originally been meant to do this or not. At a time when the self-respect and self-awareness of black people were being encouraged by growing movements, especially in America, France and Africa, this film showed only too clearly how little had been done for the black population in South Africa. The black singer from America Paul Robeson, already well known here for his role in *Sanders of the River*, sang and talked in a prologue and an epilogue. We see him, kindly and relaxed, moistening his full lower lip from time to time. In a static mid shot against a plain backing he stands in formal lounge suit and sings of banishing hate and fear:

Oh star of love, the kindly light . . .

We cut back to the initial basic shot of a road in an African township, then once more to Robeson sitting at a table facing us, reading carefully into a microphone about "my people", and how they long for a better life.

You may think they are primitive – such an idea this film will certainly help to correct.

With dignity and patience, he tries to correct our wrong ideas. There is

> no difference whatever between the capacity of Africans and Europeans. This may surprise some of you.

He sings another verse to "round off this introduction", as he explains, and we plunge into the film. This turns out to be a straight old-fashioned travel film with a continuous and deadpan commentary, illustrative visuals, out-of-date clock wipes and incongruous Western music accompanying tribal dances. But the dispassionate statement that "the natives" earn £1 down the gold mines every week to the whites' £8, the sight of the Durban beaches thronged with whites only, the negro slums, the poor whites (disapprovingly, "they have a low mentality, and can do only manual work") leads us to the question

> and what has he done for the native? He has put him to work.

The introduction of a few better educated black people, the headmaster, the solicitor's clerk and some better housing, the passing remark that "miscegenation" is illegal, combine to give a picture of Africa somewhat different from that of the usual travelogue or, indeed, feature film. Best himself was in no way part of the documentary movement. But despite a rather patronising tone in the commentary the facts have an emphasis of their own which is enough to explain Robeson's involvement in this odd production. And so,

> Africa marches on . . .

and we end with a little more song.

Summers's film of 1933, *Across the Sahara*, was another one slightly off the beaten track. Walter Summers was a professional director of entertainment films who was on location in North Africa in early 1932 for a B.I.P. film called *Timbuctoo*. Unlike the travellers and explorers who made amateur films on their expeditions, here was a professional film maker, a Fellow of the

Royal Geographical Society, who found himself in exciting surroundings. He was a strange man obsessed with questions of
courage and danger, who several times attempted to put a little
bit more thought than usual into his films. He decided now to
take advantage of the circumstances to make a personal chronicle
of the journey, which dragged on and on, to the concern of the
people back at the studio. *Across the Sahara* was a two-reeler
shot, put together and narrated by "Captain Summers". It shows
in tinted film some wild and magnificent scenery and a unique
view of the legendary desert town. Alas for poor Summers,
however, things rarely went well for him. He could expect little
encouragement from a firm like B.I.P., and indeed they even
reduced his animal and travel footage for the main film into a
feeble comedy cobbled together back at Elstree. The photography
of *Across the Sahara* did not, in fact, live up to his intentions, but
surely it must have been some saboteur who decided on a brisk
musical accompaniment from beginning to end from *Casse-
noisette* and *L'Arlésienne?*

Perhaps Summers was trying, on this North African trip, to
emulate those professional camera adventurers who had long been
peripheral members of the film industry. Frank Hurley, Cherry
Kearton, M. A. Wetherell and others had for years been making
their highly individual productions, reappearing in this country
from the wilds every so often with a fresh batch of film. Their
travels were not expeditions of scientific research or exploration,
but camera expeditions. The world was still wide open to the
traveller slightly more daring than the rest and jungle pictures,
or even dramatic stories from the exotic unknown made with
native casts, could be made to finance the way of life they liked.
Thus a few endearing loners were able to survive, not quite film
men but men using films, books, lectures and articles to pay for
their wanderings. Their films broke no records and were surpassed by those of the big American operators like Frank Buck
with his *Bring 'em Back Alive* in 1932 and the Martin Johnsons
with films like *Simba*, made in 1924–8, and *Congorilla* in 1929–
32. Nevertheless they succeeded in using the structure of the
commercial cinema for their own purposes.

One of the first was Frank Hurley, an Australian who had

been Shackleton's cinematographer on the two Antarctic expeditions on *Endurance* in 1914–18 and *Quest* in 1921–2. The result had been two true expedition films, *South* in 1919 and *Southward on the "Quest"* in 1922. He had also made travel and dramatic films in Papua, New Guinea, and the six-reel film *Pearls and Savages* made in the twenties was cut and synchronised in the thirties and used as a two-reel educational film, *The Head Hunters of Papua*. Hurley joined the Australian film company Cinesound in the early thirties, and a Cinesound film handled here by Wardour in 1931 was *Oasis*, showing a car tour through South Australia and beyond it to the north by a youngish, bright and perky-looking Hurley with his companions. It includes some wild, flat, bleak and unfamiliar scenery, and rare shots of the customs and habits of the aborigines, including the application of ritual decoration and some ceremonial dancing. Unfortunately the approach is that of the old scenic or travel film with no attempt to edit life into this unique material or widen it to a true anthropological record.

Cherry Kearton was of an even earlier vintage, having previously been, with his brother Richard, a nature photographer and a pioneer of still pictures of wild animals in their natural habitat. He had taken up cinematography in the early years of the century and among other things had filmed Theodore Roosevelt hunting big game in Africa. Later, his wife Ada travelled and worked with him. In 1929 they put out *Tembi*, said to be a fully-fledged feature film with "native cast". Far away Ben R. Hart and St. John L. Clowes, travelling and filming in the north of Norway in 1928, had also filmed a drama with local players. Kearton did not pretend to be a gifted film-maker, and had his material edited for him by the firm of Brunel and Montagu. *Tembi* was, of course, a silent film and by mid-1929 this was already a commercial disadvantage. The Hart and Clowes film with its Lapp cast, *Frozen Fate*, was also put on the market in 1929 and suffered from the same handicap. The next year Kearton made the transition to sound film with *Dassan*, a full-length film about penguins on Dassan island, again edited by Brunel and Montagu. Brunel tells how a camera fault had led to a blurring of the image every three feet or so, and how they had to doctor the film by ingenious cutting to make the most of the truncated shots.[4] A shorter film, *Mototo*, in 1932 was followed after a lapse by a full-length compilation in 1935 of all his films, *Big Game of Life*, rather grandly described by *Life and Letters Today* as a "screen autobiography" but less kindly by others as a rehash. Later he published a book of autobiography, *Cherry Kearton's Travels*, from which it is very clear that the films, along with still photographs, books, lectures, articles and later wireless talks, were simply a means to the end of living the life of a hunter. He was, as he said, quite simply a *shikari* with a camera instead of a gun: "I was the first man to put Central Africa and its varied inhabitants on the cinema screen." A conventional man writing sincerely and unselfconsciously in the clichés of the time, he accepted without cynicism the contemporary attitudes of white superiority and "kindly" amusement about the natives. He had the real enthusiasm of generations of imperial Englishmen for Africa as jungle and bush, inhabited by the animals he loved and studied. As with all our film travellers he was more interested in the animals than in man. Africa was his ground, animal pictures were his meal ticket.

Another veteran of travellers' tales from Africa was M. A. Wetherell, best known for a twenties film on the life of Livingstone which had years of non-theatrical distribution on the strength of its historical and religious content and African background. In August 1930 he was said to be returning from the Congo after a year's absence with footage for a sequel about Stanley. When this finally appeared as *Stanley*, towards the end of 1933, it was handled as a short by M-G-M, a company notorious for its ruthless disregard for quality in British quota footage, and it proved after all to be merely a film tracing Stanley's route in Africa. Meanwhile, in 1931 *Livingstone* had been reissued in sound "with many new scenes", in fact only a slightly updated version of the old film with a narrative sound track replacing the titles, but no dialogue. In 1933 he tried, perhaps a little desperately, a short story film called *Hearts of Oak*, which included parts of the 1924 war reconstruction film *Zeebrugge*. Three more African productions seem to have been his last, *Wanderlust* and a series of twelve single-reelers called *The Land of Zinj* in 1933, and *Safari* in 1937.

This last film of a safari near Kilimanjaro was described in the *Monthly Film Bulletin*, which had already been critical of *The Land of Zinj*, as slow, with photography "only competent" and a commentary which was "irritatingly facetious and often indistinct". Wetherell died in 1939, at 55. He seems to have had only a sketchy idea of the real possibilities of the film and to have been unable to meet the greater demands of the sound film.

F. W. Ratcliffe Holmes, like Kearton, was a traveller and writer rather than a film maker and had started in the silent days, but continued to work for many more years. As with Kearton, African animal pictures were his speciality, although he did also make a news film compilation called *Peace on the Western Front*. His first sound film was a production called *Interviewing Wild Animals* in 1930, with what was described as his own humorous commentary, recorded on Vocalion disc. *Never Never Land*, like the other put out as six one-reelers, was shown here the following year and was actually an Australian film using actors, as well as some interesting material about the tribal customs of the aborigines hung on a crude travel story, again with a facetious commentary delivered by Holmes himself. *On Safari* and *Way of the Wild*, shown in 1932 and 1934 respectively, were further films of Africa.

Major C. Court Treatt and his wife Stella, our modest British embodiment of the Martin and Osa Johnson spirit, had filmed their *Cape to Cairo* journey by car along an all-British route, with dumps of food and spares prepared along the way, between September 1924 and the beginning of 1926. They had been accompanied by the cinematographer T. A. Glover, always referred to as "Mr Glover", Fred Law, the special correspondent of the *Daily Express*, Stella's young brother Errol Hinds and "C.T.'s" servant, Julius. "His old native servant, Julius, was devoted to him . . .".[5] The Major, Westminster School and then Flying Corps during the war, was Cornish and over six feet tall, with moustache and pipe, and appeared the perfect English hero, strong yet gentle, to his petite and pretty young wife. The expedition was financed by C.T. himself and the film was an important part of the enterprise, for which a diary was kept by Stella. She saw things with the eyes of a romantic:

I saw myself as two separate beings – the one, modern, gay, and laughter-loving, liking the things that civilization gives, enjoying dancing, pretty frocks, and care-free companions; the other, serious and eager to do something worth while, longing to get down to the simple and big things of life, even to suffer, and play a losing game through to the end if necessary.[6]

After the film had been made C.T. and Errol were anxious to go to the Southern Sudan to film big game. ". . . and, since a 'story' is, in these days, essential as a peg upon which to hang an 'animal' picture, I had been busy on a 'plot' as my contribution to our equipment,"[7] wrote the good wife. The three of them returned to Africa alone this time, with more lavish equipment, including a collapsible darkroom. Unlike other camera adventurers they were not short of money. They devised a film which begins with what must surely be one of the most unconvincing attacks by a lion ever filmed. The dead jungle woman's baby is adopted by a nomadic tribe. After many adventures including a drought and a jungle fire the adopted son, now grown up, falls in love and becomes sheik of the tribe.

This story was published as a most romantic novel, *Stampede*, at about the same time as Stella Court Treatt's own account of the filming, which she called *Sudan Sand*. The film itself was edited at Welwyn studios by John Orton, and put out by British Instructional as a full-length feature, also called *Stampede*, in January 1930. *Close Up*, leaping to conclusions about its "modicum of story",[8] rightly pointed out that this was simply an excuse for the film. The major, foolhardily ignoring the fact that his wife had admitted as much in her book, was stung to reply:

Mr. Hinds, my wife and myself went out to Africa in order to make a film written to a definite story and photographed to a definite scenario of that story. . . . My wife wrote the story on our combined knowledge of the life and customs of this tribe. The fact that it was taken to a careful scenario ensures that the film has tempo, continuity, and rhythm and provides material for proper montage. At the same time it is a real story of the real things which have happened and are still happening in the lives of the tribe and the incidents are lived rather than acted by the people to whom these things have actually happened.[9]

This is hard to assess as the version of the film in the National Film Archive includes less than half the original footage. But this does give a clear impression that two very different tribes have been used as though one, for the purposes of the story. It is fair to question whether Stella really did know the life and customs of the people or simply imposed her own Western idea of a romantic story on the unfamiliar setting and people. The film created little interest despite a notice in *Close Up* and has since been completely overlooked, perhaps unfairly, for in spite of these reservations it was enterprising and not all bad. However, it was too late for a silent film to succeed. Had British Instructional had any faith in it they might have helped by providing a sound-track. Like B.I.P.'s cavalier treatment of Summers's material from Timbuctoo, British Instructional's failure to promote the Court Treatts was characteristic of the lack of interest shown by British companies in anything unusual. The story, after all, was hardly more unlikely than those of their own normal studio-made features. Later in the year, economically trying to get the most out of their jungle material in a more conventional way, they put out *Stark Nature*, a full-length feature with a Klangfilm sound track. Directed this time by Arthur Woods and with studio camerawork by Jack Parker, it added introductory shots of the Court Treatts and Hinds in a nightclub conversation leading by way of flashback to a jungle film about animals and a warlike tribe. This found some use as an educational film. In 1934 *Cape to Cairo* was also reissued by Famous Films in a shorter version, with a sound-track giving commentary and music.

In general the camera adventurers who felt the urge to travel and used films as a way of paying for it were well advised to stick to animal pictures. When they did turn their attention to people the results were too obviously sham. Better the modest Mr Glover of the Court Treatts' first expedition who later, with his wife, made a trans-Africa trek film of his own, *Cities of the*

Desert of 1934. When the great Flaherty had gone into the wilds to film the life of the Eskimo Nanook he had started along the same path, but his interest was in man himself, and his method was to watch and film until the material began to take on a meaning of its own, his guiding hand seeming to interpret it only. How different, then, the Court Treatts with their prepared story and their quick dash to Africa and back.

Thus our adventurers enjoyed the romance of travel but failed to understand the people among whom they moved. There were others, some of them anthropologists, who travelled less because they were footloose than because they had a serious interest they wished to study at first hand, and took along a cine camera as one of their recording tools. Indeed, the camera was becoming a normal part of many holidaymakers' luggage during the thirties. The middle classes were going further afield for their holidays, and the home movie fan with his cutting and splicing outfit and his title-making kit could make quite an elaborate record, perhaps even in colour, of the family in faraway places, the friends they made, and their own choice of picturesque views. Similar in their amateur technique were the records of many an official or unofficial expedition, by everyone from the solo lady traveller to the expert backed by a scholarly institution. Many such films must have mouldered, shrunk and decomposed in private cupboards since then, although the National Film Archive and other institutions have fortunately kept many.

Olive Murray Chapman was perhaps on the borderline between expedition and holiday. Mrs Chapman, a widow who looks young and jolly in the shots of her, bundled up in furs, taken by the local people, travelled north of the Arctic Circle between March and May 1931, and although it was hardly exploration her trip by reindeer sledge across Norwegian, Swedish and Finnish Lapland with only a Lapp guide to help her was certainly very enterprising tourism. Indeed it seems to have surprised and alarmed both friends at home and the agents and contacts through whom she arranged it. According to the book she published later, *Across Lapland with Sledge and Reindeer*, her purpose was to study the life of the Lapps in winter and get a pictorial record of the people, their dress, homes and customs in sketches, photo-

7 Australian aborigine
ritual to drive away
evil spirits (*Oasis*,
1931).

8 Tiger hunting in
India in the
mid-thirties: an
amateur film of a
hunting party
accompanied by
many servants.

9 *Kamet Conquered*,
1932.

graphs and film. She relied on a large supply of Woolworth beads to secure their co-operation, but the film is evidence that she had little gift for putting people at ease before her camera. *Across Lapland*, a one-reel film shown late in 1933 and also a longer version covering the same ground, *Winter with the Lapps*, were handled in standard and substandard versions by Zenifilms and Visual Education and although surviving copies are silent it seems possible that some form of disc commentary may have been available. As usual, the film had E registration and was therefore not useful for quota despite her hope that it would be shown in the cinemas. The introduction states that it was shot, edited and "described" by her, and the technique is basic, with simple head-on shots, mostly long shots and with the odd shudder rather than camera movement; it records the loading up of dogs and reindeer, the herding of wild reindeer, a simple tent, the boiling of snow to get water, the wooden houses, children playing in the school yard and a wedding party assembling. A blizzard exists perforce only as the title "after struggling for hours against a blizzard". There is little detail, and the continuity is simply that of the progress of her journey. Schoolchildren run wildly around the school yard until assembled for a group "photograph", whereupon a plea for movement must have been made, for they suddenly start to bob vigorously and pointlessly up and down. Yet her book is packed with the information which her unskilful film technique fails to get into these very routine film "snapshots". She continued in later years to write travel books and, though no film maker she was certainly one of the determined English lady travellers of legend.

Lions and tigers were an obvious thrill for the amateur cameraman. Many a hunting party must have included someone with his camera at the ready. Two short 16mm fragments by James Corbett, *Tigers in the Stream* and *Tiger Hunting in North India*, are representative of the hunting films of the mid-thirties. The first is smudgy and badly exposed, but shows tigers beneath the tree in which the cameraman is sitting. The second, more interesting, shows a large party of tough empire builders in their long khaki clothes and sola topis, the ladies sensibly shod, accompanied by their many Indian servants fetching and carrying.

They advance over stepping-stones and climb into machans. Several tigers, heavy and limp in death, their gleaming coats as yet undimmed, are lugged by the leg on to the backs of waiting elephants. Even a bear is caught. Elephants cross the stream, flapping and swishing, ridden by members of the hunting party. Indian servants crowd round a dead tiger, squatting on the ground in the traditional victory photograph. The film, lacking the glorious colours and exciting sounds, gives a surprisingly morbid and dreamlike impression of the hunt, a dance of death emphasising its central purpose in a rather unexpected way. Another amateur film of about 1938 shows a hunt in Nepal by Lieutenant-Colonel and the Hon. Mrs Bailey, while *Shooting a Lion in Serengeti Plains* by J. D. S. Pendlebury was followed by an article in *Sight and Sound* written by the hunter and affectionately called *Simba, the Lion*.[10]

More scholarly work was also being done. One example is the work of an enterprising young ethnographer and anthropologist from Cambridge, Dr Ethel Lindgren. She led an expedition which included, as well as herself, a local guide and translator, and a Norwegian who acted as photographer. They went to north-western Manchuria on three occasions to study a little-known and apparently disappearing tribe, the Reindeer-Tungus, unique in the use they made of the reindeer. Going first in June 1929, she delivered a paper on her work "photographing types, recording their language, and attempting to reconstruct the elements of an older social organization which they have already all but lost" to the Royal Geographical Society in April 1930. In the autumn and winter of 1931, and then in the spring and summer of 1932, the party went again, this time taking film equipment. Four 400-foot reels of 16 mm black and white film were the result. She spoke at the Royal Central Asian Society in February 1935, showing films and slides from the second and third journeys. As the Chairman, Sir Denison Ross, said in his opening remarks, nowadays it was not enough to write a book when you came home from your travels, but "every traveller seems to take a ciné-camera as part of his equipment". In further expeditions in Swedish Lapland in 1934, 1937 and 1938, Dr Lindgren herself shot three more reels of film, as well as some colour film incorporated in another reel by Colonel Andrew Croft, a colleague on the expedition.

This is only one example of what seems to have been a fairly widespread and growing practice. Such films varied very much in their quality, and also in the nature of the audience for whom they were intended, whether it was the family, schools, academic groups, people of like interests or even the commercial cinemas. But in all cases, unlike the films of the camera adventurers, they were the by-products of travel and not its occasion. Major Sherriff, Vice-Consul at Kashgar in Chinese Turkestan in 1927–9, went on botanical expeditions to Eastern Bhutan and Tibet in the thirties and forties, bringing back some 17,000 feet of film, 10,000 of it in colour. Ralph Cutler, who worked for the Tanganyikan Education Department, made films like *At School in Tanganyika* in about 1936, showing a day in the life of a local schoolboy, and a charming, amateur, fuzzy, silent one-reel film with titles and elementary camera technique, disarmingly called *A Day in the Life of a Msukuma Called Kinga Mkono Bara* and ending with a title straight from the cinema travelogue: "The moon is full and the dances will go on – *au revoir*, Kanga." It is nevertheless a serious and fascinating look at life in an African village in the thirties. Rather different was *Caves of Perigord*, a nicely made short film which achieved registration in October 1939, on the caves near Les Eyzies. Excellent film of the Palaeolithic paintings and carvings shot by Caroline Byng Lucas was dressed up with music, cloudscapes and some rather self-conscious thoughts delivered in sepulchral tones about the origins of man. *Sailing 1,000 Miles up the River Amazon*, a two-reel film made in 1936 by educational film maker Blake Dalrymple, was different again, the outcome of a journey which combined adventurous travel with an educational offshoot.

Film records of official expeditions also became increasingly frequent during the thirties. 10,000 silent unedited feet of film lie in the Film Archive under the title *Across Bolivia*, made for the Bolivian Government in 1930 by an Englishman, Julian Duguid, whose book about this jungle expedition bears the much more characteristically romantic name *Green Hell*. The young Consul-General for Bolivia in London was commissioned to explore a strip of jungle in the eastern part of the country, having nine months in which to follow the route of the sixteenth-century explorer Nuflo de Chavez and decide if the district had agricultural possibilities. He took Duguid, whose highly picturesque and readable account includes a photograph of the author, showing him as another traditionally moustached Englishman. The party also included Alejandro Siemel, known as Tiger Man, and J. C. Bee-Mason. The latter, a dedicated apiarist, had wandered into films in 1911 with a bee film. He had afterwards become a commercial cinematographer, going with Shackleton on his last journey and both Commander Worsley's and the Oxford expeditions to the Arctic, and later acting as a war cameraman. Bald, and wearing metal-rimmed glasses, he had a meek appearance not at all in keeping with his tough and outspoken personality. The book gives us a vivid impression of a man in search of a scoop. On Duguid's encountering a snake, ' "My camera !" cried Bee-Mason. Bee-Mason is a roaring mono-maniac on the question of his camera,'[11] wrote Duguid. When they discovered some man-eating piranha fish :

> "Let's prove the piranha theory for ourselves" he suggested.
> "Going for a swim ?" I asked.
> Bee-Mason fingered his beloved camera.
> "It would be a unique picture" he said.[12]

Or later :

> . . . Bee-Mason said :
> "Thank God for wanderlust", quite quietly.
> A bright colour burned in his cheeks, and he swept his arm in an upward semi-circle that embraced the river, the trees and the sky. For the first time Urrio and I realised the consuming fire that underlay the sober, priest-like shell.[13]

More successful than this mass of undigested material was a film made of the British Arctic Air Route Expedition of 1930-1, *Northern Lights*. H. G. Watkins, Gino to his friends, as a brilliant and persuasive undergraduate believed to have leadership qualities was allowed to take an expedition to Spitzbergen in 1927 when he was still at Cambridge. After this he was able to get financial backing from the rayon magnate Stephen Courtauld, with patronage from the Royal Geographical Society and collaboration from official sources, for the First British Arctic Air Route Expedition of 1930–1. Its aim was to anticipate the long flight from Europe to North America over the Atlantic by finding a suitable alternative route of shorter hops by way of Iceland, Greenland and Baffin Island. Watkins gathered a band of like-minded friends including John Rymill, L. R. Wager of the Himalayan climbs, Courtauld's son Augustine and an ambitious, good-looking friend from Cambridge, F. Spencer Chapman, who was painfully conscious of his own lack of the money and contacts that gave the others such confidence. They sailed, in Shackleton's old ship *Quest*, in July 1930. News films of the expedition showed planes landing and taking off on the snow-fields. Courtauld, who was already dabbling in films through his interest in the colour process Raycol, joined the board of Associated Talking Pictures at Ealing in March 1931 and also formed Albion Film Syndicate, which was responsible for the film of the expedition brought back by the very young Flight-Lieutenant H. I. Cozens, called *Northern Lights*. Registered in May 1932 as a short film eligible for quota, it was shown with a synchronised commentary at the Plaza cinema in London. Chapman wrote a book about the expedition, also called *Northern Lights*, which came out in 1932.

The expedition, which according to Chapman cost at least £13,000 and gained Gino the Gold Medal of the Royal Geographical Society, brought back survey details, but some members of the expedition later quoted by Chapman's biographer[14] complained of slack leadership. Several members of the expedition were allowed to sleep with local servant girls in the communal accommodation, to the annoyance of some of the others, according to this account. Even worse because of its implications of careless planning, Augustine Courtauld, who was left alone to take readings at a weather station, was temporarily lost. The news that the relief party sent to bring him back according to plan had failed to locate him appeared in the papers at

home as "millionaire's son lost", and was also relayed by the
expedition to his family. The Courtaulds promptly sent a Junkers
plane flown by a Swedish aviator, "not because our judgement
had been doubted", as Spencer Chapman claimed in his book,
"but because those at home had been anxious to do anything
that could possibly help us". Augustine was found only with some
difficulty, incarcerated under the ice and snow, almost out of food
and completely out of fuel after his five months' isolation. He
emerged dramatically, bearded and stiff, like a good-natured bear
and later wrote his own modest, restrained and generous account
of this disturbing experience.[15]

The expedition left Greenland in August 1931. Once at home
Gino was at a loose end and tried to raise money for an Antarctic
expedition. Not surprisingly he failed, despite starry-eyed support
from many hero-worshippers. However, in July, with Rymill
as well as Spencer Chapman, he decided to return to the Arctic
for further surveys, again with encouragement from the Royal
Geographical Society. Chapman's book on the earlier junket came
out in October, but by this time things had already gone wrong
with the new one. Gino, who had written a brief introduction to
the book, seems to have been a young man driven to excel. He
had earlier learnt the Eskimo technique of rolling the kayak or
canoe, a way of righting it, if it turned over in the water, by a
manoeuvre of the paddle. Not many Eskimos, we hear, were able
to roll the kayak by the hand alone, but Gino was said to have
mastered even this. However, one short month after he left
England this second time his kayak was found floating upside
down, and his body was never recovered. Letters to the papers
praised his charm and vision and spoke of the love of his companions. However, the expedition carried on without undue
disturbance under the steadying leadership of Rymill, to return
in the spring of 1933. Augustine Courtauld wrote in an Introduction to Chapman's next book, *Watkin's Last Expedition* in
1934: "Whether the Northern Air-Route will ever come into
being is a difficult question to answer."[16] Film brought back from
this expedition, excellent in quality but impersonal, also lies
unedited in the Film Archive.

In all these books there is little mention of films or filming.

Although the first expedition was filmed because Courtauld was interested it is clear from subsequent voyages and books that Spencer Chapman was not, although footage of this expedition exists under the title *Greenland Rymill 1933*. Rymill went on to survey the west coast and islands of the Falklands Dependency in 1934–7, leaving another great mass of silent unedited film under the name of *The British Graham Land Expedition* in the Archive. Again, he recorded, he did not edit. Chapman, after unsuccessfully trying to join a mountaineering expedition, went as personal assistant to the Political Officer in Sikkim, Sir Basil Gould, when the latter led the diplomatic mission invited to Lhasa in the summer of 1936 and remaining there until February 1937. This important visit opened up diplomatic relations with Tibet, hitherto hidden and secret. In an article by Chapman, *Tibetan Horizon*,[17] in which he referred to himself as a naturalist and photographer, he said that he had been able to take advantage of the rare opportunity to record this legendary and unknown country and to film such things as festivals and sacred dances, sending his film down to Calcutta for development. He had taken a Bell and Howell camera with a turret head fitted with 2-inch and 6-inch lenses, and was said to have come back with 3,000 feet of 16 mm silent film, 6,000 feet of Kodachrome 16 mm silent and 13,000 feet of 35 mm silent film, including sequences of the Dalai Lama and the Devil Dances at the Potala. A further weighty book by him, *Lhasa: the Holy City*, published in 1938, was impressively illustrated with a magnificent collection of photographs and contained much detailed information about the natural history of Tibet, but made no mention of film making. Yet a reel of silent Kodachrome film shot by Chapman and put together for Gould to show as an illustrated lecture, which includes excellent shots of the Potala, Tibetan trumpets, the town, ceremonies and processions and close shots of Buddhist dignitaries, suggests that his evident talent as a still photographer might well have extended to cinematography had he felt any interest in it. However, this was virtually the end of his life as a traveller, apart from service in Burma during the war, and it is clear that film as such had no charms for him.

The true exploration film already had a considerable past,

especially in polar exploration. Like many other silent films, some of these began to reappear with added sound tracks. Hurley's *Endurance* was issued by Gaumont-British and W. & F. in 1933, sub-titled "The Story of a Glorious Failure". It was substantially a re-edited version of the two Shackleton films of 1919 and 1922 with a synchronised lecture as previously given in person by Commander Worsley, Captain of the *Endurance* in 1914 and *Quest* in 1921. A rather bad musical score was added, and additional film is credited to Sir Hubert Wilkins. The expedition is introducd by a prologue in which Worsley, showing the film at home to a small boy, starts telling him what it is about. Herbert Ponting's *Great White Silence*, too, the film of Scott's last expedition in 1910–13, had a new lease of life in a re-edited sound version put out in 1933 by New Era. Considerably shorter than the 1924 film, *90° South*, as it was now called, had a Fidelytone sound-track. A short title tells us it is "the authentic synchronised film record of the last expedition of the great polar explorer Capt. R. F. Scott, R.N., C.V.O.". There is a short introduction by Vice-Admiral Evans, who as Lieutenant Evans had been second-in-command of the expedition, and who now stands in dinner jacket in front of a badly creased curtain and introduces us to the balding, dark-moustached figure "whom we always called Pont". The latter then also delivers a commentary similar to the lecture that he had previously given in person to the silent version, accompanied this time by music written by Sir Walford Davies. An even shorter version was issued by International Cinematograph in 1936, after Ponting's death in 1935, as *The Story of Captain Scott*. As is so often the case with these films, thanks to the excellent technical quality of the photography the magnificence of the material shines through the somewhat uninspired presentation. It is sad that after many years of wrangling over rights to the films and stills Ponting seems to have died, at 65, a poor, lonely and embittered man.[18]

Two other pioneering explorer-cameramen were Captain J. B. L. Noel and Frank Smythe, both connected with Himalayan rather than polar expeditions, and therefore both climbers themselves. Both were technical perfectionists like Ponting. Even so, their early efforts received from their mountaineering colleagues even less appreciation than the amused tolerance which was accorded the weird activity known as "ponting".

Himalayan exploration occupied broadly the place in the twenties and thirties that polar exploration held earlier. The first exploratory Everest expedition in 1921 was not filmed. But the second, or first climbing expedition of 1922, which reached within 2,000 feet of the summit, was filmed by Noel. Born in 1890, he had been bewitched by Everest ever since he was a young man in the Indian Army before the First World War. The 29,000 foot peak, shrouded in secrecy by the Tibetan and Nepalese authorities, shared the mysterious appeal which the Himalayas had for many a young Englishman during the Raj, in love as they were with a romantic image of India. *Climbing Mount Everest*, a five-reel film of late 1922, was silent but had a musical accompaniment devised out of the Tibetan folk tunes collected by Dr T. H. Somervell during the expedition. The latter had been sent by the Everest Committee of the Royal Geographical Society and the Alpine Club, who had appointed Noel as photographer; even so he sensed considerable opposition to his presence. On this occasion Mallory, Norton and Somervell reached about 27,000 feet,[19] and Noel's four cameras were taken up as far as 23,000 feet. Noel showed the film himself for ten weeks at the Philharmonic Hall in London. Next came the second climbing expedition, the fatal one of 1924 during which Mallory and Irvine were killed, which is said to have reached 27,880 feet.[20] Noel's full-length film of this, shown late in 1924, was *The Epic of Everest*. But this time he was more ambitious, aiming at more than a mere day-to-day chronicle of the expedition, and seeking to express his increasingly mystical feeling about the mountain as Goddess Mother of the World. His technical arrangements were much more elaborate. There was a base photographic party under Arthur Pereira at Darjeeling, where Noel actually bought land and put up a special building, and he had brought out improved equipment, including a Newman-Sinclair camera specially adapted to withstand the cold. He intended to fall back on telephotography when the climbers were too high for him.

"The longest distance picture I actually got was that of Mallory and Irvine at 26,000 feet at two miles range," he wrote. However,

". . . some members of the Organizing Committee and even some members of the Expedition itself seemed rather to resent the presence of the cinematograph."[21]

There seems to have been a feeling that he was an outsider who was capitalising on their exertions. In fact no one could have been more devoted to the cause of the expedition than the tall, lanky Noel, inspired by his dreams. Mallory, however, seems to have gradually relaxed his attitude and from 27,000 feet wrote to Noel, who was in Camp 3 at 21,000 feet at the time, telling him to look out for him and Irvine on the summit ridge on the following morning. Noel trained his camera on the ridge three miles away, but the tragic result of the attempt on the summit left him only with the famous shot of the blankets arranged on the snow in the shape of a cross, the pre-arranged sign of disaster. Noel's film aroused great interest at home and was followed in 1927 by his book, *Through Tibet to Everest*.

There were no more attempts on Everest for nine years after this, and meanwhile many changes had taken place. The sound film had arrived and, whilst attaching a cinematographer to an expedition had become a more elaborate and expensive affair, it had also become much more acceptable and even necessary. German expeditions up the 28,150-foot Kanchenjunga in 1929 and 1931 led by Dr Paul Bauer failed, but a four-nation attempt on the part of the Germans, Austrians, Swiss and British and led by Dyrenfurth in 1930, in which Frank Smythe took part and acted as the *Times* correspondent, resulted in a German film, *Excelsior*, in 1931, with an English-version commentary recorded on Fidelytone by L. S. Amery. The party took a large Debrie cine camera with various telephoto lenses, three Kinamo cine cameras which took 100-foot spools and could be loaded in daylight, and 60,000 feet of standard film. Together with other photographic equipment and supplies, for all these expeditions also took a large number of still photographs, the load was so great that they needed fifty extra porters to carry it. In 1931 a British Himalayan expedition of six climbers, including Eric Shipton, climbed Kamet to its full 25,000 feet, and was filmed by Smythe. The five-reel film *Kamet Conquered*, shown in 1932 with a Visatone commentary, was distributed by Smythe himself.

As seen at the first show it was what Basil Wright, writing in the first issue of *Cinema Quarterly*, called a "somewhat lecture-tour version" and the trade showed little interest. Wright wrote: "The subject was good; so was the photography. All that was needed was construction."[22]

There was some indignation in the correspondence columns of *The Times* at the lack of interest shown in the film. After this it was re-edited, synchronised and shown at the Polytechnic. Even so it failed to get a commercial booking at an ordinary cinema.[23] For non-theatrical purposes, however, it was afterwards handled by Visual Education in standard and substandard silent versions and a 16 mm sound version.

Smythe also wrote a book about the climb called *Kamet Conquered* which included an Appendix describing the filming. He had Kodak panchromatic stock, with red filters from Ilford, and used 15,000 feet of film. He took two cameras with him, a Bell & Howell Eymo with fixed focus 6-inch telephoto lens, which was clockwork and took 24 frames a second on 100-foot reels, but which broke down; and a de Vry taking 16 frames a second, also on 100-foot reels. He was able to take the Eymo to the summit. He remarks on the difficulties of working and carrying heavy loads at such altitudes without masks, which were not used on the expedition, and indeed the achievement of making a film under such conditions was considerable.

The film in the National Film Archive, apparently the improved version, starts with a dark screen and a voice proclaiming that we, the audience, are wondering why men do such things as climb mountains. "It is for Adventure." Then follow the titles, and a voice quoting James Elroy Flecker. The usual travel shots and foothill sequences around Ranikhet are seen, and the recruiting of Sherpas, a cook and two Gurkhas. We set out to the sound of the *Pastoral Symphony* and with hearty British approval of these excellent chaps. As we near Kamet the organ joins the sound-track. The gorges of the upper Ganges, its source, wild flowers, remote villages, rocky torrents and the endless vistas of mountains, and of course our excellent fellows, are all beautifully filmed. We see sixty Bhutia porters and thirty yaks being taken on. A base camp is made in the snow. Headaches and sleeplessness, we are told, follow at Camp 2. As we near Camp 4 at 22,000 feet, Tchaikovsky takes over and once we pass Camp 5, at 23,000 feet, movement gets slower and more painful. "Something kept us going, and I believe that something was the unconquerable spirit of man." The film finishes at the summit and, not for the last time, British cameraderie insists that the Sirdar should be the first man to set foot on it.

Evidently considerable effort had been made to give the film drama and shape. But the film technique is as unsophisticated as the philosophical approach, and the fine photography and composition cannot conceal that the film is put together by a traveller, not a film maker. The camera lingers on a flower or a vista which appeals to the traveller because of its rarity, but may well spoil the pace of the film. As Basil Wright wrote : ". . . what a FILM it might have been."[24] Sadly, Smythe's book shows that in seeking a reason for the disappointing reception it received he was quite unaware of what Wright meant when he pointed out that a film needed construction. Instead, he took refuge in a belief that audiences had a morbid appetite for disaster. He ended his Appendix bitterly : "The public has been so soaked in sensational make-believe that the unvarnished truth is no longer anything but boring."[25] In his disappointment he blamed the public instead of realising his own lack of a demanding professional skill, the ability to hold the interest of an audience.

After 1932 or thereabouts the Tibetan Government was willing to consider further attempts on Everest. There was renewed interest, and to take advantage of this a rehash of the 1924 material was issued as *The Tragedy of Everest.* In January 1933 the Ruttledge Everest Expedition, also sponsored by the Everest Committee of the Royal Geographical Society and the Alpine Club, left England. It was led by Hugh Ruttledge, but at 48 he was too old for the summit and Noel, now 42, was also too old to be taken as cameraman. Cine cameras, however, were taken by Ruttledge, E. O. Shebbeare and Wyn Harris. Smythe, fresh from Kamet, was in the party which also included Eric Shipton, L. R. Wager and others. In May the first assault on the peak by Wyn Harris and "Waggers" failed, and in June the second by Smythe and Shipton, during which Smythe spent a night alone at 27,400 feet.[26] The film they brought back was made into a second, but this time substandard, film called *Climbing Mount Everest*, cinematography credited to Wyn Harris and commentary to Smythe, both of whom had reached 28,100 feet.[27] Bad weather and inadequate equipment led to a film which, though made with courage and determination was said to be technically poor and of little interest. Different versions of it, in different lengths and with or without synchronised commentary, seem to have appeared. One was shown at the London Polytechnic, and one was handled non-theatrically by Western Electric. A book, *The Challenge of Everest*, was written by G. J. Cons as teaching notes to accompany the film when it was used in schools. There were further British attempts under Ruttledge in 1936, of which a 16 mm film partly in Kodachrome was made by Smythe,[28] and an R.G.S. expedition in 1938 was filmed by P. R. Oliver. But by then attention had been diverted to the Houston-Everest Expedition, and a totally different way of conquering the highest peak in the world.

Wings over Everest was an expensive commercial film made by Gaumont-British of the flights over Everest in 1933 by the Houston-Everest Expedition. In some ways it was the most ambitious British expeditionary film of the thirties, different in every way to the polar and climbing films.

Flight films struck a contemporary note. The Schneider Trophy had been won outright by Britain in 1931 and record flights were being made one after another. The Mollisons, Amy Johnson and Jim Mollison, who both broke the air record to Cape Town in 1932, were popular figures whose romance added to their appeal and they made an odd little film for B.I.P. in that year, a two-reeler called *Dual Control*. Once again written and devised by the unconventional Walter Summers, it was described by *Kine Weekly*, as "naive comedy-information" and shows the famous pair stunting and showing off their biplanes to interested youngsters. Aerial photography of, and from, the planes by James Wilson includes shots from a camera slung low as the plane comes in to land on the long grass of a field. Jim's strangled and refined stutter contrasts with Amy's awkward manner which changes to taut and practical efficiency when she is flying. ("I say, Amy, do you mind if I tell the chaps at school it was a man I went up with?" asks her joy-riding schoolboy passenger). A coda, with Jim beside his new plane expressing patriotic hopes for the future, ends with "England yet shall stand".

But this is by the way. Air transport provided the cinema with a new form of the old phantom ride. The aviator Sir Alan Cobham, who had made eight one-reelers for Gaumont-British in 1928 under the general title of *Round Africa with Cobham*, combined a genuine expeditionary purpose with professional film making in the production of *With Cobham to Kivu* in 1932. Like Watkins's expedition to find an Arctic air route it had a serious aim, to find seaplane bases up the Nile Valley and promote this form of air travel. He used a professional Gaumont cameraman, S. R. Bonnett, and apparently made a successful film. Writing in *Cinema Quarterly* Forsyth Hardy called it a pioneer documentary, which had not been properly appreciated:

> But the film is more than a pictorial record of a voyage of discovery. For the first time it seems, the aerial camera is given a large and long opportunity to show what it can do; and this aerial travelogue is a remarkable revelation of the startling effects in panoramic geography which it may obtain. . . . S. R. Bonnett, who was responsible for the photography, has achieved some outstanding and occasionally magnificent work. The film has been effectively edited, appropriate close-ups being inserted between the panoramic shots, and the commentary is informative and never stupidly facetious.[29]

The following year two more flight films appeared. Paul Rotha's important film for Shell-Mex and Imperial Airways, *Contact*, was part of the documentary movement and is described in the companion volume. Begun in October 1932, it showed a flight to Karachi and after many difficulties and disappointments was finally seen in August 1933. Meanwhile in 1933 a flight on the Imperial Airways route from Croydon to Capetown was filmed by F. Roy Tuckett as *Wings over Africa*. Tuckett produced and handled it himself and registered it in May 1933, but Gaumont-British had a 16 mm version and the narration was by their commentator R. E. Jeffrey. *Air Ways to Cape Town*, produced by Richard Wainwright with the co-operation of Imperial Airways, was yet another film on the same subject.

The purpose of the Everest flight of 1933 was to demonstrate the use of aerial photography in the collection of data for map-making. Under the highest official and geographical auspices preparations had begun in March 1932. Lady Houston, who had earlier sponsored the Schneider Trophy, was approached in September for financial backing, which she gave lavishly, and from then on it was called the Houston-Mount Everest Expedition. Lucy Houston, a plump and large-spirited, rich and eccentric lady with both the flair and the taste for lots of publicity, was accorded the dedication of the official book about the flight as a "great protagonist of aviation, whose imperial spirit and generosity enabled success to be attained". A long list of acknowledgements included the Royal Geographical Society, the India Office, the Viceroy of India and the High Commissioner for India, as well as the Air Ministry, the War Office and many, many others. The expedition was prepared and later described by Air-Commodore P. F. M. Fellowes, L. V. Stewart Blacker, Colonel P. T. Etherton and Squadron Leader the Marquess of Douglas and Clydesdale. The film rights were contracted to Gaumont-British, and the latter decided to use sound recording on location and make the film in style. It was a new and expensive approach. Geoffrey Barkas, who had already shown a talent for actuality and location filming, was sent as director with a unit of seven and kit which filled a two-ton lorry, including 80,000 feet of negative. Three Gaumont-British cameramen, the same Sidney Bonnett who had worked with Cobham and who later stayed with Barkas on some location feature films, and news cameramen Arthur L. Fisher and V. Veevers were accompanied by two sound men and an assistant. Ivor Montagu, who was in charge of the film as it reached the studio at home, was jointly credited as director. The unit had a Newman-Sinclair camera suitably modified and with telephoto lens. Experiencing great difficulties from high winds and a cold so intense it made the celluloid brittle, they were able to secure modifications on the Westland biplane in order to site their camera. They set to work to film background stuff while they waited.

Three flights eventually took place, strangely enough at the same time as the Ruttledge expedition which had left England in January, and first attempted the peak in May, was winding its way up the mountain. Clydesdale flew over Everest on 3 and 19 April, and Fellowes over Kanchenjunga on 4 April. Bonnett accompanied Clydesdale over Everest. Michael Balcon back at Gaumont-British wasted no time and had a letter in *Kine Weekly* on 6 April saying that film had been shot over Everest at a height of 37,000 feet. There was, however, a long delay before the finished film appeared. Meanwhile a book about the flights, *First Over Everest*, was published in December 1933, magnificently illustrated with photographs of the Himalayan range. It also included an anaglyph, a composite stereoscopic picture printed in superimposed complementary colours from vertical photographs approaching Everest from the south. Viewing spectacles with one red and one blue-green transparency were included in a pocket in the back cover. The book had a foreword by John Buchan, in which he referred to the mass of topographical and meteorological information brought back by the flight, and also included a chapter on the filming written by Barkas.

Wings over Everest finally appeared in the summer of 1934, a commercial four-reel film which also had a considerable non-theatrical market. With marvellous Himalayan panoramas including a comparatively close shot of the famous north-east ridge, solidly good camerawork and an unobtrusive commentary, it nevertheless was padded out with long sequences on the early preparations, work on the ground and even a reconstruction of the accident in which Bonnett was nearly killed. The three flights were compressed into one. Rotha in *Sight and Sound*, with a passing reference to the brief but unforgettable appearance of Lady Houston, found it disappointing.[30] And Forsyth Hardy could only say that the material had "value and impressiveness which would withstand the most indifferent presentation".[31] It was, alas, a familiar assessment of expedition films.

Once more, in fact, "what a FILM it might have been". But perhaps this is hardly fair. All of these films, even this most professional one, were incidental to the purpose of the expedition. Time and again we find the true explorer or mountaineer as the typical tall, good-looking moustached upper-class Englishman, allowing his beard to grow only when actually in the wilds, secure in the money and social contacts which gave him access to the testing life he sought. Forsyth Hardy and Rotha both record the laconic aristocratic British tone on the Everest flight. Clydesdale is asked about the roof of the world :

"Did you get there?"
A nod.
"What's it like?"
"Alright".[32]

The real explorers were driven not so much by curiosity, least of all by curiosity about their fellow men, as by a compelling need to prove themselves and do something that had never been done before. We are lucky that in the dreamer Noel, the eagle-eyed Smythe, the keen and diligent Ponting, and Hurley the breezy Australian, good cameramen if not brilliant film makers, we had four odd fellows who were more interested in recording what they saw than in proving anything about themselves. As for our humbler camera adventurers, none of them had the imagination of a Flaherty, or the fascination with unfamiliar lives and sensitive response to the film medium which made him unique. As Augustine Courtauld very wisely said of his companions in the snow : "They would be the first to admit that the objects of the Expedition, like most objects of most Expeditions, were the means of living the life they liked to live, rather than ends in themselves."[33]

4

Interest Films and the Independent Film Maker

Although many of the films used as educational were not originally made with the classroom in mind, an educational film was comparatively simple to define. So were other categories of film such as news, travel, propaganda and publicity, even though they might overlap. All could be interesting if they were well made. But there was something else, something called an interest film, which was none of these things and indeed could be so very uninteresting that the term became almost derogatory. The early commercial interest film at its worst was a short film essay about almost anything as long as it was non-controversial and made as cheaply as possible. But there were other films, mostly short and factual like the commercial interest film but not always, made independently by many different people with many different motives, which are difficult to classify. Between the amateur cine film made for family and friends and the rubbishy product of the cynical shorts merchants lay many impressions and observations made by beginners and amateurs, the work of the aspiring *avant garde*, and independent work by professionals hoping to do something a little more personal than usual. This independent production needed some sort of audience, some sort of economic viability. Some of the films trickled on to the market. But the operation of the 1928 quota legislation intended to protect British film production had particularly harmful results in this very area of the non-commercial short film, whether subsidised or independent.

Nevertheless a number of independent souls were intrigued by the camera's power to record the world as they saw it. More outward looking than the family cine enthusiast, ambitious and skilful as some of the latter were, these were impressionists and observers who produced a miscellany of unclassifiable films, unclassifiable that is unless we simply say they are "of interest". But first let us take a necessary look at the uninspired work of the commercial shorts merchants.

The commercial interest film was a mini-industry of its own, into which the big feature studios rarely entered except through their regular magazine films. The *Pathé Sound Magazine* which started in July 1929 and ran weekly for a few months later gave way to the *Pathé Pictorial*, which appeared weekly from April 1936. The *Ideal Cinemagazine* became the *Gaumont-British Magazine* and appeared weekly from 1930 to 1938 under its producer and editor Andrew Buchanan. *Ace Cinemagazine* later in the thirties began with twenty-six one-reelers in July 1937, with punning titles like *Brake it Gently, Snuff Said, Business is Bristling, The Write Stuff*, which suggest a light treatment of what otherwise might have been serious informative subjects. A number of companies appeared, also, which took a slightly more serious line and produced a popular form of documentary or pseudo-documentary. Throughout the thirties many of the small companies available on contract for advertising or educational production occasionally ventured a film thought worthy of registration. But the real shorts kings, whose well-known names guaranteed low prices and quality to match, were few in number.

At the end of the decade the shorts producers formed their own association, British Short Film Makers' Society Ltd. The big names were Widgey Newman, Joseph Best, Horace Shepherd and Ronald Haines. The latter was elected Chairman in June 1939. A letter from Best just after the new quota Act spoke of "Genuine, unsubsidised entertainment shorts" and sought protection from the unfair competition of advertising and propaganda films.[1] They doubtless feared that the entry of better short films in the market they had exploited so shabbily under the old legislation would ruin their business.

John Betts was a survivor from the twenties who continued

throughout the thirties with sports and racing items and films about the Armed Services, mostly three- or four-reelers or series of one-reelers. He even secured War Office approval for *The Seventeenth Lancers* in 1929 and co-operation from Gaumont-British and the R.A.F. for a crude recruiting film, *R.A.F.*, in 1935. His films were always elegible for quota.

But one of the best known and most prolific interest producers was Widgey R. Newman. Having briefly tried medicine and journalism he settled for films, and at the age of 26 registered his own company in 1929. Making many short dramatic films as well as factual shorts, he remained an independent and shoe-string operator throughout. Here again, almost all his films were acceptable for quota. Variously producer, director and writer, he was associated at different times during the thirties with pro-ducers Geoffrey Clarke and Bernerd Smith, director R. W. Lotinga and writer John Quin. In the early thirties he was working with Clarke, with John Miller as cameraman and studio supervisor, as Delta Pictures, a £2,000 company using the old studios at Bushey. When the new quota opened up the shorts market he formed Widgey R. Newman Productions and Associated Inde-pendent Producers Ltd, a grandiloquent title which referred simply to his wife Joan, the veteran director G. A. Cooper and himself. The associated company of Ace, under managing director Frank Green, concentrated on films of vaudeville turns.

In the shorts field Newman specialised in films based on newspaper series, horse racing subjects, and animals in general. For example, for some years he had an annual series of one-reelers under the title of *Derby Secrets*, and one year made a two-reeler, *Gordon Richards*, about the famous jockey at the peak of his fame, reviewed on the same day in 1933, incidentally, as another film, *A Day in the Life of Gordon Richards*, by old-timer Walter West. *Faces of Destiny*, a series of one-reelers in 1933, based on articles in the *Sunday Dispatch* by John Clennell, attempted to relate character and personality to the shape of the face. *What the Stars Foretell*, also in 1933, were twelve one-reelers made by Newman together with the *Sunday Express* astrologer R. H. Naylor and were followed later by another long series in 1938 based on the signs of the zodiac, *What the Heavens*

Reveal. His Coronation offering in 1937 was *Our Royal Heritage,* compiled in association with the *News of the World.* He also had *How to Take the Driving Test* in 1935 and in 1936, the big year of road safety campaigns, he made a film about the A.A. called *This Motoring.* With animal films he was on particularly safe ground with the British public. R. W. Lotinga, a Fellow of the Royal Zoological Society, had already made zoo films in 1934 and 1935, ahead of the famous documentary Strand series although not ahead of Mary Field, who had very early realised the possibilities offered by the Zoo as a subject for slightly humorous interest films, nor of one A. F. H. Baldry who, as a member of the Zoological Society, had made *Animal Friends* back in 1930. *Here Comes the Zoo* and *This Fishy Business* were made by Lotinga with the co-operation of the London Zoological Society in 1934 and 1935, and Newman's firm A.I.P.D. later had three films taken as quota by American companies in 1939, *Animal Moments, Zoo in Spring* and *Under Dogs. Pandamonium* was about the very popular new baby panda, Ming, in the London Zoo in 1939, and featured her and her keeper Hal Walters in a film with a slight story. The titles of these films suggest the style, informative but light and humorous. One of Newman's more interesting ventures was *His Apologies.* He had long wanted to film Rudyard Kipling's story of life seen through the eyes of a dog, *Thy Servant a Dog,* but the rights of £1,000 were high for his type of production. By the mid-thirties Kipling was more or less a recluse. Surprisingly, he approved Newman's scenario and agreed to its production on a profit-sharing basis. The film, shown late in 1935, was called *His Apologies* and Newman's assistant was Roy Boulting, his cameraman John Miller; the cast included Moore Marriott, Roma Beaumont and Violet Hopson. There was no dialogue, but the dog's thoughts were spoken by the actor Laidman Brown. Kipling himself came to the press show. According to the critic Ian Coster the film was reasonably good[2] but, possibly because of Newman's reputation as an interest film maker, it received little attention. Newman died during the war.

Another big name, a shorts king with a difference, was Andrew Buchanan. He had started the *Ideal Cinemagazine* in 1924 and continued to produce it in the early thirties and later, when it was taken over in 1935 and became the *Gaumont-British Magazine*. In 1938 he struck out on his own, ready for the new quota. Films of Great Britain and British Films were made at the Albany Street studios with Henry Cooper, formerly a cameraman, as director, Charles Frances as cameraman and James Anderson as editor. Producing, directing and editing throughout the decade, Buchanan took himself seriously, and was the only film maker not in the mainstream documentary movement who joined Associated Realist Film Producers in 1936. He wrote a stream of popular little books on film technique. An article by him in *Sight and Sound* at the outbreak of war on Britain's need to use film for propaganda purposes is full of platitudes. Writing in *Film Art* on another occasion, he describes magazine production in glowing terms. Producing one 1,000-foot magazine a week, each containing five 200-foot sequences, he boldly claims that in making some 300 items a year he achieves the technical quality of the feature film with the speed of newsreel production. He needs the skill of the journalist in his choice of subjects and their economical portrayal, estimating that he shoots 450 feet for a 200-foot sequence; he describes his practice of collecting out-of-the-way material and beautiful scenery, the building up of a large library, and his extremely careful planning of work in the studio. His account of how to make, say, a fashion sequence "different" is an exposition of the gimmick.[3] Despite his pretentions he was practical, and made many advertising films as well. *Her Crowning Glory* for Amami shampoo, for example ("Friday night is Amami night"), shows him in a rather different, cute light. A conventional tale of the girl whom nobody wants to kiss until she washes her hair with the right shampoo, it includes a fantasy figure of Buchanan himself as the ubiquitous cameraman filming "beautiful heads of hair" for his collection wherever he finds them. Undoubtedly a skilled technician and one of the best commercial shorts makers, he was treated extremely respectfully by both *Film Art* and the British Film Institute, notably Oliver Bell and Arthur Vesselo, who perhaps found him more to their taste than what they regarded as the "arty boys". *Film Art* repeatedly praised him for experiments, and wrote of him:

". . . lovely photography, compositions, and cutting that means something – in each one sequence stands out – Andrew Buchanan is an artist, his work is miles above any other shown regularly at cinemas".[4]

But views like the following jar the image : ". . . the surest way of pleasing the largest number of people is to include the smallest amount of intelligent material in the reel".[5]

London River, made for T.I.D.A. in 1939, proves to be about as competent, and as uninspired, as similar films made by Marion Grierson, perhaps the least talented of the mainstream documentary film makers. In the summer of 1939 Buchanan was interviewed by Vesselo on a new series he was planning. It is explained in the chapter on newsreels that he envisaged this as a less controversial form of depth reporting than *The March of Time*, with subjects more social than political. He explained that he was against sponsorship and wanted to promote commercial shorts.[6] Clearly his motivation was very different to the documentary ideal as understood by the Grierson school, despite the ambiguous status which he cultivated.

About 1934 a number of producers appeared who specialised in the mass production of series of very cheap "factual" films acceptable for quota, and were responsible for a considerable increase in British footage in the market supply of shorts. One of these was Inspiration Films. Horace Shepherd formed a company of his own in 1931 to make cartoon films by Norman Cobb, who had in fact already produced a few "Bingo" cartoons, but the venture rapidly failed. But between 1934 and the new quota he found a magic formula for the manufacture of films, one or one-and-a-half reels long in series, usually relying heavily on the filming of pictures of paintings – even postcards were filmed – or architectural landmarks, with strong "English" appeal and the cheapest possible production. These were taken gratefully as quota, with their Br. registration, by First National and Columbia and to a lesser extent by M-G-M, Warner Brothers and R.K.O. He has been mentioned already in connection with so-called travel pictures made to a similar formula. He poured out over a dozen such series until the minimum cost clause of the new quota caught up with him. After that he proceeded with less verve, making occasional two-reelers, until the approach of war suggested that some commercial mileage might be got out of patriotic shots of naval ships. The fate of *The Cavalcade of the Navy* is instructive. A series of one-reelers made in collaboration with Frank Green of Ace, partly in Technicolor, was shown to the press in July 1939. Based on paintings of ships, they had cost so little to make that they failed to get registration at all under the new rules.[7]

Meanwhile others, seeing the new quota as an opportunity rather than as an obstacle, were forming new companies to take advantage of it. Ronald Haines, whose real name was W. R. Hutchinson, had entered films in America and then worked in France before coming to England in 1935. Here he produced a five-reel *Lawrence of Arabia* for Ace, shortly after the death of T. E. Lawrence, largely as a compilation from records at the Imperial War Museum and with a commentary by Sir Ronald Storrs. In 1936 he made a film about Cornish fishermen called *Red Sails*. As managing director, producer and director of British Foundation Pictures, with cameraman Reg Wyer, he started making what he called "documentary entertainment shorts" in 1937. From November onwards one or two solid two-reelers appeared more or less every month, some thirty of them in two years, giving a not too serious fifteen-minute treatment of some topic of general interest. These, of better quality than most, were also used by the big American companies as quota.

Other new **firms** appeared, of which the most important was Technique Films and its associated Technique Distributors. One of the directors of this company was Harold Lowenstein of Short Film Productions, founded a couple of years earlier. It seems to have started by distributing not only various miscellaneous films, including a popular one called *How the Motor Works* which used colour cartoon and diagrams with elves and pixies to explain the working of a motor, but also their own "Reporter" series which was a more serious attempt at investigative reporting, mentioned in Chapter 2. In addition, the company became one of the principle distributors for mainstream documentary films.

Certain subjects, such as sport, were always popular, *Don Bradman in "How I Play Cricket"* in 1933, *This Leg Theory* by

10 Pavlova with her
pet and symbol (*The
Immortal Swan*, 1935).

11 A new technique,
which aroused the
suspicions of the
censors (*Tusalava*,
1929).

12 *Out to Play*, 1936.

13 The pastoral idyll, seen by the Boulting brothers (*Ripe Earth*, 1938).

14 A semi-professional film expressing its maker's own interests (*The Caves of Perigord*, 1939).

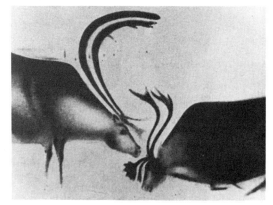

15 A Massingham short story (*Come for a Stroll*, 1938–9)

Alba Films in 1934, *Bob Bowman Calling,* about ice hockey, by Ace in 1936 were only a few of the many. Horoscopes and any form of fortune telling made good series. Animals, above all dogs, were a standby. John Alderson for British Screen Service made *Border Collie* and *Sheep Dog* in 1938 and 1939, but the feeble jocularity of their approach shows a timid lack of faith in their interesting subjects. Nevertheless these films were considered to be of a relatively high standard by the trade. Scottish Films Productions, which did scenics of Scotland as well as the Scottish sequences for *Pathé Pictorial* and British Movietone News from their base in Glasgow, scored with *The Family Life of the Golden Eagle* in 1935. Their *Sport in Scotland,* which was little more than a miscellany of shots to show how many sporting facilities Scotland possessed and how hardy the people were, was one of the films made for the Films of Scotland project co-ordinated by Grierson at Film Centre.

As a footnote to the interest film we may give a passing thought to special film shows for children, a field where many interest films, as well as entertainment films, were expected to find a second and often most prolonged lease of life. In April 1930 the Birmingham Cinema Enquiry Committee had set out to investigate children's film preferences at special Saturday-afternoon programmes. Children, of course, also went to ordinary cinema shows, and in 1932 the London County Council produced a Report based on the work of the school inspectorate estimating that 9 per cent went twice a week, 30 per cent once a week, 48 per cent irregularly and 13 per cent never.[8] Again, the usual rather obvious conclusions about preferences were drawn, but as this Report left unanswered the question of how often the children went alone or with their parents, or to special shows, it was of limited significance.

Experience of children's tastes had been gained the hard way by those exhibitors who had provided special children's shows. Sidney L. Bernstein had started them in his theatres in 1928, engaging Miss J. M. Harvey, the Secretary of the Film Society, to run them and launching the first season with a good deal of prestige publicity and appeals to parents and educational authorities. He had started with shows at four London suburban

cinemas on Saturday mornings in March.⁹ They started well
but attendances soon dropped and he stopped them in the summer
months. He tried again in October, but again felt it necessary to
stop in the summer of 1929. Only a brief season was held in
1930 in the keenest area, Enfield. His experience led him to feel
that there had been little co-operation from the educational
authorities, and that by trying to please them and the parents
the organisers had chosen films, *Peter Pan* and the *Secrets of
Nature* for example, which the children found too tame.¹⁰

Bernstein, in fact a most enlightened exhibitor, modestly
claimed that his motives were severely practical, to create a film-
minded generation, to obtain goodwill for the cinema, and to
keep children out of the ordinary shows where they occupied
seats at half price, hampered the showing of "A" films, and were
sometimes a nuisance.

Others were frankly concerned with the children's welfare. In
December 1931 the Exhibitors' Association received two delegates
from the Children's Cinema Association, F. W. Chudleigh and
the Rev. Dr Donald Soper, both of whom had organised
children's shows. The problem was one of finding enough suitable
films. Next month British Instructional, together with the large
A.B.C. circuit, inaugurated a series of Saturday morning shows in
London suburbs with the co-operation of the local authorities.
Bruce Woolfe later claimed that 20,000 children attended these
every week, and the company persevered with them. The programmes were selected by Margery Locket, and had a strongly
improving flavour. Two other schemes, different in that they
required children to be accompanied by their parents, consisted
entirely of short films and also sound rather serious. In 1934
J. S. Fairfax-Jones started a Children's Film Society at the
Everyman Cinema at Hampstead, with a winter season of six
programmes including discussions led by various celebrities. This
was a more expensive and demanding type of show but seems
to have been well attended in the prosperous and intellectual air
of Hampstead. And a season of six shows in the winter of 1934
was run by Elsie Cohen at the Academy Cinema in the West
End which also required the attendance of parents. These schemes,
however, differed radically from the adventurous, independent,

anything-might-happen air of the true local children's matinée, with its vast queues outside and its occasional rampages inside, part of whose charm for the children was that it was their own territory. Gaumont-British ran schemes after Bruce Woolfe and Miss Locket had joined them, partly of educational shows, but in 1936 they also had a series of entertainment shows at six London cinemas organised with the help of the London Head Teachers' Association and the L.C.C., and were said to be actively seeking films of "high cultural and technical level".

Ken Nyman, Chairman of the London and Home Counties Branch of the Exhibitors' Association, gave shows for some 2,000 children aged between 7 and 11 in poor areas like Bethnal Green. A vigorous campaigner on many exhibition matters, Nyman took a hard commercial line about his motive, which he said was to show what the children liked in order to make a profit.

In 1934 Bernstein had also tried again, this time with greater success. Disenchanted, he no longer sought the approval of educational or local authorities but had his shows run firmly by the cinema managers, "Uncles" with nerves of steel. He later said that between October 1935 and September 1936 his Saturday-morning shows had 650,000 admissions, running successfully although at a small financial loss. He seems to have felt that he had found the secret of success. The average age of the children was 9, with few over 13; community singing led by "Uncles" let off steam; the popular films were all action, including serials, Westerns, cartoons, sport and hobby films; popular stars were Joe E. Brown, Jack Hulbert and Cicely Courtneidge, and Richard Talmadge; not only were sentimental pictures unpopular but also the jungle pictures so much approved of by parents and teachers; programmes, he concluded, should consist of a feature, the news, a serial, a short comedy and a cartoon or interest film.

Thus as experience was gathered it became clear that there was a shortage of the type of films children really wanted to see. The Child Welfare Committee of the League of Nations, formed in 1925, took up the question in 1935 on the initiative of the British representative, S. W. Harris, Assistant Under-Secretary at the Home Office. At his request the British Film Institute appointed a committee which prepared a memorandum on the subject, and this was discussed at Geneva in April 1936, the Institute being represented by A. C. Cameron. The Public Morality Council and the Cinema Christian Council also held a conference on the subject in 1936. And in November of that year the Institute held its own important Conference on Films for Children, which received wide attention from the press. Ninety-five religious, social and educational bodies and the film trade were represented by some 300 people, under Cameron's chairmanship. It was addressed by Harris, by Simon Rowson who was chairman of the Institute's Entertainment Panel and President of the Renters' Society, and by Dr Emmanuel Miller, a child guidance expert. Others present included exhibitors Nyman and Bernstein, Eleanor Plumer representing the Mothers' Union, and John Grierson and others interested in the effect of the film from many different points of view.

It was estimated by Rowson that some 500 cinemas out of a possible 4,500 now had regular children's shows, catering to some 600,000 children, mostly in working-class and industrial areas. Children in more prosperous neighbourhoods and in rural areas, it was thought, had better things to do than go to the cinema. But however much the children enjoyed it, from the pushing and shoving outside to the frank reactions and possible rough-house inside, the exhibitors felt that for such an unprofitable business as this was bound to be, at admission prices of 2d or 3d, they received woefully little support from the community. There were problems. The children were hard to handle and sometimes destructive, but the main difficulty was still the scarcity of suitable films. As with the educational cinema, the absence of special films and the absence of an assured market interacted. The percentage of current features which was truly suitable was small enough, and after their profitable life, estimated at some eighteen months, they were junked or at best shelved and were unlikely to be kept on hand for uneconomical single bookings, at possibly low prices, for the children. Rowson, characteristically firm, optimistic and sweeping in his calculations, estimated that if the shows could be trebled in number it would be economically practicable to produce films specially. But most people agreed that this was not likely for the moment and Bernstein, more realistic, agreed with the

Film Institute's 1936 Memorandum suggesting the establishment of a special body to centralise booking. He felt this might be a non-commercial body actually acquiring films, and eventually building up a collection and keeping them in circulation at moderate fees; he also spoke of cutting and re-editing some "A" films which were not suitable in their commercial form but could be made so by comparatively small alterations; and of perhaps being able eventually to commission production. J. Arthur Rank, who in 1944 was to be the one to take practical steps to remedy the lack of entertainment films for children, was not yet deeply enough involved in either production or exhibition to be a participant in the discussions.

A report on this conference came out next year, and in July 1937 the Institute brought out a first list of entertainment films recommended for children's programmes. Eighty features both suitable and available were listed, as well as shorts and interest films. A second list was published in April 1938. The Institute also sent a questionnaire to cinemas on the problems of running children's shows. Although exhibitors continued to claim that the shows did not pay, many continued to run them, and Odeon Cinemas set up a special department in the autumn of 1937 to run their Mickey Mouse Clubs, which were estimated to have over 100,000 members. Clearly it was with some pride that Oliver Bell, when he attended the Child Welfare Commission of the League of Nations in Geneva, claimed that by May 1938 such matinées were attended by 700,000 every week.

The basic assumption underlying the film lists, thousands of copies of which were sent to exhibitors and many organisations of teachers, parents and others, was that a great extension of special cinema shows for children was desirable. As is so often the case, the many different and even opposing interests represented at the Conference had come to an agreement which was more apparent than real. The showmen wanted films the children would enjoy and pay to see, whilst a lot of other people wanted films that would do the children good, aims not necessarily incompatible but certainly not identical. It seems to have been an easy slip of the mind to think that if you helped to overcome the scarcity of films suitable for children in the sense that they would actually hold their attention and give them fun, you would be doing something for film appreciation and would raise the standards of taste. The thinking might have been clearer. However, for once the Film Institute must have felt on very safe ground, doing the children good and not offending the trade.

Whatever they showed the children, it was obvious that a miscellany of second-rate interest films was not going to be good enough for this very demanding audience. But, if the interest film was on the whole the dullest of all films, much of the miscellaneous production going on outside the formality of the big studios was very interesting indeed, embracing a fascinating band of impressionists and observers, many of them with a wistful eye on a slot in the "full supporting programme". After all, who wants to make a film for no one else to see? And some sort of economic return was usually needed, although film making could still be treated as an expensive hobby by a small minority.

Many families were beginning to use their home cines for purposes other than the recording of holidays, weddings and the other set pieces of life. *Priestley and Friends at Home* resides in the Film Archive and the films of Amy Johnson's family have come to light and many, many other families, celebrated or not, have their own reminders of social occasions. British families, living and working in many parts of an Empire then vast and run without guilty misgivings by a huge body of armed forces, civil servants and commercial houses, brought back collections of films some of them personal, some of them of general interest. Some have survived, some, alas, have not. Some were mere snapshots but others were photographed and edited with care and knowledge. At home, too, many were making with varying degrees of skill quite elaborate films about people, hobbies and activities that interested them. Because Harry Price was concerned with the setting up of the National Film Library his amateur shots of the Pulborough carnivals of 1932 and 1933, with their floats and maypoles, ended up in the Archive. But they were in no way unusual. As Honorary Secretary of the Council for Psychical Investigation he also edited a twelve-minute silent film called *Magic*, which showed an attempt to do the Indian rope trick in a Hertfordshire field in 1935; a group, including

Professor C. E. M. Joad, incredibly carrying out the rites of a ceremony intended to turn a virgin he-goat into a young man; and a fire walk in a respectable garden at Carshalton. Every now and then some undergraduate at Oxford or Cambridge would be stirred by a desire to tell the world all about it. Amateur scientific films, like *Power*, made at Cambridge in the summer of 1932 by Gordon Taylor and Maurice Harvey, might even get wider distribution. *Pond Life*, a silent single reel made by G. H. Higginson of the Bolton School of Art, with microscopic work by R. G. Slater, received a prize at an International Amateur Film Contest in Hungary in 1934. Again, these are only isolated examples but they are signs of a great deal of activity. The celebrated dramatist and producer Maurice Browne made a two-reel *Domesday England* in 1934, which was distributed non-theatrically by Western Electric. J. S. Fairfax-Jones, as well as running the unusual Everyman Cinema in Hampstead and Denning Films, which distributed rare and foreign films with specialised appeal, in 1936 made *Happy Hampstead!* about the amenities and history of this London borough. The later B.B.C. film critic E. Arnot Robertson also tried her hand. In 1934 she and H. E. Turner made *Young Things*, described in a review as a host of irresistible young animals. Later, directing, scripting and editing although not shooting, she made *Low Water* about the sailing barges of the Thames Estuary. According to William Farr in *Sight and Sound*[11] it was an "intelligently conceived, well made, good-looking film". It showed an out-of-work barge mate who got a day's work on a barge; the question of whether he would remember all the details of his former craft provided an imaginative continuity thread. In this respect it was a contrast to Commander Hunt's *Our Island Story*, a commercial film with quota registration. The same reviewer, in the same issue of *Sight and Sound*, found Stanley Holloway's interruptions in the latter film, to explain naval manoeuvres in his part of chief yeoman of signals, a crude device and an irritating intrusion on otherwise pleasant photography. Finally, the plight of the amateur film maker is well illustrated by *Plane Sailing*, a film about gliding. Made during weekends over a period of three years by enthusiasts Philip Wills and Bosworth Goldman, with a commentary by

Alan Howland, it was said by *Sight and Sound* to be "sheer delight".[12] It secured distribution, but with the usual handicap of an E registration.

A major interest film by an outsider was *The Immortal Swan*, the film about the great ballerina Anna Pavlova made in 1935. Much of the footage was earlier and came from abroad and it was registered as a foreign film, but it was put together here, four years after her death. It was directed, written and arranged by Edward Nakhimoff, who had become a naturalised British citizen as a very young man in 1932. Victor Dandré, her manager, and according to her biographer[13] her husband possibly since 1914, supervised the production, which was an act of homage. It is introduced by a reconstruction by the *corps de ballet* of her production *Chopiniana*, and ends with an epilogue of the company dancing around a sentimental portrait of her in the centre of the stage, to the accompaniment of choral singing. Within this framework, devised by Pavel Petrov and her dancer Algeranoff, the film uses still photographs of her when young, various conventional programme-cum-travel montages, cine and news films of her on her travels and at home at Ivy House in north-west London, and a number of films of her dancing popular numbers from her repertoire like *Californian Poppy*, *Fairy Doll*, *Dragonfly* and others, part of *Rondino* filmed out of doors in slow motion, and finally her *chef-d'œuvre*, the *Dying Swan*. Most of these dance films had been made in 1924 when, already 43, she was staying in Hollywood with Mary Pickford and Douglas Fairbanks, and had been made not for public showing but as tests for her own private study. For these silent, simple one angle shots of her dancing on very much too small a stage, the difficult task of sound synchronisation and editing the film, shot apparently at varying speeds, was performed bravely by Julia Wolf, with musical direction by Vladimir Launitz. The results were technically distressing, being impossibly fast or jerky in many places. Nevertheless a surprising amount of information comes through the very unfavourable conditions of production. In the casual films of her with friends she appears cool and composed. With her high forehead, fine jaw and muscular legs, she has tremendous poise, gracefully slinking along with those large elegantly splayed-out 1920s feet and fluttering voiles. Conscious of every gesture, she is vivacious without warmth, fondling birds and animals but not children, a dominating presence. Her voice is heard once, briefly, murmuring to her swans from the side of the pool. The content of the dances is popular and demands little from the audience, the dreamy *débutante* of *Invitation to the Dance*, the scintillating *vivace* of *Variations Classiques*, the skimming and darting of *Dragonfly* with its pretty costume and the ingenious closing petals of the costume she designed for herself in *Californian Poppy*. Dimly perceived through the technical inadequacies of the film is an impressive technique, but it is perhaps only in the final signature, the *Dying Swan*, that the breath-taking grace of gesture and expressive power she had at her best can be glimpsed.

Another film made out of sheer enthusiasm was the two-reel *Table Tennis Today* of 1929, but Ivor Montagu was a many-sided film maker as we may assume it was a fully professional film. Rather different were the signs of an aspiring *avant-garde* to be found in, for example, the activity of the Pool group. Studio Films' *I do Love to be Beside the Seaside* made in 1929 by Oswell Blakeston – poet, writer and artist associated with *Close Up* – had music composed by Edmund Meisel to accompany it. And the abstract film *Light Rhythms* which Blakeston made as assistant to Francis Bruguière had a musical accompaniment by Jack Ellit. It has been described as "an attempt to create the illusion of movement entirely through 'mixes' and moving lights without altering the position of the forms employed"[14] and it was shown at the Film Society in April 1930. Blakeston maintained at the time that emotions, characters or scenes could be portrayed entirely with light, and he dreamt of fantasy films made with moving lights only.[15] Kenneth Macpherson, editor and owner with his wealthy wife Bryher of *Close Up*, made the six-reel Pool film *Borderline* featuring Paul Robeson and his wife Eslanda in 1930. By this date Robeson was already lionised in left-wing circles in England, and had a house in Hampstead, a bust of himself by Epstein, and friendly relations with many of the intelligentsia. *Close Up*, with such correspondents as Robert Herring, Jean Lenaur, Kraszna-Krausz and Harry Alan

Potamkin, was influential intellectually but it would seem that its wealthy owners wanted to play film makers as well. Macpherson had already made a film called *Monkey's Man* in 1929. With Robeson to star, he now wished to make an important advance in film technique.

The "book of the film" of *Borderline* shows it to have been set vaguely in an imaginary border town, but the events seem to have been of secondary importance. Claiming to have started making *Borderline* before Eisenstein's "theory of overtonal montage" was known to him, Macpherson replied to critics who complained of the film's obscurity and vague symbolism that he had wished to make a film "to insist on a mental condition. To take the action, the observation, the deduction, the reference, into the labyrinth of the human mind", and he boldly claimed that it was "perhaps the only really 'avant-garde' film ever made". He had in any case a low opinion of mere comprehensibility, which he described as a demand for concessions. He defended the film against the charge of being chaotic: "It was intended to be. But over this chaos rings and reverberates one pure, loud, sullen note. I had no specific name for it, but now we know it is overtone."[16] Since no one else seems to have noticed this pure, loud, sullen note, some audacity was clearly needed to defend the film. It does not seem to have saved the day. The film does not appear to have been shown publicly and is not mentioned in biographies of Paul Robeson.

Another unusual experiment was a three-reel film of 1932 called *The Dump*, directed by Benjamin Artz, "a young man who has wandered around the world and is still wandering", and shot by the British cameraman William Shenton who, though not an experimentalist, was no stranger to the seamy side of life. This seems to have been an impressionist film about what it was like to be down and out, using an experimental sound-track. Although it was given an encouraging hand by Grierson in the first number of *Cinema Quarterly*, it turned out to be yet another film leading nowhere. Grierson's description gives an idea of it:

Sequence 1 is concerned with feet tramping into the drabness of a dump. Sequence 2 beats up their coughing and plays it over pans of monotonous walls. The coughing goes on and on with a certain brutal insistence. It is rag-timed on visual images of doors, walls, corridors. The sequences which follow flit back and forth between the poor and the rich, using symbols in sound and mute to cross-section society. A child cries and goes on crying: the rich in their clubs are disturbed, move uneasily, are a trifle disgusted: the poor on the park benches do likewise. They are all similarly reading the "Daily Telegraph". Artz seems to be making some commentary on herd instinct, and the infant yell symbolises presumably The Cry of Humanity. A child laughing is similarly used at a later stage. The feet-tramping and coughing sequences are repeated in identical form (duped) to demonstrate that dereliction is as desperate (and hell as hopeless) to-day as it was yesterday.[17]

But Grierson suggested that the use of symbolic sound became monotonous because of the inadequacy of the visuals, and left it an open question whether this was a "richly felt experience" or not.

More fruitful, of course, was the abstract work of Len Lye and Jack Ellit, which started independently but became part of the mainstream documentary movement despite its very different character. At the beginning, *Tusalava* was made by Lye with the help and backing of the Film Society and the writer Robert Graves, with a sound score by Ellit, and shown at the Film Society in December 1929. Drawn on film, the squiggles, rings and dots writhe and wriggle, splitting and joining in a way strangely reminiscent of the films Dr Canti was making of cancer cells at approximately the same time. They develop into a vaguely creature-like shape which is attacked, stabbed and thrust, filled in, emptied and twisted by another shape of similar fluidity which finally whirls, shrinks and disappears. It is an impressive and alarming little piece, shattering rather than enjoyable. Possibly suspecting some sexual meaning, the puzzled but ever watchful British Board of Film Censors demanded an explanation, to be given Lye's famous statement: "The picture represented a self-shape annihilating an antagonistic element."[18] After this Lye was adopted by the documentary movement, and his later films are described in the companion volume to this book.

The other art periodical, *Film Art*, was edited by B. Vivian Braun with Irene Nicholson and Robert Fairthorne, and had Herbert Marshall and Marie Seton as Moscow correspondents. They, also, dabbled in film making. The first Film Art production, *Beyond this Open Road*, made in 1934, was described by some as a hiking film but by Braun and Nicholson, who made it, as a "symphonic treatment of the open air".[19] In 1936 Irene Nicholson, with Bryan Montagu, were said to be making a film in Trinidad for the *Trinidad Guardian*. Later Braun made a film about the work of a lighthouse called *Danger at Sea* which was registered for theatrical showing, though not for quota. It was made with Harold Lowenstein, who made further films under the name of Short Film Productions. Of these perhaps the most notable was *Out to Play*, which he directed together with Philip Leacock. The latter had entered films in 1935 from school at Bedales, and was later to become a director and associate producer in the feature industry. This charming film, credited with a "visual script" by Kenneth Martin, is a one-reel impression of children's play in city streets complete with evocative shots of coal cart, barrel organ and stop-me-and-try-one toffee-apple cart, and delightful shots of children at their most natural. One member of the documentary movement remembered *Film Art* with some disdain, but was prepared to concede that Lowenstein, at least, had talent. In the spring of 1937 he made *Kew Gardens*, supervised by the Director of the Royal Botanical Gardens at Kew and again directed by Leacock, with photography by Braun and music by Brian Easdale. This film, showing both public and behind-the-scenes aspects of Kew, seemed a success and Lowenstein later attempted a short story film set in a Cornish fishing village and made in Dufaycolor, *Once Upon a Time*. When the sponsored documentary became eligible for quota he was actively engaged in promoting its distribution as Technique Film Distributors, which handled a number of mainstream documentaries.

It would seem that there were wealthy amateurs able to dabble in film making, and although *Out to Play* is such a lovely film, dilettante or not, that we can only be grateful for it, this could not be said of all of them. Would more effective use have been made of the talent if professional survival had been necessary? Leacock later became a successful professional film maker. But there were other groups such as the Socialist Film Council whose aims were political rather than artistic, and to them professional standards were at that time of secondary importance.

Not only were there people outside the industry who were anxious to express something important to them through the film, but those working in the industry itself also parted company with the established framework from time to time, to try something a little more individual. In 1933 the director Geoffrey Barkas's name was on a three-reeler called *A Symphony of the Sea*, showing a windjammer in a storm, herring fishery girls, anxious wives waiting, the Royal Navy and the various moods of the sea. Barkas was already keenly interested in outdoor and location filming, but this sounds rather like a mishmash of library material. The editor Daniel Birt made a film called *Silt* in 1932 under Pool auspices which was shown at the Film Society in January 1932, and which was described as an "attempt to recapitulate the process of silt precipitation in a river through the association of sound with corresponding images".[20] Ronald Steuart of Steuart Films, most academic of film makers, made *Vanishing Sails* in 1935. Produced, directed and shot by him on the Medway sailing barges, it was a personal film made as a plea for this vanishing form of transport. And Roy and John Boulting, soon to become well known as fiction film makers, made *Ripe Earth* with the co-operation of the controversial left-wing priest of Thaxted in Essex, the Rev. Conrad Noel. This seems to have been shot silent, with music and a commentary by actor Leo Genn added later, and is simply a film about the harvest, with lovely shots of corn, stooks, wheels, tractor, horses and carts, fences, the Morris Men dancing their annual dances at Thaxted, the harvest supper and the Thanksgiving service inside this most beautiful and unusual church.

This was only one of many nostalgic English pastorales. Gaumont-British Instructional used the country theme for a series of their best instructional films, and Rotha liked to begin films with an idyll of an earlier rural environment. In 1937, also, Lewis Jonas produced, directed and shot a three-reel film about the English farm at harvest time, a film regarded as somewhat pretentious by *Kine Weekly*, called *The Earth Remaineth*. Jonas had shot, and John Gifford produced, *Shrimp Fishers of Gravesend* and *Turning her Round*, registered in November 1932 and January 1933 respectively, the latter showing the Cunard liner *Majestic* refitting at Southampton. Both were reviewed in the *Monthly Film Bulletin* in March 1934 as two parts of a production *Betwixt Land and Sea*. *Shrimp Fishers* was called "a little gem of a film – and thoroughly English".[21] Related in spirit was a film called *And Now they Rest*, which was produced, shot and distributed in 1939 by two professionals who worked for G-B I, Brian Salt and the biologist J. Valentine Durden. This clear, admirable two-reeler about the decline of windmills in Britain was made under the auspices of the Cambridge and Suffolk Preservation Societies. Trees and clouds in the wind introduce us to windmills from the year 1175 onwards. Some two hundred were still working when the film was made. The post mill, Dutch or smock mill and the tower mill with its six or eight sails are shown and explained. With the idea of arousing interest in mills and making a record of them while they were still in existence the film, with no music but with a commentary spoken by actor Carleton Hobbs, avoids the documentary technique which later became widespread of presenting its subject as a controversial issue, and simply confines itself to an interesting account of the subject, beautifully shot.

One unusual outsider with a strong motive was the coal miner Charles Hanmer, who fulfilled a dream of many years when he made *Black Diamonds*. This five-reel film of 1932, made without professional resources or studio and with an extremely rough sound-track recorded on Edison Bell and Asdic, desperately patchy lighting and a wild hotchpotch of material, was Hanmer's bid to tell the world about the dangers of mining. Miners on the skyline and that inevitable silhouette of a wheel at the pit-head lead in to newspaper headlines about mine disasters and a title telling us John Morgan started down the mine when he was twelve. When he grows up he goes, cloth capped, to Westminster to plead for money to make a film about conditions among miners, an interesting continuity device which enables Hanmer to show us the conditions of which Morgan is complaining. He persuades the London sceptic Martin, complete with spats, gloves and umbrella, to come and see for himself, where upon he is involved in a roof collapse in the mine. An operation to save his sight after this accident opens his eyes in all senses, and 'THE WORLD *SHALL* KNOW!' he cries, and the miner can go ahead and make his film. Back to our initial skyline, and Welsh voices singing:

> They are Britain's Black Diamonds,
> Men, to whom respect is due,
> Modest heroes from down under,
> Men who toil for home and you,
> Oft in danger you will find them
> But their duty they must do
> Just to keep the home fires burning
> In a land so brave and true.

Roof falls and explosions are shown with brave ingenuity but an absolute lack of credibility; stock film of the work of the mine, an open air concert in the park and the Miners' Welfare – "the miner is just like other men" says Morgan – play their part in an ambitious continuity which despite the appalling technical quality of the film manages to convey its message by its sheer urgency. Naturally enough, it had difficulty in securing a distributor, but was eventually trade shown by Wardour. Next year a shorter and somewhat more professional film which had something in common with it was attempted by another independent. C. H. Dand, a journalist and publicist who had been working as scenarist for the film company A.S.F.I. at Wembley, made an independent short film about Welsh slate quarrying in the summer of 1933 called *Men Against Death*. Written and directed by him, it was shot by James Burger. It, also, was intended as a realistic account of a dangerous industry with some dramatic content, and was referred to as a "dramatic reconstruction". It was generously given testimonials both by *Kine Weekly* and by Grierson. But the lack of adequate finance led to poor photographic quality and a serious anticlimax when the crag whose threatened collapse was the crux of the story did not, in fact, fall. After all, their resources hardly covered the dynamiting of mountainsides. Dand handled it himself and it was eventually shown on the Gaumont-British circuit and elsewhere,[22] but with only an E registration the film was handicapped and made too little money for production to continue. The fate of films like these two, compared with the mass production of the cynical shorts merchants, added fuel to the demand that there should be a shorts quota in the forthcoming legislation.

Richard Massingham, later to become a prolific and popular professional in the documentary movement, was a doctor, and was Resident Medical Officer of the London Fever Hospital when he made his first film *Tell Me if it Hurts*, in 1934. It was not until 1940, after some years of making occasional contributions to the G.P.O. Film Unit in his own very individual style, that he abandoned medicine for films.

Tell Me if it Hurts starts with the music of the "Blue Danube" accompanying a sequence which, with the extreme economy of the silent film, uses close and angle shots of such things as a wine glass, bottles and food, to suggest a high-life diner-out. As he breaks a tooth on something the music jars and grinds down, breaking its sugary theme with pops and jolts. We see him, but do not hear, as he phones. When he looks at the bill he says, voice-over, "But this is ridiculous." The camera tilts up to his face before he has finished speaking but the voice and mouth are not synchronised, and throughout the film music and effects predominate. Except in this one case care is taken not to show dialogue. The clock ticks in the silent waiting-room of the dentist. Heavy mock-ominous music takes us on the long walk through to the surgery. Our hero slowly sits in the dreaded chair, which is lovingly examined by the camera. The dentist's voice says "Yes, I think that must be the one", and we have a large close up of a brilliantly lit drill twirling ever upwards on the dark screen. There follows old-style montage of trains, cars, water, wheels and shots of the squirming patient, his mouth stuffed with impedimenta, while the voice says: "This won't hurt. . . . Now, now – that didn't hurt, did it? I don't *think* this'll hurt. . . . This may hurt a little", then vigorously, "I'm afraid this *will* hurt."

More montage, this time of animated dots, squiggles and

shapes, and then the punch line as the dentist says to the exhausted patient: "I'm sorry. I tried to save the tooth but it'll have to come out." Patient's disappointed face, to another burst of the "Blue Danube".

Making the film cost £400 and it was shot during the week-ends over a period of nine months, using a handturned 35 mm camera, a Newman Sinclair with a 2-inch lens and a 6-inch lens adapted from a still camera, and six 500-watt lamps.[23] It was post-synchronised at Imperial Sound Studios. Made in 1934, it was shown in 1935 but not trade shown and registered until January 1938. According to one report[24] it was delayed by the British Board of Film Censors because it ridiculed the dental profession. Produced, written and directed by Massingham, it was shot by Karl Urbahn and featured the young actor Russell Waters as the patient. Careful and observant in the selection of detail, it is basically in silent film technique, the poor lighting adding to the sleaziness of the whole. It is not so much a comedy as an impression of the grotesque, a painful picking over of the unpleasant in the form of a neatly turned sketch.

His second film, *And so to Work*, was made by the same team and appeared commercially before the earlier one, being trade shown in November 1936. It conveys the horrors of rising and breakfasting in a slatternly boarding-house. It uses slow-motion, lots of angle shots, strange disembodied voices repeating ". . . wanted on the telephone", ". . . get up", and a pan along the early morning tree tops which halts sharply when the wakening knock on the door is heard. It dwells fondly on the sour and the disgusting, the competition for the bathroom, the slip of the razor, the blood which drips on to the basin, the dusty grovel on the floor for a lost stud, the sticky marmalade jar, the under-boiled egg, the dirty ashtray, the wet bathroom.

Massingham was personally liked and these widely known films were repeatedly shown at Fairfax-Jones's Everyman Cinema and at film societies. They are entirely individual with a fresh and original approach, although hardly experimental in technique for their date. They show a fascination with the ugly and unpleasant in a prosaic everyday world, a sort of attraction to the repulsive. While *World Film News* described *And So to Work*

16 The all-rounder
Moholy-Nagy tries
his hand at film
(*Lobsters*, 1936).

17 An amateur's
cheap and ingenious
faking of a coal
mine disaster (*Black
Diamonds*, 1932).

18 Industry's picture
of itself (*From
Coal Mine to Road*,
1931).

as brilliant comedy and noted the excellent direction,[25] *Kine Weekly's* reaction was quite different: "Pretentious novelty featurette . . . The high-faluting treatment limits the short's appeal to the highbrow."[26] Certainly Massingham's style in these two early films was somewhat arty. The son of a well-known journalist, he was a man of great charm and integrity and many social contacts, and one of the growing band of intellectuals interested in film. His work was enthusiastically accepted by others of the same class, and he later became a sort of honorary Griersonian by adoption and almost a cult figure. Although his later films retained a quirky character of their own he became more conformist with greater experience. A third personal film which was shown about 1938 was called *Come for a Stroll.* Well photographed by the professional S. D. Onions and using full sound-track with dialogue, it is considerably less mannered. But even here Massingham could not resist such set pieces as a close shot of two silhouetted heads face to face in conversation, swinging in chorus in and out of frame as they laugh, a shot which stands out obtrusively in the more modern and less self-conscious style of the rest of the film. This is an anecdote about a writer taking his revenge on a stereotyped figure of fun, a fat man with big moustache and glasses, plus-fours and loudly striped and checked clothes, who brashly criticises the other's books for their lack of murder and sex appeal. They go for a country walk, during which the writer subtly conveys the suspicion that he is planning to murder the vulgar fatty. The ambiguity and suspense is cleverly maintained but the humour is heavy-handed and cruel, and the film did not become a repertory favourite like the other two. Massingham made three films for the G.P.O. Film Unit before the war, and registered his own company, Public Relationship Films, in 1938.

Another charmer who was, briefly this time, taken up by the intelligentsia in London was the Hungarian László Moholy-Nagy. He was a highly intelligent and talented all-rounder; his interests spanned painting, photography, design, sculpture and architecture, education and social philosophy; and he was a member of the Bauhaus group from 1922 to 1928. His interest in film led him to plan a "Dynamics of a Metropolis: a Film Sketch" in Berlin in 1921, long before Ruttman made his *Berlin*. From about 1921 he worked, with an anonymous mechanic, on a kinetic light sculpture known as a Light-Space Modulator or, in Germany, "Das Lichtrequisit". This is described by his biographer as a six-foot "apparatus of moving aluminium and chrome-plated surfaces driven by an electric motor and a series of chain belts".[27] Best displayed in a dark room, where changing spotlights produced dissolving and moving shadows, it was shown in Paris in 1930. It is interesting that Blakeston and Bruguière were theorising about light rhythms at about the same time. The machine was also the subject of a grand film project by Moholy and his wife Sybil. The film was to be in six parts, the first four dealing with light and lighting effects of every possible sort, the fifth leading into a light-display machine, and the sixth, which was intended to have a musical score, to dwell on the machine in action. This was the only part made, and called *Lichtspiel, Schwarz, Weiss, Grau*. This silent single-reel was shown at the Film Society in November 1932, and has since become a standard curio under such names as *Light Display: Black and White and Grey* or *Lightplay – Black/ White/Grey*. Rights to it were acquired by Grierson, who used sequences or shots in film trailers and poster films, according to Rotha. It appears, most oddly, in a 1933 telephone film called *The Coming of the Dial*. Discs, tubes, wires, spirals, inclined planes and perforations revolve, sometimes wobbling slightly, reflecting light and shade and new angles and perspectives.

An amateur film of an Architects' Congress shot by Moholy was shown at the Film Society in 1933, and he himself followed to England in 1935. He lived here for a while, on friendly terms with Herbert Read, Henry Moore, Barbara Hepworth and many other artists and writers, did some design work and photography, and held an exhibition at the London Gallery in 1937. Alexander Korda, always on the lookout for talent and prestige, particularly from Hungary, commissioned him in 1936 to contribute to *Things to Come*. Some sequences of special effects were made but not used in the film, although according to Kostelanetz[28] they were shown separately. However, with Korda's backing Moholy did make a short film in 1936, put out in late 1938 by Bury Productions as *Lobsters*.[29] This was directed by Moholy together with

John Mathias, with advice from Professor Daniels of the Marine Biology station in Port Erin, Isle of Man. Moholy shot and edited it himself. Musical direction was by Korda's own Muir Mathieson with music by Arthur Benjamin, and the film was eventually distributed theatrically by A.B.F.D. It begins with a lovely sequence of sea, sky and Sussex lobster fishermen making and setting their pots of willow. Six families depend for the season on their hundred pots, and it seems for a moment that a little social significance is creeping into the film, but despite Moholy's stated interest in movement the film is made so obviously with the still photographer's eye for the picturesque that it looks almost unreal. The sequence is accompanied by brisk traditionally based music, but once the pots go over the side we sink beneath the sea, or more accurately into a tank, and into another world. Weird and unfamiliar music accompanies what some critics felt was too much static close photography of the lobsters. There is a third sequence, a magnificent stormy sea above, and a final shot so surprisingly out of place it is almost surrealist, possibly not the work of Moholy himself, of a menu with a lobster appearing through it like a circus horse through a paper hoop. The registered version, it may be added, was about 1,000 feet shorter than the original 2,400 feet. Moholy made a second film in Britain in 1936, the silent 16 mm *New Architecture at the London Zoo*, before leaving in 1937 for the U.S.A., where he later opened a school of design and in 1946 died of leukaemia.[30] Moholy-Nagy was an important theorist. He was seeking new forms of art, and earnestly exhorted artists to abandon the old "easel picture", to go abstract, to examine optics, kinetics and acoustics and find the "new culture of controlled light".[31] His visit was welcome and stimulating. Yet the films he made, apart from the Light Machine, were strangely traditional.

Bury, the firm under whose name *Lobsters* came out, also made a film called *The Grey Seal* in the Hebrides, *Birds*, and *Zetland Birds* in the Shetlands in the years 1937 and 1938. John Mathias, who had helped Moholy, was the director and Cyril Jenkins acted as cameraman, with light musical accompaniment by John Reynders. The wild Scottish islands had great attractions for the location film maker. Dr Werner Kissling made a two-reel film called

Eriskay in 1935 with the assistance of the John Gifford of *Betwixt Land and Sea*. *Rugged Island*, a three-reeler of 1934, was a comparatively ambitious attempt at a documentary story acted by Shetlanders in their own setting. It was made and shot independently by Jenny Brown, a graduate of Glasgow University who had already made several 16 mm films and spent a year in the Shetlands making this one. It was treated with some respect by *Cinema Quarterly*[32] as an example of what independent pro-duction could achieve if you had a little money, but was remembered by Rotha with little enthusiasm.[33] It dealt with changing conditions in the islands and the dissatisfaction felt by young people with the old traditional ways, dramatising this in a story about two families. It was made before *The Turn of the Tide* of 1935 and Michael Powell's *The Edge of the World* of 1937, two much-admired feature films with which its theme had something in common, and at the same time as Flaherty was making his *Man of Aran* off the West coast of Ireland. Made by a flexible amateur unit of ten, it was registered as eligible for quota. Next year Jenny Brown was in Canada where, with the Canadian Griersonian Evelyn Spice, she made *Prairie Winter* about a day in the life of a Saskatchewan farmer. This was handled here by Kinograph, ready as usual to give the inde-pendents a break.

At the other end of the scale was the big-time professional Alexander Korda, who had helped Moholy-Nagy as he did so many other compatriots. He had earlier made an abortive sally of his own into the actuality field. It was announced in October 1934 that he was going to produce shorts "to be supervised by Winston Churchill", but this proved to be only one of his many highly publicised prestige plans which came to nothing. Shortly afterwards, however, he sponsored Julian Huxley in the making of a lovely short film of 1935, *The Private Life of the Gannets*. This was shot by the Korda cameraman Osmond Borrodaile at an island off Pembrokeshire.[34] Editing was by Korda's Philip Charlot and musical direction by Muir Mathieson. Zooming into the map and thence to an overhead shot of Grassholm, the beauti-ful shots of this island, white with birds against the dark sea, and the sequences of birds in flight, diving, and in slow motion are accompanied by Huxley's commentary. The film includes unusual close shots of gannets and of their eggs hatching, as well as extra material on seals and puffins. "And so, once more to Grassholm with its snowy patch of brooding birds, to say Good-bye." It was greatly admired, well reviewed by Rotha in *Cinema Quarterly*,[35] and gained an Award from the American Academy of Motion Picture Arts and Sciences for the best short subject in 1937. It was expected to be the first of a series, and by implication a challenge to Gaumont-British Instructional, but in fact had no successors from the Korda studio. Informative as it undoubtedly was, the ceaseless commentary was criticised by *Sight and Sound*,[36] and the film is really an exceptionally interesting and beautiful illustrated lecture.

A pleasing minor project allowed to go ahead almost unnoticed by the large Korda organisation was a two-reel film called *Wharves and Strays* early in 1935. This, directed and shot by an assistant cameraman at the studio, Bernard Browne, used no commentary but relied entirely on the visuals and a score by Arthur Benjamin and Musical Director Muir Mathieson. It was an attempt to show the London dockland scene, the loading and unloading of cargo, the work of tugs, barges and dockers, by following the adventures of a homeless dog. This was Scruffy, a shaggy mongrel who was London Film Production's "studio dog" and appeared in several feature films. The film was well reviewed as an independent short in *Cinema Quarterly*[37] and had a non-theatrical distribution.

The long production story of Korda's *Conquest of the Air* is one of the most tangled in the field of factual or semi-factual film. Still with the idea of backing up his features with his own documentaries, he planned a full-length film about how man had learnt to fly. Said to be nearing completion at Worton Hall in November 1935, it was described in Rotha's book *Documentary Film*, which was published in January 1936, as a documentary in the theatrical style with scenario by John Monk Saunders and Hugh Gray, cinematography by Hans Schneeberger and editing by William Hornbeck. A version was prepared with a large cast, Wilkie Cooper was added to the credits as cameraman, and Zoltan Korda, Lee Garmes, William Cameron Menzies and

Saunders himself as directors. This version, weighed down with talents, was eventually shelved. In 1937–8 it was taken down and handed to Donald Taylor at Strand to do what Rotha has called a make-do-and-mend job. This new version, of six reels, was shown in March 1938 but not officially trade shown. Documentary director Alex Shaw, cinematographer George Noble and editor R. Q. McNaughton, as well as the composer Arthur Bliss, had pulled it together and made a film covering flight from man's earliest efforts to the rockets of the future. As might be expected it made a bitty film, spanning lyrical shots of sky, birds and statues, some diagrams, stock shots, the original expensively staged historical *scenas*, shots from newsreels, technical information, model work and all. Although it was well treated in *World Film News* Korda was not satisfied with the film and it was not released.[38] Korda's interest in anything but the fully-fledged studio feature was slight, however, and probably did not survive his irritating experience of the leisurely and expensive Flaherty method during the making of *Elephant Boy.*

From the most commercial to the least, we must not overlook the fact that in this welter of film making there was a serious, academic strain making highly specialised demonstration films. Overlapping teaching films, they included for example several hundred short silent films in the Kodak Medical Library, made from 1928 to about 1933, showing mainly surgical procedures demonstrated by senior British specialists at hospitals all over the country. The hospitals sponsored the films, which were photographed and put together, sometimes with stills and diagrams, by the Kodak Medical Department. The National Film Archive also contains such miscellaneous fragments as *Twitching Feet*, showing foot movements of patients suffering from neuritis, filmed by C. C. Ungley; and *Virus Diseases of Plants – the Formation of Intracellular Inclusion*, shot by Percy Smith for the Rothamstead Experimental Station. Both these films were made as early as 1930. *Stasobaso-Phobia*, shot in 1933, shows a patient suffering from a psychiatric disorder during which he found it impossible to stand or walk, and ends with shots taken several months later when, after encouragement, he was able to take faltering steps. In 1935, again, Dr K. H. Pridie made a three-reel silent 16 mm film at Bristol Royal Infirmary Fracture Clinic to show his own technique of *Functional Treatment of Fractures*. The Amalgamated Dental Company had a series of films of from one to four reels, all 16 mm silent films, for exhibition to the dental and medical professions only, demonstrating dental procedures. Less specialised was *Vitamins*, a two-reel film made by the future professional film maker Geoffrey Innes after leaving Cambridge in 1937, giving a history of research and a survey of the importance of vitamins in the diet. At this end of the scale the films overlap both interest films and documentary.

At the other extreme of academic filming was the unique work of Dr Canti, later the subject of an interesting monograph by Professor G. E. H. Foxon. Ronald George Canti was Clinical Pathologist at St Bartholomew's Hospital in London. He worked on the use of radium in the treatment of cancer, and was at one time Scientific Secretary of the British Empire Cancer Research Campaign. He became interested in using film during the twenties, not merely to demonstrate his results but actually as a research tool. Building his own equipment at his home in Hampstead, he was the first to apply time-lapse cinemicrography to cells and tissues to show the effects of exposing cells to rays from radium. By photographing both normal and malignant cells with time-lapse cinemicrography he made it possible to see what happened in various circumstances, research which was hardly possible in any other way. As St Bartholomew's had a link with the Strangeways Laboratory at Cambridge, which was working on the effect of X-rays on cells, they collaborated with Canti by preparing the material to be filmed and sending it up to him in London. He showed his first two films at the Tenth International Congress of Zoology at Budapest in 1927, where they created a sensation. These were *Cells in Tissue Culture (Normal and Abnormal)*, 908 feet, and *Irradiation of Living Tissue by Beta and Gamma Rays*, 560 feet, and Canti was awarded the Röntgen Prize of the British Institute of Radiology in 1928 on the strength of the second one. More professional equipment was provided for him by the British Empire Cancer Campaign, and he made several more films before he died in 1936 at the early age of 53. It is important to remember that, unlike almost any other film maker, research was his aim rather than record or demonstration. The films were sometimes shortened, renamed or altered and the titles and lengths, including those of the important first two, are subject to minor variations.[39]

Serious work was also being undertaken by Dr Townend of the National Physical Laboratory. As early as 1934 Robert Fairthorne noted "the extraordinary film of Townend which, by stroboscopic spark photography, demonstrated the flow of air through pipes".[40] This film was shown at the Fourth International Congress for Applied Mechanics at Cambridge. A couple of years later Strand, with Arthur Elton as producer and Stanley Hawes as director, made a film for the Air Ministry using some of this visible air flow photography of Townend's. Called *Air Flow*, the film showed air flow round various parts of aircraft.[41] Not a documentary film in the usual sense, its aim was to show some methods of aeronautical research used in Britain, and it included shots of some of the apparatus at Farnborough in operation. The Air Ministry liaison was by Robert Fairthorne, and the film was shown at the American Institute of Aeronautical Sciences in December 1936, and at the Royal Aeronautical Society in January 1937.

A performance arranged by the British Film Institute in January 1937 included *Air Flow*, as well as some of the more technical and scientific Gaumont-British Instructional films and such productions as the Forest Products Research's *Box Testing*, *Wind Pressure on Buildings* from the National Physical Laboratory, *Fusion Temperature of Coal Ash* from Fuel Research and others. It was not suggested that the film camera had been a tool in the research rather than a witness to it. In his use of film for research Dr Canti stood almost alone although, according to W. H. George, Lord William Percy's early little film *The Norfolk Bittern* proved for the first time that the bittern cleaned its feathers in the same way, with a powder coming from their roots, as the heron did.[42] Short lengths of film taken by the G.P.O. Film Unit just before the war, also, by showing how differently reinforced basements collapsed when blown up, could also be described as research rather than record.

Down to earth again, it must be repeated that these are but

fragments of the immense amount of activity as people learnt how to use the new medium of expression and communication. But even these few individualists and independents on the fringe of production are enough to refute the idea that the documentary, movement, important though it was, was the only worthwhile activity outside the industry itself.

5

Commercial, Moral and
Social Persuasion

Early in 1935 there were tantalising rumours of the subliminal
possibilities of the cinema. H. J. R. Lister with his Process of
Synoptical Kinepsycotherapy and Kinesynoptical Multisuggestion
was said to be working on the idea of conveying a message to the
subconscious minds of the people in the audience, by printing
superimposed words on the screen "in terms of contrasting and
changing colour light beams". There seemed no end to the
possibilities and, although it was noted in passing, with some
satisfaction, that films could thus be assured of commercial success
by telling people's subconscious minds how good they were,
idealism suggested uses far beyond the merely mercenary. It was
reported that Lister wished to use his system "to treat criminals
and lunatics" and to further international peace. A suitable peace
message superimposed on entertainment films, with governments
paying a possible £5 per 1,000 feet, would lead to the mouth-
watering prospect of £5,000 extra on 200 copies of a 5,000 foot
film *"with no damage to the entertainment value of copies so
treated"*, as Lister emphasised. He even wondered if the League
of Nations might take it up. Alas, no more was heard of this
tempting project.

But there was plenty of more humdrum manipulation of minds
going on. Take the ingenuous approach of the young Sydney
Box, working at the time as a writer for Publicity Films:

Today film propaganda is a world force of inestimable power –
inestimable because at least two of its principal manifestations
are ingeniously camouflaged as entertainment, news, or interest
pictures. Political, or semi-political propaganda, and publicity
for great industries are being disseminated regularly in this
way.[1]

That was written in 1937. The direct film advertisement,
extolling the virtues and pushing the sales of a named product,
had existed for many years. Cinemas booked them through
agencies, and the advertiser paid for screen time in proportion
to the size and character of the expected audience, which
depended on such things as the size and situation of the cinema
and the time of the year. These films ran for up to five minutes
and exhibitors found there was a limit to the number the public
would tolerate. There was evidence that they had already tried
the patience of audiences in America.

Younger Publicity Service, founded in the twenties, was one
of the chief agencies in this country. Under Harry Adley, it
controlled the advertising rights of some five hundred cinemas all
over the country by 1931. Box claimed that several commercial
firms in Britain allocated over £10,000 a year to film publicity
and that it cost approximately £1 per thousand people reached.
He gave four anonymous examples, showing production and
booking costs and the kind of audience attained. The first, a
historical film about tyres, had cost £1,125 to make and the firm
spent £4,875 buying space at 404 Grade A cinemas, including
in this figure the cost of copies and transport. A story film with
two stars popularising a household product had cost £1,000 to
make and £3,500 to book to 362 middle-class suburban cinemas.
A documentary about industrial Britain made on behalf of a
brand of petrol had cost £850 plus £4,100 for 229 bookings and
one of a film star promoting a beauty preparation had cost £1,000
plus £2,716 for 514 working-class area bookings. In general,
according to him, an advertising film by 1937 could cost anything from £500 to £7,000, colour cartoons costing from £3 to
£5 per foot.

Sound was adopted quickly by the advertising men. A film of

1929 made for Rowntree's chocolate, *Meet Mr. York! – A Speaking Likeness*, claims towards the end to be the "first advertising talking cartoon that has ever been made, lip synchronised". In it, "Plain Mr. York of York, York" is brought to life from a well-known hoarding poster, animated and given speech in a mixture of live action film, showing artist and film technician, and a rather crude black and white cartoon.

This short film was produced by an old-timer, Bertram Philips, for "British Publicity Talking Films in conjunction with S. A. Benson". There was a hinterland of film makers and agents, largely unknown to the rest of the film industry, arranging for the production and dissemination of publicity films which ranged from the simple local advertisement to a background promotional film about a whole industry like *The Wee Blue Blossom* made for the Irish Linen Guild. There were many such films during the decade and it is possible to identify only a few. Nor is it quite as easy to define even this simple category as one might expect. Although films made for commercial purposes are easy enough to distinguish, they were frequently used as educational films, interest and magazine items and even documentaries. There were uses within the sponsoring firm, such as training and instruction of staff, morale building, or showing to customers or shareholders. Several companies included vocational training films in their work. The films were booked extensively as educational films. In 1933 G. H. Sewell, writing a handbook of *Commercial Cinematography*, gave a list of people using film publicity which included aircraft, aluminium, boot polish and electrical gear manufacturers; motors, oil, paper, scientific instrument makers and many others; hospitals, building societies, garages, laundries, press agencies; steamship and tram companies, missionaries. The list seemed endless. The films to which he referred, in fact, were those which three or four years later William Lally was to gather together in his encyclopaedic list of "educational films". And the descendant of the early industrial, the background film about an industry or large firm promoting goodwill and a familiar image, was so much more geared to information than persuasion that it was much nearer to documentary than to advertising. The National Film Corporation, and later Younger Film Productions, were producing

19 A social warning
(*The Road of
Health*, 1931).

20 "Suffer me to
come to thee . . ."
(*In Our Time*, 1933).

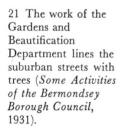

21 The work of the
Gardens and
Beautification
Department lines the
suburban streets with
trees (*Some Activities
of the Bermondsey
Borough Council*,
1931).

associates of Younger Publicity Service with a small studio at Great Windmill Street in London where longer and more ambitious advertising and propaganda films were made.

As the substandard film developed during the decade a new outlet for these films opened up, different from either the cinemas or the schools. In 1933 Sewell observed that the United States were ahead of the U.K. in the use of substandard film by business, for free films were being distributed to home movie shows, clubs and institutions of every sort. But four years later Box, whilst still regarding the cinema as the largest market, also spoke of a large non-theatrical audience in this country, supplied by film libraries and road shows. Both Western Electric and Gaumont-British ran important road show services. Sound Services, founded by Western Electric, claimed to have given over 40,000 shows of sound film programmes between 1934 and 1937 and were prepared to undertake single shows or whole national film campaigns. Road show audiences were distinguished by the trade as to whether "invited" – in other words gathered together specially to see the films in question in hired cinemas, halls, shops and trade exhibitions – or "existing", as in the case of a group already meeting regularly and booking the films whether from a special interest in the subject, or, more likely it must be admitted, as an inexpensive form of entertainment. W. D. & H. O. Wills, makers of a cheap brand of cigarette called Woodbines, had a substandard one-reel sound-on-disc film called *How Woodbines are Made* which they calculated in 1934 had been shown in some 8,000 working men's clubs. Groups included film societies, churches, Women's Institutes, Mother's Unions, Townswomens' Guilds, Girls' Societies and Clubs, the British Legion, the Conservative, Liberal and Labour Party Clubs, Friendly Societies, works clubs and sports clubs. Box estimated that there might be twenty million people in such audiences. The size of this non-theatrical market is of some importance in view of Grierson's famous dictum that the audience outside the cinema was bigger than that inside it, which is frequently cited as the reason for his change of direction about 1933 and his subsequent interest in non-theatrical distribution. The fact is that it was not one audience at all. The potential school audience for good educational films, which was part of it, was certainly very large, although in this country it was hardly tapped during the thirties. But for publicity or persuasive purposes the overall impact of a single countrywide booking to a major circuit of cinemas, with its large unspecialised audiences, would undoubtedly have been far greater than even a large number of bookings to the small, miscellaneous groups which comprised the fragmented and casual non-theatrical audience. The concept of a large audience outside the cinema was more or less meaningless until the advent of mass television.

Unlike educational films, most industrial films were by their very nature specially shot rather than made from library material. Who made them? Some firms tried their own hands. The Croydon Gas Company, for example, made an hour-long amateur film about gas on silent substandard stock to be accompanied by a lecture. Vickers Aviation had had a cinema unit since 1914, and their chief cameraman, W. G. Carrington, made films for publicity as well as for technical purposes. The best known of these was in fact a silent compilation of 1932 called *Historic Flights*, showing famous British air achievements which had used Vickers aircraft. Morris Motors had a film unit consisting for the most part of people with other jobs at the Cowley works including R. W. Barnes, a jig draughtsman who acted as cameraman, and W. M. W. Thomas as scenarist and editor. They made a number of sound two-reelers for free loan and also had four road show units of their own. The films were aimed principally at agents and salesmen, but like so many others figured in many educational lists. *Michael Faraday* was registered in 1931 as having been produced by British Thompson-Houston, and *Write Thro' the Ages*, a one-reel history of shorthand, by Sir Isaac Pitman and Sons. The Bristol Development Board had a half-hour 16 mm film in 1937 called *Bristol, City of a Thousand Years* made by a local firm, and the Isle of Man Publicity Board had *Where Dreams Come True*. Both these films, however, were of a type which was gradually being taken over by T.I.D.A.

More typically, publicity films were either made or farmed out by the big advertising agencies which were a growing feature of the commercial world of the thirties. Dorland Advertising, for example, had a film director called C. R. Stilwell who used the

Pathé studio at Welwyn. Pritchard, Wood and Partners made advertising films and later in the thirties formed a film company of their own. This was Spectator Short Films, under its chairman and managing director Fleetwood C. Pritchard, other directors including Sinclair Wood and film men G. F. Noxon and Ivan Scott. They had a comparatively large professional staff, including the editor and scenarist Michael Hankinson and the cameraman George Noble, and a studio in Old Burlington Street. They made the *Point of View* series discussed under news films and other more documentary films, as well as contract work.

Publicity Films, the biggest producer in this field, was a subsidiary of the London Press Exchange. It had a studio at Merton Park, built about 1929, with a small stage of 66 feet by 72 capable of taking two small sets and fitted with R.C.A. sound. S. C. Leslie, the publicist, worked for the London Press Exchange in the early thirties, when it handled the gas industry account, and he was an early enthusiast for the prestige film not directly about the sponsor's own product. He was unable to convert the firm to the idea of the documentary with some sort of social significance instead of a purely commercial appeal, and left them in early 1936 to work directly for the gas industry, where he was instrumental in the sponsorship of some of the most important mainstream documentaries of the decade. Publicity Films stuck to a more conventional type of film, and had a very large output of high quality advertising films for many companies. They made several for the Dunlop Rubber Company. *The World Rolls On* was directed by Ralph Smart (who later became a feature director), shot by James Rogers and written by Box, and was a brief account of the invention and history of the wheel, including the rubber tyre invented by the Irish vet Dunlop; *Dunlop "90"* showed the manufacture of a car tyre; and *From Acorn to Oak* was a shorter film made to celebrate the jubilee of the invention of the pneumatic rubber tyre for bicycles. This was directed by Montgomery Tully, who also later became a feature director, and again it was shot by Rogers and included well staged historical sequences.[2]

It was at Merton Park that Walter Creighton, after his unsatisfactory experience with the Empire Marketing Board, made his

Cadbury Films. Cadbury Brothers had long favoured publicity films, unlike their rivals J. S. Fry and Co., who sponsored only a few. In 1932 Creighton and the cameraman Rogers visited West Africa for them and made several films which were shown in 1933. *Castles and Fisherfolk* about the Gold Coast, *Message of the Drum*, and the long film about cocoa from its growth on the Gold Coast to its manufacture in the U.K. called *The Night Watchman's Story* were apparently felt to be nice-looking films but were said to lack the deeper significance which would have lifted them into the documentary class, and to be marred by an over emphatic style of commentary. However, the first was shown at the Film Society, and all were well reviewed in *Sight and Sound*, which said: "Creighton has a flair for screen pictorialism which puts his work into a class of its own among publicity films."[3]

Creighton had also received some praise for the second of his E.M.B. films, *A Southern April*, and seems to have made something which sounds from the title as if it might have had more documentary content, *Me Proper Black Man*, a one-reeler about village life on the Gold Coast. But nothing was subsequently said about this film and he does not seem to have pursued the course it presented. From all this material Cadbury's was later able to supply the National Film Library with *Cocoa from the Gold Coast*, a silent educational film made under the supervision of the B.F.I.'s Geography Committee. Publicity Films continued to make Cadbury films, including a training film for retailers in the form of a five-reel story film, *Sweet Success*. *Country Fare* in 1936 was a two-reeler about the production of eggs, milk and barley in the Cotswolds and was directed by one of the mainstream documentary directors, Evelyn Spice. *Workaday*, also in 1936, was a four-reel treatment of twenty-four hours in the Bournville works directed by Ralph Smart and shot by Rogers, and *Plantation People*, also of 1936, was a two-reeler about cocoa growing made in Trinidad in Technicolor. It was directed by Bournville executive A. R. Taylor and was said to have been shot by Hollywood cameraman Ray Rennahan, who was in Britain in mid-1936 to shoot the first British Technicolor feature, *Wings of the Morning*. Like *Country Fare* and *Workaday*, it was of sufficient importance to be reviewed not only by *Sight and Sound* but by *Life and Letters Today*, yet it proves to be a rather amateurish film, with disappointing colour and a typical John Reynders light musical score, surprisingly making no use whatever of the local music. It is larded with complacent remarks about the "native workers . . . contented in the sunshine" and "happy in their neat little houses". *The Night Watchman's Story*, too, although ambitious in conception, proves on examination to be pedestrian in style.

Another firm associated with a press agency, in this case the Topical Press Agency, was the Commercial and Educational Film Company with its small studio at Red Lion Court, Fleet Street. During the thirties it made topical and magazine items and publicity films, including a number for the London Midland and Scottish Railway, and prospered to such an extent that by 1939 it was using Highbury Studios as well as its own. The anonymous people who produced these films would hardly have been regarded as film makers at all by, for example, the mainstream documentary élite, and Harry Watt is slightly scathing about an L.M.S. railway film director who actually appeared wearing a bowler hat.[4] Yet the films, unimaginative and without conscious social significance, are clear and interesting and show a firm and workmanlike attention to their own purpose. *Engine Shed*, for example, is a one-reel film of dos and don'ts for railway staff, and wastes no time in sugaring the pill. The upper-class, positive, authoritarian voice of the commentator exhorts staff not to waste the company's money. All mistakes would waste money, and to show them what not to do the film impolitely pictures the men foolishly making one mistake after another, each with its inevitable consequence. "Not too good, is it!" he says grimly. Using music only at the beginning and in the final sequence of the speeding train, the film seeks simply to be businesslike, yet is full of interest. *Study in Steel*, a two-reeler about the construction of an engine at the Crewe works of the London Midland and Scottish Railway, was made in 1935.[5] It starts with a sequence of busy music, railway puffing and hissing noises, trains rushing about with strident mood music to accompany the message of how much society needs them; the main body of the film begins more calmly with plans and specifications, materials and works, and with steady, lucid continuity we follow the building of Loco No. 62007, the casting of the cylinders being an exceptionally clear sequence. Written with knowledge and spoken with affection by a commentator quite unlike the usual educated and uninterested outsider, it is a most beguiling fringe film with its quaintly conventional ending: "Here's to you, No. 62007, here's luck and good running." After the new quota legislation opened up the theatrical market for shorts, a number of Topical Press Agency films made earlier were registered for theatrical booking.

The important advertising agency J. Walter Thompson was behind the production of four colour puppet films for the Horlicks Malted Milk Company by George Pál. A Hungarian, Pál had started making films in 1932 for a German cigarette firm, and had made *The Ship of the Ether* in 1934 and a non-advertising film, *Ali Baba and the Forty Thieves*, in 1935 in Holland. By 1936 he had a studio at Eindhoven and was making advertisements for Philips Radio.[6] He first made a Horlicks film for J. Walter Thompson in 1936 whilst still in Holland. This was *On Parade*. In Gasparcolor, it made play with the Horlicks advertising catch phrase "night starvation". It was much admired both by trade and critics and was shown at the Film Society. After this, still in Holland, he made *Love on the Range*, *Sky Pirates* and *What Ho! She Bumps* in 1937, and *South Sea Sweetheart* in 1938, all for J. Walter Thompson. All five films were made to the music of Debroy Somers and his popular dance band, and all except the early one *On Parade* were in Technicolor. The Gasparcolor of the first, more diffuse and glowing than Technicolor, brighter and more colourful than Dufay, stressed amber-red and torquoise-blue and gave the images a softly-shaded, gem-like quality. This very attractive process was a subtractive one and used acid dyes. Invented by Dr Bela Gaspar, it was expensive to use and seems to have been suitable only for animation films with their single exposure method. It was used for advertising films by Carreras, Parke Davis, Cadbury and Euthymol as well as Horlicks and a Len Lye film for BP and Shell-Mex, and was later managed in this country by the inventor's brother, Imre Gaspar. The Technicolor of Pál's other films is very different, flatter and paler, perhaps more manageable but certainly less decorative. New wooden puppets were carved for each stage of the animation and thus appeared very flexible, even rubbery.[7] They were clever and sophisticated films rather than lovable ones and the general effect of these "Puppetoons" was bright and professional. They cheered up many a drab supporting programme. Horlicks's rival bedtime drink, Ovaltine, seems to have preferred radio to film as an advertising medium. *The Home of Good Health* was an Ovaltine film, but it was their pervasive jingle "We are the Ovalteenies, Happy girls and boys", sung on the commercial radio of Luxembourg, that was heard everywhere.

A variant of the advertising film was the magazine. A short film put out by "Kirwan Film Service" in the mid-thirties, for example, shows the pretty actress Enid Stamp Taylor flying to Blackpool, visiting a pub, discussing cars with a Blackpool car dealer, seeing over a clothing factory, talking brightly throughout and managing to plug Blackpool itself, United Airways, Ford cars, a pub, a motor dealer and a manufacturer of overalls in quick succession. Other firms which used film included Lever Brothers with a four-reeler about their manufacturing garden city, *Port Sunlight*, and *The Romance of Soap Making*. Mabie, Todd & Co. had three films made by Blunt & McCormack, with Leslie Eveleigh directing and L. C. Rudkin as cameraman; these were a fifty-minute film showing the manufacture of fountain pens, *Making a Swan Pen*, and two shorter films, *Brewing Ink* and *Then Came the Swan*, the latter a history of writing. The United Steel Companies had several detailed films showing some of the technical processes involved in making steel. Bassett Lowke had *Real and Model Railways*, which they hopefully described as "a good film for boys". Various films were made for the Ford Motor Company by Pathé, including *Your Driving Test* and a more direct advertisement, *Power Farming by Fordson*, which demonstrated how a tractor could find uses on the farm right through the year. Clear and persuasive as it must have seemed at the time, it is for us today an interesting document about farming in the thirties. A couple of silent substandard films directed by Marcus Cooper and shot by Harry Waxman were the one-reel *Down Dagenham Way* and the two-reel *Ups and Downs*, the second showing the touring prowess of four popular models of car. Another Ford film which encouraged car touring, *Westward Ho*, was almost a travel film, and *By the Water's Edge* is a half-hour tour of the Ford works. Gibbs Dentifrice had *Ivory Castles*; Steuart Films made *Making Records* for H.M.V. Gramophone Co.; Cine Equipments made *Optical Glass Manufacture* for Chance Bros; and Lyons and Co., the catering and restaurant company, had their *Noona be Nippy*, a long film showing their waitresses how to behave and, like the L.M.S. railway film, mercilessly demonstrating the wrong methods at the expense of what the National Film Library catalogue called the "clumsy girl", who fared badly compared with her defter colleagues. Fox Photos, a commercial advertising and press photographic agency started in the twenties, was said to be making substandard silent films for Talbot Motor Works and Winsor & Newton, the artist's materials supplier, in 1933. The British Road Tar Association had an early film, *The Highway*, produced by British Films and directed by James Fenton, with musical background by Horace Shepherd, which told the history of British roads from two thousand years ago to the modern tar-surfaced roads.[8] Another British Road Tar film of the early thirties was the two-reel *From Coal-Mine to Road*. This, showing the processes from the mines to the final tar macadamising of the roads, is another example of the strange charm of the fringe film. In sepia, with a mixture of titles and commentary, it appears to have been put together from old silent film, some of it almost certainly foreign, vast vistas of dim factory with sunbeams slanting down through the haze, and a charming and courtly commentator using such unexpected phrases as "the unsuspected wonders of tar", and speaking of "a general view" or a "top view" and "more about that anon".

There were usually between fifty and sixty firms available to make advertising and commercial films, but an Advertising and Industrial Films Association was formed in the early part of the thirties, significantly enough "to promote confidence in the industry and promote members' prestige", and of this association there were said to be only twenty members in October 1934.

The Executive Committee included G. E. Turner of Publicity Films, Harry Adley of Younger Publicity Service, and E. P. L. Pelly of Western Electric. Other members were S. Presbury & Co., a busy firm in Charing Cross Road; W. Devonport Hackney of the Garrick Film Company, which also did cartoon work; T. F. Aveling Ginever, whose company Gee Films had been making films for Austin Motors before 1930 and who also made a few religious films; and H. Hales Dutton of Gaumont-British. Gaumont had, of course, very early experience of industrials and Gaumont-British Screen Services had been formed for publicity production at the same time as Gaumont-British Instructional and Gaumont-British Equipments in 1933. They were in a good position to handle advertising films on their large circuit, and rapidly became one of the leading firms in the field. Other names were Morgan Film Service with its managing director Philip de Solla, which had made early films for Robeleine, Lloyds Bank, Boots the Chemists, Gibbs Dentifrice, the *Daily News* and Eagle Star and British Dominion Insurance; and Publicity Picture Productions and Cartoons, which was another early and durable company under film directors A. E. C. Hopkins and R. H. Dyer and editor M. J. Samuel, which specialised in colour and cartoon work. British Utility Films under John Alderson, with Mrs Florinda Kingdon-Ward and cameraman James Burger, made advertising, educational and industrial films for a short while in the early thirties, including two sponsored health films, and had a high reputation in the trade. And Revelation Films used several different studios and made educational and commercial films and colour cartoons for a few years in the mid-thirties, changing its name to Cartoon Films about 1937–8.

It was Revelation which produced a seven-minute film called *See How they Won* in 1935 for the Boots Drug Company. This was a colour cartoon in Brewstercolor, showing disease germs being driven from a suburban house by a "white-coated army of young men from Boots the chemists".[9] It was said to consist of 7,000 drawings and to have taken 170 people seven weeks to make, but, whereas the story and sketches came from the U.K., the animation was done in Hollywood by the well-known and experienced American cartoon maker Ub Iwerks. It was important enough to be mentioned by *Life and Letters Today*[10] but the reliance on American expertise speaks for itself.

The few cartoon makers in this country subsisted largely on advertising work and animated diagrams for educational or documentary films. Horace Shepherd had tried the comic cartoon in 1930 with a few "Bingo" cartoons but had abandoned it and transferred his attention to interest films. Len Lye's early abstract film, *Kaleidoscope*, shown at the Film Society in late 1935 and reviewed by *Life and Letters Today*[11] and many others, was used as an advertisement by Churchman Cigarettes. In Spicer colour, it was animated though hardly a cartoon, and was credited as "painted and designed" by Lye and "charted and synchronised" by Jack Ellit to the music of a beguine. Travis Jackson, with Travis Jackson Productions at Morecambe, was a prolific producer of cartoon films for publicity and also had a series of "Jackatoons" of his own. He had one sound and two silent stages, with facilities both for animation and microphotography. Apart from the Hoppin-Gross cartoon, *The Fox Hunt*, backed by Korda in 1936, and some films made by Cyril Jenkins using animated puppets ingeniously made out of curled and rolled paper, animation in this country was rarely used in films for entertainment only. But by far the best known British cartoon maker was Anson Dyer, who managed to produce a well-known series of comic cartoons as well as a number of publicity films.

Dyer, who by 1936 was already 60 years old, was a veteran of the British film industry and had worked at the Walton studio for some years. A tall, bony, dapper man with slick silver hair and dark bushy eyebrows, he had started as a stained-glass artist before turning to film cartoons at the end of the First World War. In association with Nettlefold, who had taken Walton over from Hepworth, Dyer was at work in Jermyn Street in London during 1935 on a colour series for Nettlefold's new firm Anglia Films, which had some twenty-five draughtsmen. He worked at first in a two-colour system, Dunning Colour, and used Visatone sound with pre-synch recording, animating the drawings to fit the sound track. His key men were D. Mikkelsen and J. Myller, and his technical expert S. Griffiths. His series was based on, and accompanied, the famous comic monologues of actor Stanley

Holloway, delivered in north-country accent, about a working-class character called Sam.[12] During the next few years he made *Sam and his Musket, 'Alt, Oo Goes Theer?, Carmen, Beat the Retreat, Sam's Medal, Drummed Out, The Lion and Albert, Gunner Sam* and *Three Ha'pence a Foot.* The first of them was shown at the Film Society and they had considerable popular success, partly as a result of Holloway's identification with Sam on radio and record. In June 1937 Anson Dyer Productions was registered with a capital of £2,000. He made advertising films, for Cocktail Cigarettes among others, but chiefly for Bush Radios. *All the Fun of the 'Air* shows gaily dressed costers going to the fair on Hampstead Heath, and ends with a riotous version of the song "Down at the Old Bull and Bush", the name of a Hampstead pub, the bush being used as a symbol for the film's sponsor, Bush Radios. The animation is adequate and the simple stylised visuals are pleasing, the Dunning Colour softly emphasising green and yellows.[13] Although both Dyer and Anglia were said to be doing well there were no more Sam cartoons, and early in 1938 both companies were in voluntary liquidation. In July 1938 Dyer and his key men, now using Technicolor, started a new company at Riverside Studios purely for advertising films. Two Bush films, *The King with a Terrible Temper* and *The King with Terrible Hiccups*, are colourful and well animated although narration is preferred to dialogue. The stories, which both rely on visual surprise gags, lean heavily on a traditional fairy-story formula, and are as alike as the similarity of their titles would lead one to fear.

In the car industry, we have seen that Ford Motors preferred the strictly commercial film. But B.S.A. & Daimler employed Bruce Woolfe's British Independent Productions with Paul Rotha and the cameraman from British Instructional, Jack Parker, to make a two-reeler, *Roadwards*, in 1933. In the same year the Humber-Hillman Car Company had a one-reel film made by Steuart Films, with J. B. Holmes, later also a mainstream director, cameraman Jimmy Rogers and music by Clarence Raybould, called *Where the Road Begins.* This, explaining roads from blue-print stage to the road itself, lacked the social theme of more advanced documentary but was rather more than mere product advertising, and in fact both of these films were potential documentaries. The Austin Motor Company, however, a very big user of film, went to the small commercial firms for ordinary publicity films as Ford did. In 1930 they sponsored a five-reel film called *This Progress* to show to their customers, which was made by Ginever with cameraman Walter Blakeley; this was later re-edited as a three-reel version for theatrical showing and called *Men and Machines*. Other Gee films were *Wheels Then and Now* and *Building Britain's Dependable Car*, showing some of the processes at the Longbridge works. During the next few years a very large number of short films were made for Austin by Publicity Films. Available variously in 35 mm sound and 16 mm silent film, they took the form of interest films. Dealing partly with the manufacture and use of cars, they also included a number of travel or touring films. *Men Who Work* was even said by Lally to be about the "human aspect of modern motor car production", but it is far from the documentary spirit that this implies. Examination of the film shows it to be a very ordinary interest film about the 19,000 men working at Longbridge, with loud insistent and irritating music, and a bright travelogue type of commentary.

But there were areas, particularly in transport and the public utilities, where the commercial advertising film and the Grierson documentary were seen to be alternative approaches. And, whereas railways stuck to the commercial firms, air transport largely preferred the documentary; electricity, the commercial; gas, mainly the documentary; Cunard White Star, the commercial; the Orient Line, the documentary.

A number of private commercial firms in the electricity industry sponsored early films made by British Instructional Films, silent films that were in fact little more than lantern lectures with long, informative titles replacing the lecturer. We have seen that British Thompson-Houston were more enterprising, with their historical *Michael Faraday*. But it is important to realise that during the decade the effects on society, and on individual living, of a greater use of electricity were at least as important as those brought by gas. Yet, although the British Electrical Development Association were also responsible for a number of films, these were all made

by commercial rather than documentary film makers and
B.E.D.A. does not seem to have appreciated the social significance
of its role as the gas industry did. Whereas the British Commercial Gas Association could sponsor a film like John Taylor's
outstanding *The Smoke Menace*, the B.E.D.A. film on the same
subject sounds dull and unimaginative in comparison:

> The Blight of Coal Smoke and a Cure – the Evils of
> Atmospheric Pollution (1 reel, silent):
> The evils of atmospheric pollution by the wasteful burning of
> coal in London and the industrial areas are clearly shown, and
> the help which Electricity can give in abolishing the smoke
> nuisance is illustrated by views of various methods of using
> Electricity for heating and other duties. This film includes
> amusing cartoons.[14]

Other films were *Coal Heap to Consumer*, *Electricity* about the
work of the Central Electricity Board and *Power*, a long silent
film about the construction of the National Grid. B.E.D.A. seems
to have been content with an older style of film making. Percy
Nash, who was 70 by 1930 and had completely dropped out of
the film industry itself, made a silent 16-minute *History of
Electricity* for them. And another veteran, Joseph Best, made a
four-reel silent film about the uses of electricity in the country
districts which circulated in a full-length version called either
Rural Electrification or *Country Currents*, with a one-reel version
also called *Country Currents*. This film, clearly made in the
middle or late thirties, is old-fashioned in its cutting, its choice of
camera angle and its general approach. Even so it is a competent
professional job within its limitations and it is only fair to say
that, as was so often the case, this simple approach gives a good
clear look at a facet of the life of the time. The contrast between
the old kitchen and the new electric one is a document of social
history brought to life. B.E.D.A. also had a number of acted
films directed by Alexander Esway, meant to be more popular and
made in 35 mm sound film for the cinema, with slightly whimsical
titles such as *Plenty of Time to Play*, a vision of a labour-saving
future; *Well I Never!*, in which everything goes wrong but is put

right by electricity; *Wizard in the Wall*, a historical treatment; and also a warning film about correct wiring called *Edward and Eda*. The T.I.D.A. film of 1939, *News by Wire*, put out for the B.E.D.A., was a general film about the grid system and the use of electricity in industry, transport and the home. The only time this important industry used the documentary idea was when Hugh Quigley of the Central Electricity Board agreed to sponsor the film about England which Paul Rotha already wanted to make. This was accordingly linked to the idea of changes made possible by the contemporary extension of the national grid, and became *The Face of Britain*, an important film described in the author's book on the documentary movement, but this isolated venture into true documentary was not repeated. The gas industry, on the other hand, although it had its commercial shorts made by Publicity Picture Productions and the animated figure of "Mr Therm", a cheerful star-shaped personification of gas energy, was carried by the influence of S. C. Leslie into the forefront of the documentary movement.

These snatches of information are enough to suggest the enormous number and variety of commercial publicity films. Those made in 35 mm might or might not be in substandard versions as well, and many were made in both sound and silent versions. The films that remain, and the titles and descriptions of many, many more, show us a large number of people using film, not by any means amateurishly but very competently within the limits of their own purposes, to promote their goods or services.

But commercial firms were not the only ones to have discovered the persuasive power of the cinema. Another category of motivated films which show vividly how the idea of using film to communicate and persuade spread during the thirties was that of the religious film. In earlier times there had been many silent imported films with a religious theme such as passion plays, biblical stories and spectacles. The more grandiose were usually given special exhibition in theatres and concert halls, and a special pseudo-reverent note crept into the promotion. Even so there seems to have been less interest in them here than in Catholic countries or in America, and the attitude of the British Board of Film Censors was not favourable to their use in cinemas. They had been made to exploit a rather special vein in the audience but were still commercial ventures within the entertainment framework. By the early thirties they were far less numerous. On the other hand religious groups, like so many others, were beginning to wonder how the film could be of service to them as a means of communication.

Thus in 1932 a non-denominational body called the Guilds of Light was formed "to encourage the religious use of the film", according to R. G. Burnett.[15] The Established and Free Churches joined together with branches in different parts of the country and in late 1933 and early 1934 formed the Religious Film Society to assist in the production and exhibition of religious and other films which Burnett calls "definitely Christian films". The Catholic Film Society under Father Ferdinand Valentine was formed separately in the summer of 1934. And Dr Donald Soper, the Methodist, had been speaking independently in support of the film and its possibilities for several years.

The Methodist millionaire flour miller J. Arthur Rank, according to his biographer, had seen "the possibility of using modern techniques of propaganda and the Press to preach to the irreligious mass of twentieth-century Britain"[16] and had already entered the field of journalism by buying the *Methodist Times*. He then became interested in the idea of showing films in churches and was one of the people behind the formation of the Religious Film Society. He was Joint Honorary Treasurer along with Norman Spicer, and the Chairman was Thomas E. Marks; others on the committee include the Reverend Benjamin Gregory, who was also to have a hand in the affairs of the British Film Institute. Another was the Reverend Thomas Tiplady who, as superintendent of the Lambeth Mission, had established the first "cinema-church" in London. According to Burnett alterations to the church cost over £10,000, and the minister used hymn-slides and a 60-minute film.

A film called *In Our Time* had been greeted in 1933 as the first religious sound film to be made in this country. It was produced at Wembley by Thomas F. Aveling Ginever as a David MacKane production. Ginever had been in films since about 1928, and had recently been making advertising films for the

Austin Motor Company. He and David MacKane Watt registered David MacKane Productions in June 1933 as a £100 company. The film was described as "the first serious attempt to use popular cinema as direct religious propaganda".[17] In it a mysterious stranger in a long black cloak, his face in the shadow of a big black hat, interrupts an argument in a pub about the state of the country, between a rich man with his whisky and a poor man with his pint, asking them "Why blame each other?" A panorama of the country in our time, the glorious countryside, poverty and depression in ugly cities, waiting and listening crowds with the Salvation Army speaker, the minister and the politician build up to the message that faith is what the country needs. In the second reel things look up and the film, which uses every sentimental cliché possible – the shaft of sunlight through the clouds, the little girl at her innocent prayers – and mixes a strong patriotic note with the religious one, ends with the rich man accepting a half-pint from the poor man after the mysterious stranger, departing against the light, turns and says "Courage, my friends, we shall meet again." Completely carried away, the *Monthly Film Bulletin* discovered "touches of genius".[18]

As he was known to be searching for religious films of a sufficiently high quality to suit audiences accustomed to the standards of the commercial cinema, Rank was shown *In Our Time* and introduced to Ginever. The film was technically adequate, even if its content was poor. As a result Ginever made *Mastership* for the Religious Film Society, at a cost of £2,700.[19] This two-reel film, trade shown and registered for renters' quota in April 1934, took a week to shoot at Merton Park studios with a professional cast and the well-known minister from the slums of Poplar, W. H. Lax, as himself, preaching a sermon about several conversions he had witnessed in his Poplar mission work, and appealing to the audience to submit to the mastership of Christ. Rank's arrival in the film world was marked by the credit "scenario based upon material supplied by Rev. W. H. Lax and J. A. Rank". But, according to Wood, Rank later described this film as "lousy", and certainly the vignettes, the redemption of a drunk and of two burglars, sound melodramatic and banal. As for *In Our Time*, it seems to have disappeared from view and figures in none of the contemporary lists of religious films.

It is most unlikely that Rank found these films satisfactory. Being the man he was, he was drawn step by step into the industry. In July 1934 he registered a £6,000 private company, British National Films, which originally seems to have had leanings towards a patriotic, religious and educational style of film making. Other directors were fellow industrialist Major J. S. Courtauld, already dabbling in films in A.T.P. and Raycol, and Lady Yule, an extremely wealthy widow with an inherited fortune from the jute industry. Wood tells how Rank and Ginever fell out, although a further Ginever film for the Religious Film Society, made after the formation of British National, came out in the winter of 1935. This was *Service*, a three-reel moral tale described as follows:

> Depicting an attempt to serve Christ, but failure follows the first temptation. Restitution is made and the hero is strengthened for more successful endeavour.[20]

Other British National religious films for the R.F.S. were made, but they sound equally unimpressive. *Inasmuch*, the story of St Francis of Assisi and the beggar woman, with Donald Wolfit as St Francis, was criticised in *Sight and Sound*.[21] And one can imagine *The Common Round*:

> Boys first seen at school grow up to find adventure in a remote African Mission and live up to their school-master's exhortation to "stick it out".[22]

During 1935 British National became a full commercial feature producer with *Turn of the Tide*. Although it retained some of the characteristics of moral purpose, sincerity, simplicity and realism, this was a commercial feature film and after it British National went on to produce ordinary entertainment films. Ginever had left and was by now working for Pathé. The R.F.S. continued, however, opening a small studio of its own at Norwood in South London in September 1937. Films included *Peter Smith*, a modern version of Peter's denial of Christ, *In his Steps*, *Te Deum*, *Barabbas* and *William Tyndale*, all made in 1936 or earlier. Of

a later group the best seems to have been *The Life of St. Paul,*
later called *Faith Triumphant,* made at Pinewood by the professional director who had made *Turn of the Tide,* Norman
Walker. It should be added that although *Barabbas* was about
the crucifixion the figure of Christ was not shown. Films like
The Royal and Ancient City of Canterbury were also distributed
by the R.F.S.

Rank became more and more absorbed by the commercial film
world, moving from studio ownership to exhibition and eventually
to production on a very large scale. But this unusual man, who
continued to teach at his local Sunday school even when he
was the biggest film tycoon in the country, did not give up his
interest in the religious use of film and continued to work for the
R.F.S., now under the Cinema Christian Council, of which the
Archbishop of Canterbury was President. The Western Electric
company, in its promotion of non-theatrical and substandard
shows, was campaigning for the use of films approved by the
Religious Film Society. Gaumont-British Instructional, Gaumont-
British Equipments and Gaumont-British Screen Services were all
formed at about the same time. Rank gave hundreds of GeBeScope
projectors to the R.F.S. and during the purchase of projection
equipment from Gaumont-British he was able to interest Ian
Cremieu-Javal of G-BI in the production of religious films. They
had already made *Biblical Palestine* in 1934, a three-reel tour
with relevant commentary by Lord Lee of Fareham, edited by
Andrew Buchanan. This film was usually included in lists of
religious films although it was in fact more geographical and
historical. But it was not until 1937 that G-BI actually went into
the production of religious films. There were plans for six in
September 1937, and *The Sower, Where Love is God is* and *As
we Forgive* were made at this time. The G-BI director Donald
Carter made *What Men Live by,* a four-reeler based on a Tolstoy
story and starring Esmond Knight, which was started in 1937
but not trade shown until December 1939. They made several
moral-tale films suitable for religious use, with greater care and
professionalism than were to be found in most religious productions, but although the technical standards may have been
marginally better than those of other producers it is unlikely that

22 The commercial film maker stresses not the insanitary past, but the welcome baths to come (*The Great Crusade*, 1936).

23 "The Y.M.C.A. sees that no boy lands in Canada without at least £1 in his pocket" (*Farming for Boys*, 1930).

24 Conservative propaganda for trade protection, referred to as "that there safe-guardin' " by two actors in unconvincing working class accents (*Yorkshire Woollen Workers Discuss Safeguarding*, 1932).

much money or talent was lavished on them. *Breakers Ahead* was directed by Vernon Sewell, an experienced all-rounder who had joined the company in 1937, from a story written specially by Leo Walmsley. Belle Chrystal starred in a story set in a Cornish fishing community with a moral about the importance of forgiveness. The story had something in common with Walmsley's *Turn of the Tide*, previously filmed by British National. *All Living Things* was a moral anti-vivisection drama based on a story by Nell St John Montague, and was directed by Andrew Buchanan. *Two Minutes* starred Walter Hudd and Edana Romney in a pious reflection on the Armistice at the end of the First World War. And *Prince of Peace*, a film about the birth of Christ, starred the attractive Ostrer daughter Pamela Kellino as Mary.

The Catholic Truth Society seems to have made only actuality films showing ceremonies and processions, and supplied projection units and films to schools. A popular Kodak film, *The Sacrifice of the Mass*, was probably of American origin. The Oxford Group had *Youth Marches On* made for them by Eric Parfitt and George Fraser, and also used a film made by Parfitt in Denmark in 1936, *Bridge Building*. The Missionary Film Committee under T. H. Baxter supplied road shows, consisting mainly of travel or geographical films of the countries where missionary work was carried on, many of them amateur films made by the missionaries themselves. And Michael Wayman, as World Commonwealth Films, made a film called *Triumph*, on a non-profit-making basis; this was a mixed bag of real and imaginary incidents in the life of Christ himself and of people inspired by Christ.

The underlying problem was how the film could best be used as an auxiliary to worship. Not many went as far as the Rev. Brian Hession. As curate of St Margaret's at Blackheath he had toyed with the idea of making a film in church in 1935.[23] Later, at Holy Trinity Church, Aylesbury, he persuaded the R.F.S. to record him conducting a service complete with hymns, prayers and lesson, but replacing the sermon with the popular 1935 feature film *The Passing of the Third Floor Back*, in which Conrad Veidt played a mysterious Christ-like stranger who transformed the lives of the inhabitants of a boarding house. Remarks by the minister interpreting this story concluded the filmed service. Hession founded the Dawn Trust in 1938 and continued to be active in the field of religious film for many more years.

There were, of course, two different motives for using films. Those which set out to persuade and convince were one thing. Burnett claimed that the cinema was a good tool for evangelism, which had been degraded by the film industry. What he vividly described as "half-clad women, lurid suggestions of sensuality, sadistic hints at scenes of vice and cruelty" seem to suggest that his idea of the commercial cinema was even more jaundiced than that of the British Board of Film Censors. But unfortunately the kind of film he wanted to see, such as Bible stories, temperance stories, the lives of saints, martyrs and morally inspired people, when made specially for religious organisations, turned out to be of deplorably low quality. The professionalism of the later film from Hollywood, *The Song of Bernadette*, was not to be found in such productions. But there was another motive. They sought, if not to fill the churches, at least to prevent them from emptying as the flock drifted to the cinemas. For this, many different films could be useful, from the excellent G.P.O. documentaries to a minority of worthy feature films. Burnett, writing in 1934, made a strong plea that people should overcome their prejudices against showing films in church and accused a fellow minister of having a closed mind for saying that if you wanted films you should go to the cinema itself. But, having started in the church hall and the Sunday school, the projector was now being used more and more in the actual churches. By 1938 the film trade was becoming uneasy at the potential opposition, especially in areas where Sunday opening of cinemas was not allowed. By May 1938 some fifty feature films had been approved by the R.F.S. for church shows, and between fifteen and twenty more were expected to be approved during the next season. In some parts of the country difficulties arose with watch committees as to whether licences were necessary, and the Exhibitors' Association watched suspiciously. But on the whole, except for the few recommended features, the films were of poor quality, and while the movement could get no one but hacks to produce for them it was unlikely to be much of a threat to the cinema.

Thus film was being used on behalf of commercial companies and at the same time on behalf of Christianity. But there was a middle area where organisations promoting moral and social causes of all types now found it valuable to use film persuasion. Bodies of the most varied views now had their production or two, which might be called good cause films. The dividing line between social and political motivation is arguable. Socialists may campaign for better housing, for example, in the belief that socialism is the method to achieve it, but Conservatives may also be concerned about bad housing and seek to achieve improvement within their own political system; others may simply campaign for better housing because they deplore bad conditions and wish to improve them, without political overtones. Without entering into a discussion of definitions, let us simply examine some films made for social causes whose campaigns were not backed by, or necessarily connected with, organised political parties. As in all the other categories of film, these were not a completely new phenomenon, but for various reasons both their production and their dissemination increased during the decade.

Films were made for causes all the way from elementary cleanliness to scouting, cremation and teetotalism. Every sort of idealist and reformer was turning to film. The spread of newsreel theatres in the early thirties encouraged many to think of sneaking in a 35 mm interest film with a message, and the interest slot in the supporting programmes of cinemas was also a temptation, while the existence of the British Film Institute and the Central Information Bureau for Educational Films was opening up the non-theatrical field. The films were considered to be educational. Indeed, from their minority standpoints, each was an attempt to teach people how to live, or to teach them about the world in which they lived, and in this they corresponded to Grierson's own belief in civic education. Some were made by big companies like British Instructional, some by amateurs, but by far the largest number were made by the many small firms available for advertising or educational production on contract, and as far as one can tell from the few examples which still survive the standard of film making was usually rather low.

There was a large body of films about dirt and infection, teaching the basic rules of hygiene with a strong emphasis on prevention. The Central Council for Health Education acted as distributor for films of the many associations which made them, and organised exhibitions, health weeks and meetings in collaboration with local public health authorities. One of the groups was the Health and Cleanliness Council in Tavistock Square, which had its own travelling cinema vans and a number of one- and two-reelers in 35 mm sound and silent versions as well as some in substandard, dealing with the simplest rules of personal cleanliness mainly by way of humorous stories and cartoons. *Dirty Bertie*, for example, is described as "Pictures and rhymes – Bertie becomes a bathroom convert".[24] *Ten Little Dirty Boys* is a black and white cartoon using a great deal of repetition, irising in and out of sequences, in each of which one more of the boys is converted from the muddy football and fighting life to one of shining cleanliness; it is a moral tale rather than a comic film, and it is rather hard to imagine it having the desired effect on any child. *Silver Lining*, a two-reeler made for them by John Alderson of British Utility Films and previously called *Sunshine and Shadow*, showed the effect of rehousing on the health of a slum family and included an epilogue by Sir Kingsley Wood, M.P. A series of cartoons featured an evil little black character called Giro the Germ in simple instruction about things as basic as hand washing. Again the animation was crude, with many passages repeated for the sake of economy, and the lesson was contained in a jingle which appeared as titles in the silent version or was sung in the sound version.

Another such body, the British Social Hygiene Council, was concerned with sex education and a campaign against venereal diseases. They had a number of more serious films, all silent, in three categories. Like the other group, they had their own vans and were prepared to conduct a campaign on request. They had a number of one-, two- or three-reel dramas made for them by British Instructional about how venereal diseases are transmitted and detected and the importance of getting treatment. These were intended for the public showings arranged by the

Council. Interestingly, *Any Evening After Work* was "for audiences of men" and *The Irresponsibles* "for audiences of women". *Deferred Payment* was a three-reel drama directed in 1929 by Mary Field about a young couple who have neglected to get treatment and whose baby inherits syphilis. A dramatised anecdote rather than a story, it is made very respectably and coolly and although it contains long informative titles is not really explicit. *How to Tell*, made in 1931, is an honest, slow, serious and unsensational film, this time about the importance of proper sex information for children. The idea that parents should give honest answers to children's questions as they arose was not as acceptable in 1931 as it later became and, although the films appear dated and discreet to later eyes, they were courageous and badly needed at the time. In this case the titles are dialogue titles, as the young couple discuss the problem of sex education and talk to their son at various stages in his upbringing. There were several more films of this type.

A second category of film was the teaching demonstration designed to be shown at conferences of various types. *The Gift of Life* was about the biology of reproduction made for parents, teachers and – part of it only – for school-leavers; *Life* was a simple treatment of the human body specially made for showing in Africa; *The Ways of Life* showed what was called the evolution of self-preservation and race-preservation from a single-cell creature to man and formed the introduction to a course of lectures; and *Youth and Life*, for parents, teachers and club leaders and with special versions for young people, was about "the physiological basis of the laws of personal hygiene: the relation of mind and body: adolescence: physical and mental difficulties dealt with: hints for self-management".[25] The Council also had medical films made with the help of the Ministry of Health for post-graduate and medical teaching, a five-reel *The Diagnosis and Treatment of Gonorrhoea in the Male* and a ten-reel treatment of *The Manifestations, Diagnosis and Treatment of Syphilis*, as well as a two-reeler for nurses and midwives, *Social Hygiene for Women*. Production was taken over by Gaumont-British Instructional when it inherited the British Instructional unit, and the later films were made with sound.

G-BI's early films *Breathing, The Blood* and *Circulation* are described as simple rules of hygiene in everyday life. In 1937 Vernon Sewell made a one reel film for G-BI about venereal disease called *A Test for Love* and in 1938 their animator Brian Salt made *The Road of Health.* This combines a dull, over-emphatic and foreboding tone with a careful educational style. A doctor figure gives a lecture, a section of microscope film shows us what we are dealing with, and then an animated sequence begins with magic drawing of a road through the country, with a large dark forest area marked "V.D." The road is crowded with people walking, but every now and then someone wanders off along paths marked "Prostitution", "Delinquency", "Drink" and "Broken Homes". The British Social Council for Health fights back, and makes a bridge for them to return to the road. Then in 1939, hoping to avoid the ignorance which had facilitated the spread of venereal diseases during the First World War, the Council made *A Medical Talk on a Serious Problem* for the Central Council of Health Education, consisting of a lecture by Sir Drummond Shiels. Much more frank and informative, it consists simply of a desk and walking-about lecture, apparently in a consulting room, and emphasises that free and confidential treatment centres are available.

The National Association for the Prevention of Tuberculosis, also based at Tavistock House, had its own vans as well and a collection of one- or two-reel silent films. Some, serious explanatory documentary films rather than dramas, were for general audiences and some for medical and teaching staff. They included an old film on the subject, *The Story of John McNeill, Makers of Men* about the Burrow Hill Training Colony for boys in Surrey, and *Stand up and . . . Breathe*, a film made by British Utility Films. In addition, the Welsh National Memorial Association had its own one-reel film about TB and what was being done about it in Wales, *Crusade.*[26]

Other specialised health and hygiene interests also had their films. The National Ophthalmic Treatment Board had *Do You See* and *The Eyes Have it*, both one-reel sound films whose slightly flippant titles and general interest subjects suggest that they were intended for general distribution. The Dental Board of the United Kingdom had a number of silent films about the care and importance of teeth, most of them aimed at children. The Central Association for Mental Welfare had a two-reel silent film called *Training of Mentally Defective Children*. Pests, on the whole, received surprisingly little attention. Gaumont-British Instructional's 1936 one-reeler *The Red Army*, directed by Andrew Miller Jones, was about the bed bug, and was made with the co-operation of the medical officers of health of some London boroughs. And the Ministry of Agriculture and Fisheries sponsored a two-reel silent *The Rat Menace*. It was a prolific amateur group, the Manchester Film Society under Peter le Neve Foster, who made *Sewage* in 1935, a sub-standard interest film with sound on disc made with the collaboration of a member of the Manchester Rivers Department.

Films made on behalf of hospitals included another by the Manchester Film Society, *Miracles Still Happen*, made in 1935 for the Centenary Appeal of the Royal Manchester Children's Hospital; and *The Missing Record*, made for the National Hospital for Diseases of the Nervous System in 1936. Films made for King Edward's Hospital Fund for London included *A Century of Progress*, a one-reeler of 1933 in which methods of coping with an accident in that year were compared with those of 1833; *A Century of Hospital Progress*, a one-reel 35 mm silent film listed in the B.F.I. Catalogue and the Lally list as a survey of modern conditions showing the growth of the voluntary system between 1922 and 1934; and *War Without End*, a sound film put out in both 35 mm and 16 mm, and in both a 35-minute and a one-reel version, which was directed by Francis Searle for G-BI in 1937–8 and surveyed the work of a modern hospital. This had a historical introduction and showed an operation, X-ray treatment, fractures, dentistry and ophthalmic work, and ended with the Duke of Kent presiding at a management committee meeting.

Film was also used by groups and individuals with more unusual views concerning health. Preventive medicine in the form of diphtheria immunisation was represented in two short silent 35 mm films, C. W. Hutt's *The Three Card Trick* and E. H. T. Nash's *Diphtheria Immunisation*. The Peoples' League of Health sponsored a short silent film called *Working for Dear Life*, which compared periodical medical checks to car maintenance. *Arise and Walk*, a three-reel silent film made in 1929 for the Central Council for the Care of Cripples, put forward the theory that faulty treatment was responsible for much unnecessary crippling, which correct care could have put right. It was made by Oxford Films, John and Terence Greenidge's production unit, which used professional cameramen Randall Terraneau and Frank Canham. The Eugenics Society had two early films, *Heredity – Master or Servant?* and *Prevention of Human Waste*, both silent two-reelers. Later, Julian Huxley, together with the Eugenics Society and G-BI, made two films called *Heredity in Man* and *Heredity in Animals*, and a longer film called *From Generation to Generation* which used material from both films but especially from the first. *Heredity in Man* shows Huxley, as a lecturer, very much at home in front of the camera, giving a continuous dissertation on the inheritance of characteristics. He demonstrates this by using several families, from the highly talented and famous to a distressed family with a high proportion of mentally defective members, urging that those who are healthy should marry and have enough children to "keep the stock up" and noting, sadly, that the others would have been luckier if they had never been born. The interesting material and the assured skill of the lecturer make this a valuable document despite its flat and verbal technique.

The Food Education Society had *Confessions of a Cold* and *Food, Digestion and Air*; the National British Women's Total Abstinence Union, a three-reeler about total abstinence, *Safeguarding the Nation*; the Cremation Society, *Far Better*; the Sunlight League, *A Winter's Day at the School in the Sun*; and the Wytham Country Classrooms scheme, a long amateur production made in 1934 and called *The Door in the Wall*. Obviously everybody from the conventional teacher to the mildly cranky now realised that film was a good way to grind the axe.

The Health Propaganda Department of the Bermondsey Borough Council was unusual in having a group of short films of their own make, presumably because of the enthusiasm of one of their staff, W. H. Bush, and his cameraman "Mr. C. F. Lumley". Made between 1929 and 1932, these amateur films are silent yet

have a freshness and directness which give a curiously vivid sight
of this working-class London borough around 1930. The titles
are unpromising : *The Preparation of Ambrosia Full Cream
Devonshire Dried Milk*, *The Production of Grade "A" (Tuber-
culin Tested) Milk*, *The Shirley Schools*, all made in 1929;
Maternity and Child Welfare and *'Oppin*, the latter about the
Kent hop picking which used to make a working country holiday
for so many poor London families, both in 1930; *Germs*, which
is described as "elementary bacteriology to popularise Schick
testing and immunisation" and *Some Activities of the Bermondsey
Borough Council* in 1931; and *Children's Exercises* and *Consumption (Tuberculosis of the Lungs)* in 1932. The latter dealt
with the causes and symptoms of TB, the work of a TB dispensary
and scenes at the Papworth Village Settlement.[27] *Some Activities . . .*
is a particularly diverting little film, showing exactly what the
titles suggests, for example the planting of seven thousand trees
by the Gardens and Beautification Department, and is strongly
evocative of the quiet streets and horse-drawn vehicles still to be
found in a humble area like Bermondsey at this time.

While Bermondsey's Mr Bush and Mr Lumley worked away
on their own, the Education Committee of the Borough of
Willesden, a similar London borough, commissioned Steuart
Films to make their 16 mm silent film on technical training and
various vocational possibilities to interest school leavers and
parents. This was *Success*, directed by J. B. Holmes early in the
thirties and shot by Ronald Steuart. They also sponsored
Efficiency, a film about the importance of being clean, fit,
punctual and tidy at work. Self-improvement rather than beautification in Willesden, it seems.

Some of the good-cause films overlapped the interests and
themes of the Grierson school of documentary. The National Milk
Publicity Council, for example, wanted films to promote the
consumption of milk, which might just as well have been contracted to the Empire Marketing Board Film Unit in the days
when it was meant to popularise the use of Empire foodstuffs,
but which in fact were made by commercial units in a more
conventional way. *Balancing the Budget* shows a family, suffering
from the national depression, who discover from their doctor that

25 The ex-soldier clenches his hands as the gentlemanly interviewer questions him about gas in the 1914–18 war (*Forgotten Men*, 1934).

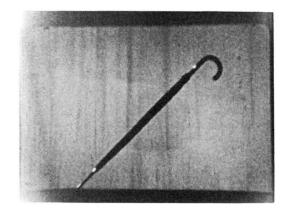

26 By 1939 the umbrella was an easily understood symbol for Neville Chamberlain (*Peace and Plenty*, 1939).

27 Lord Beaverbrook, at his most persuasive (*My Fight for Prosperity*, 1934).

a greater use of dairy products gives them more economical nutrition. *Milk* "deals with milk from the cow to the consumer". There are other interesting cases of the same social issues being treated by both mainstream and commercial units. We have mentioned *A New London* as part of the campaign against slums in another connection (see Chapter 6) but it, also, was essentially a good-cause film, made as early as 1930. We have also seen how *Silver Lining*, used by the Health and Cleanliness Council, showed the effect of rehousing a slum family. Although it lacked the depth and brilliant innovations of the mainstream *Housing Problems* made for the British Commercial Gas Company, it was on the same subject and made at the same time. Moreover, after *Housing Problems*, the Ministry of Health commissioned Pathé Pictures to make one of their own commercial blockbusters, *The Great Crusade*. Subtitled "The Story of a Million Homes", it presents the government case in a short but professional film assured of a commercial distribution through Pathé. Acknowledgement is made to J. B. Priestley for assistance with the scenario, and the material, about the government campaign to build and replace the slums, is good as far as it goes. But only one side of the issue is presented and the end, with *Land of Hope and Glory* and shots of bonny babies, is complacent and optimistic. It begins with the picturesque shots of rustic beauty and the English hills and dales so familiar as an introduction to films of industrial and urban squalor. But there follows a creditably honest, if staged, sequence about two children, Molly and Lenny, going home from their nice modern elementary school in a poor London district to a shocking slum and their worn, dispirited mother, with three kids in the bed and little Molly sleeping on the floor amidst the leaking pipes and rats. There follows, however, the construction of houses and flats and a boom in building, and finally Molly and her family in their new home, with a few happy words from mother. Clearly derivative in style and corrective in aim, it probably had more real propaganda effect on public opinion through its wide distribution and easily understood style than the Elton-Anstey film, although the latter had an incalculable effect on a minority audience and above all, of course, on documentary film technique itself.

Road safety was another topic of growing importance in the thirties. The National Safety First Association had a 35 mm sound four-reeler in the summer of 1933, *Alert Today – Alive Tomorrow*. By 1936 road accidents were a national problem and the Minister of Transport, Leslie Hore-Belisha, mounted a campaign of public education, as well as instituting pedestrian crossings with "Belisha beacons" to mark them. Two films of 1936, Rotha's *Death on the Road* and the commercial production *The Highway Code*, aptly illustrated the difference between the two approaches. Rotha's film, made under the aegis of Gaumont-British Equipments and the *News of the World* for the Ministry of Transport, and often referred to just as "the Road Safety film", was imaginative and forceful and used drama and editing technique to evoke an audience response. *The Highway Code* was in total contrast to this very urgent and rousing piece of advice. Made by Charles Barnett of the commercial company National Progress Films, it was sponsored by the Pearl Assurance Company together with the Ministry of Transport. Less than one reel in length, it was registered later the same year for cinema showing. Like the other film, it had a short speech from Hore-Belisha. Nothing could be more ordinary, with its conventional commentary from John Watt. Yet strangely enough, with its complete unselfconsciousness, like many unambitious and unassuming factual films it is interesting just because so much of the material is allowed to speak for itself. It is an evocative picture of the suburban streets of the thirties. It begins with a child in a street accident in which the producers try to match Rotha's fast cutting to give a visual shock, but this attempt at cleverness fails disastrously and the collision is weirdly slow and unconvincing. After the usual speeches by Hore-Belisha and Sir George Tillett of the Pearl, however, the film proceeds to illustrate each rule of the highway code by enacting what happens if it is not followed. Here it is competent, clear and interesting, while the street settings casually show us scenes of the world as it was, with none of the motivated selection of either the mainstream documentary, the newsreel, or the so-called working-class films.

Did the Ministry, perhaps, prefer plainer and less original films? Is it possible that as the members of the mainstream documentary movement became more experienced, assured and independent their films became less acceptable to the official world which they had begun by serving? There were other commercial competitors besides Bruce Woolfe to whom an unadventurous Civil Service could turn. National Progress in particular, a firm run by Edward Wyner and Philip Weiner for contract advertising and commercial films from the mid-thirties onwards, seems to have made a bid for the official film. They had engaged Charles Barnett after he had made a film called *The Voice of London* which had been promisingly described as a day in the life of a London worker. His highway code film, also, although not remarkable, had its virtues. But their next attempt to enter the field of public service backed by the same courtesy sponsor, Pearl Assurance, was *The Health of the Nation* and it proved disappointing. It was registered early in 1937 and may perhaps have been a further attempt to rival the mainstream, as it came shortly after the second outstanding film made for the gas industry by Anstey, *Enough to Eat*. It was made with the co-operation of the Ministry of Health and the Board of Education as well as being backed by the Pearl. But this time the film was completely routine. It starts with health services and sports facilities for children, with brisk backing music, followed by the worst sort of static desk interview with the President of the Board of Education, Oliver Stanley, who faces the camera but carefully looks elsewhere throughout; a staged sequence shows a humble, ignorant and of course regionally-accented mother being taken in hand by the posh ladies of "the welfare"; library stuff follows with a hearty, brisk and positive commentary by John Watt about how good school and PT is for "the lads" who are, after all, a "national asset"; finally an executive of the Pearl Assurance Company, even more desperate than Stanley to avoid the eye of the camera, gives us another desk chat. There was a third film directed by Barnett for National Progress, the Ministry of Health and Pearl Assurance, *One Hundred Years*, about the improved health services in Britain, but the early flickering of promise was not renewed. Whether it was from a desire to be fair to the commercial producer or a belief that they were more likely to secure theatrical distribution, or merely a mistrust of originality, some authorities seemed to be turning to the commercial units.

We have been looking at some of the films made to plead for special interests, but as in all the categories in this book they are only a few of the many. There were innumerable groups making films to arouse support for good causes. The Royal Society for the Prevention of Cruelty to Animals sought to show people in an amusing and entertaining way how to treat animals properly with such films as *A Day on Applecombe Farm*, *Our Friend the Horse* and many others, including a silent film, *Old Tom's Story*, the life story of a pony, and *A Little Help is Worth a Lot of Pity*, which describes the work of the Society. The National Canine Defence League, also, had a film on how to look after dogs, *Let Dogs Delight*, which was made for cinema showing in 1936, and the International Committee for Bird Preservation had a film called *African Adventure* shown in 1937. This was a long silent film of birds and animals shot by the veteran nature photographer Captain C. W. R. Knight and was shown as a morning performance at the Regent Street Polytechnic with Knight as lecturer. The National Farmers' Union Mutual Insurance Society also had a handful of silent 16 mm shorts, which included actualities of the Royal Agricultural Show for several years and *Future Farmers*, about the activities of the National Federation of Young Farmers' Clubs. Richard McNaughton, the G.P.O. editor, made a compilation for the Shipwrecked Mariners' Society in 1937 called *There is Sorrow on the Sea* and Peter Collins made a 16-minute film, *Firefighters*, for the London Fire Brigade in the same year. Even more ambitious was a film planned by Anthony Asquith for Guide Dogs for the Blind, a Dufaycolor film to be called *Blind Dogs* with a cast which was to include Leslie Banks, Vivien Leigh and Lee Tracy.[28] A one-reeler was made by Michael Powell at Denham for the Embankment Fellowship Centre, and called *Smith*; this featured Ralph Richardson, Flora Robson and others, and was about the story and aims of an organisation formed to help unemployed ex-Servicemen from the last world war. It was shown at the House of Commons just before the outbreak of the next one.

28 The phoney politician, "surrounded as we are by enemies . . ." (*Thunder in the Air*, 1934–5).

29 The militiamen of culture (*Spanish A.B.C.*, 1938).

30 The propaganda film stresses the educational work of the Government rather than the fighting (*Spanish A.B.C.*, 1938).

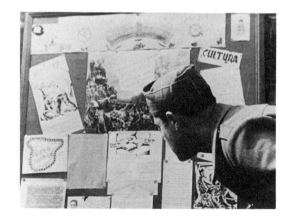

People trying to help young people were especially likely to use film. More important than most of these films was one made in 1937 by the mainstream Realist Film Unit together with the feature film producer and director Victor Saville, appealing for homes for the 4,000 Basque refugee children here from the Spanish Civil War. This was *Modern Orphans of the Storm*. It was made by Basil Wright and Ian Dalrymple, who gave their services free, on behalf of the National Joint Committee for Spanish Relief and it used some of the footage from the Progressive Film Institute, especially from *Madrid Today*. The appeal was made by the Duchess of Atholl, a formidable lady of Conservative background and views whose indignation over the plight of Republican Spain led her to stand for Parliament as an independent. Known as the Red Duchess, she was not elected.

The Youth Hostels Association had a four-reel silent 16 mm film, *Youth Hails Adventure*, which was described as a "miniature epic of youth and the countryside".[29] The Boy Scout and Girl Guide movement had a large number of films both for and about them. Ronald Gow and the County High School for Boys, Altrincham, had made *The Man who Changed his Mind* for them in 1928, and J. H. Martin Cross made *The Lone Scout* and a five-reeler, *When Scouting Won*, both silent and both registered in late 1930. They also had several stories and a number of actualities about scout jamborees, cruises and camps. These were Scouts' newsreels in much the same way that films of hunger marches and strikers were workers' newsreels. The Guides had *The Fourth Law*, a three-reel story about a Canadian Guide who comes to Britain, and *The Wiltshire Trail*, about a fund-raising "Trail of Service" organised by the Guides in 1933. These were all silent films, but 35 mm sound films were made of an *Address to Parents and Boys* by Lord Baden-Powell, the international 1933 *Jamboree at Godollo* and *The Chief Scout* talking about the movement for the Guides. In 1938 *Campanions* was made by feature producer Herbert Wilcox, who the previous year had made a film starring Ralph Reader and his Gang Show. Reader now made this short scouting film distributed theatrically through Wilcox's associates, RKO-Radio. Starting with the song "Riding along on the Crest of the Wave" on the sound-track, it shows boys at a country camp and is made with the hearty jollity of Emmett's commentary and the ringing tones of Ralph Reader and his Gang's

> Keep your eyes-on
> The distant hori-zon . . .

A camp-fire concert, with groups of foreign Scouts, is followed by what was described[30] as an "eloquent epilogue" by Lord Baden-Powell, in which he recalls the birth of the $2\frac{1}{2}$ million strong movement with just twenty-five boys twenty-seven years before. He is seen superimposed over massed marching boys from all over the world.

Finally, a chilling note is struck by two organisations to promote the emigration of children. The Child Emigration Society had a three-reel 35 mm silent film early in the period called *Fairbridge*, showing the Society's work in "transplanting" children, achieving "Empire Settlement through Child Colonization". And *Farming for Boys*, a silent split-reel also made in the early thirties, speaks poignantly down the years, despite its very primitive technique, of how little the ordinary people of Britain expected from life during the depression. It was made for the Y.M.C.A. and the Liverpool Education Committee, to show how boys were taught the elements of farming to prepare them for emigration under the auspices of the United Church of Canada. Meant as cheering and encouraging news of a great opportunity, the long packed titles, the simple camera sets-ups and the long static shots manage to be eloquent of the humility and resignation not only of the youths but also of their meanly dressed parents and even of the officials running the scheme. Perhaps no little films of the thirties have quite such a power to shock and grieve.

6

Political Propaganda

The film industry was capitalist, or, as Paul Rotha put it,[1] "in the hands of the owning classes". Far from thinking that the picture of the world it presented in features, newsreels and even short films was right-wing propaganda, the film industry simply assumed that the existing order of society was right and proper. Apart from special election films and an occasional outburst like the housing film *The Great Crusade*, "propaganda" was regarded as something rather unpleasant in which the political left indulged. The vast majority of Hollywood and British films showed a world, as Rotha saw it, in which the underprivileged, especially servants or coloured people, were either comic or sinister; where poverty was picturesque; where love surmounted all, even want and deprivation. This was not essentially altered by what he called "bluff films", which seemed courageous because they tackled serious social issues, but which trivialised these by treating them as conflicts between individuals. It was not the banality of the commercial film which bothered the political left so much as its unquestioning acceptance of the conditions of the time. There were groups, however, from aristocratic rebels, academics and professional people to the politically conscious working class, who saw in the cinema a valuable means of communication monopolised by one side of the social and economic struggle. After all, was it not Lenin who had pointed out its importance?

It is not, I believe, correct to include the mainstream documentary movement here. Although a few people, Paul Rotha and Ralph Bond among them, were members of the mainstream and at the same time anxious to make radical changes in society, and although reformism and the sense of inquiry led other members of the movement almost sideways into the exposure of serious inequality and injustice in society, the true Grierson spirit accepted the social and political structure of the time. Grierson's basic position was that for democracy to function properly people had to be shown how to use it; but he does not seem to have questioned the nature of democracy or whether it had in fact already arrived in Britain.

But various left-wing groups, starting from the premise that great changes were necessary, sought to use film to further their cause. The process actually began when the politically active thought they could to some extent counter the capitalist ethos of Hollywood by showing the latest films to come out of Soviet Russia. From attempts to show the great silent Russian films they graduated into the making of films themselves. Both exhibition and production were facilitated during the thirties by the development of substandard and safety film.

The Film Society in London, founded in 1925, had enabled its members to see interesting films from many countries, not only the Soviet productions. During the next few years the film society movement spread, more as a protest against the inferiority of the ordinary commercial product than against its generally right-wing political assumptions. There was, however, a minority with political as well as artistic reasons for admiring the Soviet films. They believed that the British working classes would benefit from seeing these, the only films made by and for a culture that was not capitalist. The firm of Atlas was founded in 1928 by Ralph Bond and others, primarily to import and distribute the Russian films. Late the next year he and Ivor Montagu and others of the political far left formed the Federation of Workers' Film Societies, among them the London Workers' Film Society, to further the showing of these films in areas, and at prices, accessible to the working class.

But the right of private clubs to show films in premises which required fire licences without obtaining a film censorship certificate had not yet been established and, as the films were on inflammable 35 mm stock, licensed premises were essential. The result was curious. Although of outstanding importance for their innovations in film technique, the great Russian films were not really likely to set the box office on fire with revolutionary sentiment. But no newsreel coverage came out of Russia, and the mysterious "Bolshies" were figures of almost superstitious dread to many people. Had these serious, silent, often slow films about problems quite remote from British audiences appeared at the local cinemas, they would almost certainly have emptied them in favour of the latest Hollywood success down the road. Yet the Pictures Committee of the London County Council recommended that permission should not be given the L.W.F.S. to show films "of special worker interest" because they would be "mainly of a propagandist nature". Harry Day, M.P., an indefatigable harrier of Home Secretaries on all cinema matters, raised the question of legislation allowing film societies to show uncertified films privately, with the usual reply that it was a matter for the local licensing authorities. Almost immediately after this another society, the Masses Stage and Film Guild, was refused permission by the L.C.C. to show *Mother* at the Regal, Marble Arch and when they sought permission to put it on at the Piccadilly Theatre the Lord Chamberlain also refused. The Guild had intended to show *Mother*, *The Battleship Potemkin*, *Storm over Asia* and *The New Babylon*, all of which had been refused a B.B.F.C. certificate, as well as *Ten Days that Shook the World* and *The General Line*, which had not yet been submitted.

A meeting of interested M.P.s was called at the House of Commons in February 1930 by Fenner Brockway, one of the founders of the Guild, and an all-party committee appointed which included him, Ellen Wilkinson, George Strauss and W. E. D. Allen to investigate the matter and form a deputation. One strange result of this was that for several years a group of sincere liberal-minded people pressed for an official film censorship to be set up, in the belief that it would be fairer and more subject to control than the anomalous system then in existence. In the end, they were unsuccessful. At the time, it emerged that the B.B.F.C. was genuinely under the impression that these Russian films were likely to provoke a breach of the peace, one of their stock reasons for rejecting films, whether shown publicly or "privately where admission is easy to attain". In other words the low subscription of the workers' film societies, unlike the higher cost of the Film Society, made them virtually public performances. Whilst the actual film technique of these films was certainly revolutionary, it is hard to believe that anyone could regard the films themselves as dangerous. But in March the L.C.C. approved its Theatres and Music Halls Committee's recommendation to refuse permission. As if to pin-point the absurdity of the position, it was shortly after this that the West Ham Council, which was Labour, passed *Mother* not just for private shows but for cinema exhibition. This time it was the Conservative Sir Kingsley Wood who questioned the Home Secretary, J. R. Clynes. Once more he replied that it was a local authority matter and nothing to do with him. In May 1930, however, the Theatres and Music Halls Committee reported to the L.C.C. recommending that film societies should have the right to show films without licence, under conditions similar to those of the theatre clubs. But the position continued to be difficult, and the Manchester Watch Committee, for example, turned down the request of the Workers' Society to show *The New Babylon* and *The Blue Express* in November 1931.

The first Annual Conference of the Federation of Workers' Film Societies was held in September 1930. Meanwhile a two-reel film called *A New London*, made by Michael Hankinson, a film editor who later became a director and producer, and shot by Jimmy Rogers, attracted attention from Ralph Bond. He reviewed it favourably in *Close Up*.[2] This was part of a campaign against slums and is in the "good cause" category rather than a political film, but Bond, who was already the London correspondent of the American magazine *Experimental Cinema*, must have been familiar with the existence of the Workers' Film and Photo League which started in New York in 1930, going into production with a *Workers' Newsreel*. Between 1930 and 1932 they were active in production in America with the professed aim of recording the world as it really was in *Workers' Newsreels*. The word "Workers" was dropped from the group's title. (A National Film Conference was held by them in Chicago in 1934.) As Bond wrote in *Close Up* in December, all film societies were having censorship trouble but especially the Workers' Film Societies. Production must have seemed to open up new possibilities.

He and the London Workers' Film Society had accordingly hurried into production in 1930 with *Glimpses of Modern Russia*, a silent one-reel compilation which he edited from film available here and which included scenes of Moscow, housing estates, factories, a steelworks, the Baku oilfields, unloading cotton, scenes on a collective farm, athletic meetings, a parade in Red Square and Lenin talking to a friend.[3] A second film, *1931*, was also made by Bond and was shown in 1932. According to Stephen Clarkson in *Experimental Cinema*, it was made at the request of the Annual Conference. Although still a compilation, and using stock shots for factory interiors, it was a more ambitious production and was meant to popularise a Workers' Charter by depicting hardship and unemployment. To show the exploitation of the workers, the "imperialist character of British capitalism is emphasised with shots of slave labour in China and the suppression of native revolts by troops and warships". Clarkson writes, surprising though it may seem, that this was "valuable as a historical document" and was "shown throughout England and was acclaimed by the workers as a vivid depiction of their misery and struggle".[4]

Like the American Leagues, the Federation of Workers' Film Societies also tried news film production. Theoretically, not being subject to the B.B.F.C., newsreels should have been easier to handle. According to *Experimental Cinema* they made three issues of the *Workers' Topical News* which covered May Day demonstrations, the international Day of Struggle against Unemployment, a strike of the Lancashire textile operatives, and unemployed hunger marches. According to Bert Hogenkamp[5] the first issue was shown in March 1930 and showed a demonstration at Tower Hill organised by the National Unemployed Workers' Movement. And according to Victoria Wegg-Prosser[6] a fourth news film on 16 mm, apparently shown although not complete, lay in a can called *Against Imperialist War, May Day 1932*, as well as a reel called *London May 7th 1933* showing the planning of a Hyde Park rally against the National Government, which does not seem to have been shown.

These irregular news films, of strictly limited subject matter and strongly political intention, do not of course exhibit the general characteristics set out by Baechlin and Muller-Straus in their interesting attempt to define newsreels.[7] These characteristics are that the films should appear regularly at relatively short intervals, that each issue should include several topics not directly related, that these should concern current events of general interest, that they should be of standard length and use a straight-forward, not an interpretative or didactic, presentation. The occasional films under discussion substituted a lopsidedness of their own for that of the commercial newsreel. Made to correct the politics of the latter, especially on unemployment, labour disputes and the attitude to Russia, they are occasional news items rather than newsreels, and contain no more background informa-tion or reasoned argument than their commercial counterparts. Shown as they were to groups already in agreement with those who made them, they can have had but little effect. They represent, however, a grass-roots movement and an attempt against overwhelming odds to correct the way the newsreels misinterpreted or, almost worse, ignored whole areas of acute national problems. Some of the films, it is true, extolled the glories of life in Russia, but most drew attention to the protests being made against the misery and degradation of mass unem-ployment here, and resentment of the extremes of poverty in Britain. But the idea of socialism being achieved solely by a cloth-capped "workers' movement" was already becoming out of date and power was beginning to show itself in more sophisticated guises. Bond himself now joined John Grierson at the Empire Marketing Board Film Unit and from 1931 pursued his aims as a trade union leader whilst working as a professional film maker. Some of the steam went out of the original amateur film movement when he moved on.

Meanwhile, however, the political right wing had not totally ignored the possibilities of the film for outright propaganda. A Conservative and Unionist Films Association had been formed in 1930 on the advice of renters Sir Ernest Gordon Craig and Albert Clavering. *Red Tape Farm* and *The Right Spirit* are typical short silent, crude animated cartoons issued by the Conservative Central

Office for the election of 1931, by which time they owned ten daylight cinema vans. *Red Tape Farm* begins with a series of titles containing the message: "Farmers and Landworkers. Do you know your job? or would you prefer to be taught and controlled by officials? The Socialist Policy is to transfer all land from private to public ownership." This was followed by a cartoon showing the ignorant official Mr Nosey Parker creating havoc down on the farm, and ending with a long title suggesting that if farmers do not want to be overrun by officials they should vote Conservative, for "Help, not Interference". *The Right Spirit* is a pun referring to the petrol necessary to get John Bull's car going, and shows Ramsay MacDonald asleep at his petrol station but Baldwin, keen and efficient, filling the car at his. The next year, after their election success, they were putting out short films explaining the case for trade protection in simple terms. *The Price of Free Trade*, for example, shows a Belgian being refused work in the British steel industry and going off laughing, with the question title "Why did the Belgian laugh at us?" and the answer that although he is not allowed to work in Britain the steel he makes in Belgium, and which we could have made ourselves, is allowed into the country, bringing ruin to British steelworks. Protection, called "safeguarding", is also the subject of a conversation between two extremely unconvincing "workers" with theatrical "ee, lud!" accents in *Yorkshire Woollen Workers Discuss Safeguarding*. Although over-simple, the film does attempt to explain an economic issue in a way that could be understood by anybody. In *My Fight for Prosperity* Lord Beaverbrook, the outsider, has his own film in which he appeals for his hobby-horse, Imperial Preference for Empire products. Shown in close and mid-close shot in front of an opulent marble mantelpiece this extraordinary man, with an expression of artless innocence, with rhetorical questions and a quizzical air, is by turns pleading and persuasive, confidential, emphatic and theatrical. Ending every sentence with a flicker of half-smile that dies instantly, he consciously uses his personality; but at the same time, like the other films, this short item pays the audience the compliment of presenting them with an argument, however simplified, rather than with emotive shots and slogans.

Free trade or protection was an issue of great importance to the Conservative Party, just as unemployment, the means test and strike legislation aroused the passions of the left. But underlying all other issues during the thirties was that of war or peace. In 1930 the Great War was still sufficiently close for the thought of another one to be abhorrent. Pacifism in the sense of a refusal to fight at all, in the belief that if enough people did this there could be no war, was not a widely held opinion but at first was tolerated as respectable if over-idealistic. Most people pinned their hopes on disarmament. Gradually prospects of this faded and with the rise of the two European dictatorships, especially Germany with its obvious bid for territory and its repressive and anti-Semitic measures, it was seen that the preservation of peace was a more complex matter than had been supposed. Even the idea of collective security implied the use of arms. After the failure to use it to stop the Italian conquest of Abyssinia a demand for the rearmament of Britain spread, cautiously at first. Grierson and the documentary movement, immersed in social documentation and investigation, remained silent on international affairs, at first finding it impossible to reconcile their belief in peace with their dislike of dictatorship. Films were made in the early thirties on the simple theme that war is hell; films about the loss of liberty in the dictatorships were made only by the extreme left, in fact by the Communist Party, until the Russo-German pact put an end even to that; several crude but powerful commercial films appeared; and finally, especially towards the end of the period when rearmament against Germany was openly admitted to be necessary, the straightforward patriotic recruiting film made its appearance.

From the mid-twenties, archive film of the First World War became available to commercial users. In 1930 Ratcliffe Holmes made a short feature called *Peace on the Western Front*, partly compiled from actualities of war and reconstruction with a commentary by himself, and partly acted, with Moore Marriott as a father explaining what war was really like to a little boy playing with toy soldiers. But the first film maker to draw attention to the threat to peace involved in Hitler's rise to power was the former Stoll screenwriter J. B. Williams, who made

Whither Germany? as early as 1933 for Mansfield Markham, using a small film company, B & N, which made sponsored films. Rotha welcomed it in *Sight and Sound*; Forsyth Hardy was more cautious in *Cinema Quarterly*. Presented as an interest film covering the years from just before the war to the present, according to *Kine Weekly* it showed "how the coming of a dictatorship . . . is likely to cause a repetition of history and a future war".[8] *Sight and Sound* commented on the "triumph of armed Fascism with all its attendant brutality and oppression".[9] This, it should be noted, was after the newsreels had started their conspiracy of silence about German anti-Semitism. The film was a compilation of newsreel and archive material including footage from Germany. According to *Sight and Sound*, the idea and much of the material came from France, re-edited for Great Britain. Although the B.B.F.C. had no formal power to censor newsreels, a compilation of them challenged their authority and they stepped in and refused to give it a certificate. The L.C.C., however, followed by some other local authorities, allowed it to be shown.[10]

Meanwhile in amateur political film making the initiative had temporarily passed from the Labour movement to a group of left-wing intellectuals, educated, socially privileged and for the most part wealthy socialists. A letter in *Sight and Sound*[11] in 1933 from the historian Raymond Postgate announced plans for a Socialist League Film Centre. This led to the setting up of the Socialist Film Council. Its figurehead president was the aged pacifist socialist leader George Lansbury. Members were Postgate, later well known for his championship of good food and wine; Naomi Mitchison, a writer who was also one of the founders of the Hampstead Children's Film Society at the Everyman Cinema; and Terence Greenidge, socialist and pacifist and one of two literary brothers who had founded a film production society when at Oxford – the dust-jacket of one of his slender but exquisitely produced books was later to refer to England's "self-imposed vulgarity". The director and cameraman was Rudolph Messel, film critic of the left-wing *New Clarion* and writer, in 1928, of a book called *This Film Business*, which was enthusiastic rather than informative.

Unlike the early film leagues, they were to use 16 mm film.
One grand plan, for local amateurs all over the country to send
in films of their own lives and surroundings, to be used to show
the world as it really was, does not seem to have materialised as
planned. But two silent films were shown in the summer of 1933,
including *What the Newsreel Does Not Show*, which according
to Victoria Wegg-Prosser starts "This is an attempt by a group
of Socialists to show the true picture of the world today", which
was, of course, also the aim professed by the *Workers' Newsreels*
made in America. According to *Cinema Quarterly*[12] it showed
work on the Five-Year Plan in Russia. Their major film was
The Road to Hell, of the same date. This was a drama, and an
attack on the means test; but the story was so unlikely and the
characters so spineless in their behaviour as to cause Basil Wright,
writing in the same issue of *Cinema Quarterly*, to deplore the
defeatism of the film although he warmly praised its construction,
acting, lighting and direction. Rotha took a more critical view. In his
autobiography he quotes one of his own letters of the time, which
called it and the other film "amateur and immature. . . . He uses
a few friends with cultured accents to speak dialogue for factory
workers. . . . In other words, they stink."[13] The film was praised
as an example of what could be done for an expenditure of £66,
but this figure presumably hid advantages such as the best
equipment and plentiful time and transport. They next planned
to make an anti-war film, and to use sound. *Blow, Bugles, Blow*
was made in 1934 and shown at the Labour Party Conference,
receiving a kindly notice in *Kine Weekly*. In April 1936, as a
seven-reel sound film, it was trade shown again by the Progressive
Film Institute but was of course not granted a certificate by the
B.B.F.C., dealing as it did with the beneficial results of a successful revolution. A melodramatic and involved story about a
newspaper editor, his unfaithful wife, a warmongering press
baron, a young reserve officer and his betrayed wife who remains
true to the cause of trade unionism and peace, its main objective
was to show how war was averted between England and France
because the trade unions on both sides of the Channel united to
strike against it – ". . . the troops are suborned and the mutual
strike is a complete success with the workers marching into

Downing Street to turn out the Cabinet. Revolution is an accomplished fact".[14] It was described as amateurish. The camerawork was said to be fair and imaginative, but in general it was artificial, especially the acting, and some instances of what *Kine Weekly* called "Russian cutting" were noticed. It was put on the market again in 1938 by British Cine Recording, a commercial services company specialising in rerecording and other sound servicing, which suggests that it may have acquired an improved sound-track. But portraying France as the enemy and pacifism as the issue in 1934, to say nothing of 1938, hardly says much for the group's grasp of international affairs.

While this somewhat dilettante group were discovering that it takes more than political conviction to make effective films, the professionals had tried again. In 1934 British Movietone, although generally considered to be in the pockets of the Conservative Party, made three films produced by Leslie Landau intended to examine the great issues of the time with some fairness, featuring people who were by no means right-wing. *Will Civilization Crash?* is a one-reeler in which Professor Joad, youngish and bearded, sits in his comfortable room and tells us that civilisations decline and fall, and that our world is being ruined by its own productivity. "We must distribute what science produces" and, moreover, without war, as "man is so dangerous he must learn to live without quarrelling". *Peace or War* was a symposium in which four "famous women", who turn out to be the Countess of Oxford and Asquith, Dr Maud Royden, writer Storm Jameson and actress Madeleine Carroll, each in her own characteristic setting of furniture and clothes and in her own vastly different style, appeal to women to use their power to prevent war. And in *Europe Today* the Liberal foreign correspondent Vernon Bartlett discusses the current issues in European foreign affairs. These films, in standard and substandard versions but aimed primarily at non-theatrical audiences, were welcomed by many. John Sydney in *Sight and Sound*[15] describes them as imaginative antiwar propaganda, and Rotha felt they might presage a "politicisation" of the newsreel, facilitated by the spread of the newsreel theatre movement, with different companies able to express different editorial viewpoints in detailed treatment of current events. Others, however, including the film critic C. A. Lejeune and many exhibitors, showed anxiety at the use of film to express political opinions of even so modest a nature.

J. B. Williams now tried again with *The Soul of a Nation*, a six-reel film described as a "documentary drama" covering English history from 1901 to 1931 in a "pictorial cavalcade". It was said to be all actuality material compiled with a commentary by Felix Aylmer, and was acquired for distribution by A.B.F.D. But from the fact that it was praised by *Kine Weekly* and used for ordinary distribution with a U certificate we must assume that Williams had learnt his lesson and taken care not to say or show anything unpalatable to anybody.

At the end of 1934 there came an anti-war blockbuster from an unexpected quarter, B.I.P., a large studio company run on very commercial lines by Walter Mycroft, who has been described as almost fascist in his views. This was *Forgotten Men*, a full-length feature film compiled from official archive material of the 1914–18 war from the U.K., France, Germany, Italy and Russia, including material which had already been used in *Der Weltkrieg*, made in Germany in 1927. To be against war was about as controversial as being in favour of peace and prosperity, and there was certainly no hint in the film that a possible source of danger might be the rising dictatorships. It was a highly professional film made by Norman Lee with the help of editor A. C. Hammond, and cameraman Bryan Langley for studio shots. Lee was an experienced professional not averse to a bit of sensational work. In 1929 he had, for example, made *The City of Shadows*,[16] in which Elizabeth Baxter, a well-known social worker among down-and-outs on the Embankment, appeared as herself in a thin story devised to show the danger, especially for young girls, of coming to London without a job. This film had considerable trouble with the censor and it is difficult to avoid the impression that the motives of Miss Baxter and of Lee may not have been identical. The sole message of *Forgotten Men* was that war was wasteful, a proposition hardly likely to raise an eyebrow. It conveyed it with considerable impact, however, showing in sometimes shocking detail the terrible absurdity of the struggles back and forth over no-man's-land during the First World War.

But no solution was suggested, and the general tone was respectful to government and military leadership and careful to dissociate itself from what it called "the peace-at-any-price brigade". The film took the form of a question. How should later generations remember the men who fell in the war? General Sir Ian Hamilton, the very picture of the traditional English military gentleman with his strangled, slow and careful introduction, may perhaps have expected the answer to be a more conventional glorification. The commentary was taken over by war historian Sir John Hammerton, more at ease, sitting at his desk and from time to time interviewing a group of former soldiers. The short prepared questions and answers, with the uneasy and respectful rankers helped by the kindly upper-class officer with no great gift for interviewing must, however condescending, represent one of the first attempts to get ordinary people to talk about themselves on sound film. More sensational was the horror of the battlefield, on which it dwelt so much that *Sight and Sound* wrote : "Some of the scenes are so terrible that nobody under twenty should be allowed to see the film."[17] A man writhing grotesquely in agony in no-man's-land, a headless body, an unregarded infant crying helplessly on its back among the ruins, are presented with cold and casual authenticity. Distributed by Wardour, after some delay it received an A certificate. Working up to a culmination of explosions towards the end to horrify and stun the audience, it subsided conventionally and even comfortably into montage, a cemetery, some poetry and a hymn. Safe, obvious, it was an attempt to exploit the issue of war and peace commercially rather than to propose a solution. But as a way of reminding people that war was not a thing to play with it must have been emotionally effective, and it ventured into areas where neither the newsreels nor the documentary movement ever strayed.

Whilst these professional films were being made, new developments had taken place in left-wing amateur film production. Since its introduction in the early twenties 16 mm film had made great strides, and by the autumn of 1933 the American Eric Knight wrote in *Cinema Quarterly* that even direct sound filming was possible for amateurs, after a fashion, now that R.C.A.-Victor had a reasonable substandard sound camera on the market. With it had come safety stock, and an easing of the censorship problem. Since films on safety stock could be shown in premises which did not require licenses under the fire precautions they thus, absurd as the system may seem, escaped any form of censorship. In December 1933 Kino was founded by Ivor Montagu and others as a section of the Workers' Theatre Movement, to acquire substandard rights for Soviet films and issue them on safety stock. The first to be so issued was *The Battleship Potemkin*. Kino also had hopes of making films of its own.[18] Their production followed the model of their American counterpart, the Workers' Film and Photo League, which also did much to import foreign films into America. Kino was registered in March 1935 "to promote sociological education by means of the cinema". In the winter of that year they announced :

Kino . . . is an organisation of amateur film-workers using the film as a medium of propagating Communist philosophy. It has an active news-reel group operating much the same as the commercial companies. Two news-reels have been produced dealing with several demonstrations, including the one at Olympia, Air Display, Gresford Colliery Disaster, International Workers Sports in Paris, etc. Another group is engaged in producing an Anti-Fascist film, and yet another group in the production of features. The last group has made the film *Bread*, described as a drama of the Means Test. . . . A film hire service is now in operation for the distribution of Soviet films.

And on the next page :

The Workers' Film and Photo League . . . has been formed to produce its own films recording the industrial and living conditions of British workers and the struggle of the employed and unemployed to improve these conditions; to popularize Russian films . . . etc.[19]

According to the detailed research by Hogenkamp and Victoria Wegg-Prosser to which the reader has been referred, the word "Workers' " should already have been dropped from the title by this date, as it had been in America, and it was the League itself which had been engaged in production, not Kino, four "news-reels" having already been made between August 1934 and the summer of 1935. Whatever the explanation of these discrepancies it seems that production continued until 1937, where at a joint Conference it sought to involve Left Book Club groups in film production and exhibition. A large number of films was made by the Film and Photo League and related units, some actuality and some dramatic, on subjects such as unemployment, the hunger marches, the means test and strikes. With the use of substandard and the now familiar home cine, many a gathering was recorded and many a small descriptive or didactic film was made. Among them, *The Busmen's Holiday* was made in 1937 in silent 16 mm film by the Green brothers of the North London Film Society's Cine unit, about an unofficial strike by the London Busmens' Rank and File Movement neglected by the newsreels. It shows the processions gathering, the rows of stationary buses, placards and clenched fists, and eventually the strikers having a day out on the comfortless shingle beside the sea with community singing, accordion and brass. Little more than snapshots, it tells us nothing of the issues at stake but something about the people. The interesting faces, strong and for the most part good-natured, marked deeply by experience, are the faces not of actors playing workers whether heroic, sinister, comic or anything else, but simply themselves. The same film makers' *Jubilee*, showing the crowds, flags, processions and Westminster Abbey doors during the 1935 Silver Jubilee of George V, contrasts them with the slums, the endlessly waiting unemployed, the war wounded, recruiting posters and marching soldiers. "Progress", they say, and "Progress towards war". This well made, sour film was perhaps unusual in that it made a point, and made it well. But for the most part the movement gradually drifted away from the strictly communist Kino, towards the milder and more intellectual socialist climate of the Left Book Club groups. The Green brothers, we are told, were schoolmasters, and the phrase "working class movement" used by Hogenkamp does not seem altogether appropriate in its English usage.

Meanwhile in the commercial cinema a hard hitting anti-war

film made by Hans Nieter during 1934, *Thunder in the Air*, was distributed by Butcher's Film Service with an A certificate. Born in Washington but educated in England, Nieter had worked in Germany for Ufa and at several large English feature studios. This off-beat film, part compilation and part acted, was made by a company called Freenat formed by Nieter to make films for the League of Nations Union. As early as 1925 a League of Nations Union Committee had sponsored a two-reel film, called *The Star of Hope*, for educational purposes. It had consisted of newsreels, material from post-war relief organisations, and maps and diagrams to show the work of the League, and was accompanied by a pamphlet for history teachers. Considered a successful beginning, it was shown at the British Association Educational Section by G. T. Hankin, and led to a more ambitious four-reel production called *The World War and After* made by Nieter to teach children about the League. This was finished by November 1926, and had been revised three times by June 1930.[20]

The new production was made, with personal conviction, to promote the idea that collective security was needed to remedy the absence of machinery to enforce the Kellogg Pact. It begins in an idyllic garden, "Anywhere, 1914–18", with a young soldier played by Ralph Richardson parting from his wife and baby; in close-up he stares with glassy-eyed horror over a double-exposure of the battlefield; the image of his face whirls clockwise with a montage of horror shots, a still drawing of flames, the figures "1918" and finally a cut-out shape of Europe which pans over a sea of white battlefield crosses. The commentary, which is by Vernon Bartlett, now enters with a remark about the "war to end war" over shots of cemeteries, the returning soldiers, the unemployed. Close-ups of faces are intercut with bread, coffee being shovelled into furnaces, poor children sitting on the kerb, an old woman riffling through a dustbin. "There never has been such folly in the world as since the war."

The young wife learns that her husband has died to make the world a better place. Shots of a shouting demagogue are accompanied only by a whu-whuing on the sound track, and scenes of rioting lead into military preparations in Moscow, Rome, Berlin and Paris, with shots of the leaders of each country. The same actor in the uniforms of each in turn repeats the identical exhortation: "Surrounded as we are by enemies, we must *prepare!*"

Flashes of the real leaders are intercut with the shots of this dummy in his various guises, and "We will lead you to a glorious future" leads to a pan over graves, and a phoney memorial to "the unknown armament manufacturer". Further sequences assert that war is big business, that the things people really want out of life are simple and small, and that we must fight for peace if we want it. The young couple's son, now grown up and off to war in his turn, bids his sorrowing mother goodbye with "This is a war to end war . . . isn't it?"

Shown at the beginning of 1935 this film, with its stress on collective security, was half-way between the pacifism of the early thirties and the rearmament moves of the late thirties, and probably pleased few. True, it is technically weak, the acted sequences are stilted and the dialogue recording is amateurish. But it is made with the lively attack of a journalist and even in some places the associative technique of a political cartoonist. Journalists were later to have a new medium of expression in television. But at this time very few of them turned to film except as commentators. This production, and Cavalcanti's *Yellow Caesar* made early in the war by Frank Owen and Michael Foot, both Beaverbrook editors in their time, were rare examples of the whole-hearted and original use of film with a journalist's attitude. It was Nieter's company Freenat which handled Rotha's Peace Film of 1936, also a plea for collective security: no newsreel caution or *March of Time* pretence of objectivity here. Despite a very wide circulation it is worth noting that the C.E.A. members in Bolton decided against showing Nieter's film because it was too controversial and they did not want cinemas to be associated with propaganda. In *Kine Weekly's* words, they were not "advertising agents" and must avoid things "which might tend to cause argument among patrons".[21] The newsreels' caution was justified, it seems.

In 1935 there was another general election and the National Government planned to make even greater use of film than before, with hour-long programmes for travelling cinema vans.[22]

Films prepared by Conservative and Unionist Films for the coalition included short speeches in close and mid shot from Ramsay MacDonald, Neville Chamberlain, Walter Elliott, Sir John Simon and Stanley Baldwin; so-called documentaries on British agriculture and Emipre Free Trade; as well as films on Scottish industry and agriculture and two "music hall" numbers. One of these was a turn by Arthur Prince, an aggressively "Naval" type with a large cigar which conveniently hid his mouth, with his ventriloquist's dummy Jim. The other was *Sam Small at Westminster*, in which Stanley Holloway visits the House of Commons and is told about the wonderful things the National Government has done. Mention is also made of a story film called *Without Prejudice*.[23]

A maverick amateur production distributed by Kino at this time was Norman McLaren's pacifist film *Hell Unlimited*. McLaren was a student at the Glasgow School of Art, where he met Grierson in 1935[24] when he was in Scotland to adjudicate at the Scottish Amateur Film Festival. McLaren's film *Seven Til Five* won first prize at the second Scottish Amateur Film Festival held in Glasgow, where Andrew Buchanan adjudicated.[25] His *Colour Cocktail* won the *World Film News* prize at the Scottish Amateur Film Festival in 1936, and he was impressively reported to be at work on a whole series of amateur films dealing with social and political problems such as the relation of slum conditions to juvenile delinquency and the expansion of colonial power, and also one on Russian reconstruction made after a visit to the U.S.S.R.[26] *Hell Unlimited*, a one-reel 16 mm silent indictment of armament manufacturers, was made by McLaren with Helen Biggar in Scotland, received a prize at the fourth Scottish Amateur Film Festival,[27] and was distributed by Kino. After going to Spain with Ivor Montagu to film the Spanish Civil War in the autumn of 1936, McLaren joined the G.P.O. Film Unit, but it was not until he worked for Grierson in Canada during the war that he found his real *métier* in the creation of experimental abstract films.

Meanwhile *Hell Unlimited* was clearly made by a group of young people with the absolute minimum of resources but with all the verve and shock tactics of youth and passionate conviction. It is a

violent tract against war, and even more against armaments manufacturers. Its point of view is elementary, and is conveyed crudely
with a heavy touch of satire here and there, but in view of their
resources it is a *tour de force*.

Starting with a dedication to the people who are compelled to
pay for their own destruction, it takes us through the idea that the
"war to cnd war" had led simply to depression and a world where
the destruction of crops could exist side by side with starvation,
while the villainous armaments firms, which are fiercely named,
grow fat by manipulating the politicians.

It ends with an appeal to the audience to

WRITE
[shots of letters being addressed to M.P.s]
IF THAT FAILS
DEMONSTRATE
[shots of crowds and speakers]
IF THAT FAILS
THEN
MASS RESISTANCE IS BETTER THAN MASS MURDER
STRIKE
[more speakers, then a map of the world with, written over it, the
word]
STRIKE

Then follows a finale in which a strike brings the armaments race
successfully to an end.

The ingredients are many titles, some very long and some broken
up : headlines, a tear-off calendar; graphics of a skull, a gas mask;
maps, a few with some animated lines; close-ups of a large thermo-
meter symbolising the state of the arms race; stock shots of the 1914
war, factories, scenes of devastation; and brief acted flashes in
which the very young film makers play all the parts of elder states-
men, demagogues and the hated arms manufacturers. A close up
of a villain's head turns into a hand grenade, which in turn
becomes a "£" sign. The word "TAXES" is followed by a hand
squeezing fruit, intercut with shots of theatre tickets, cigarettes and
other taxed items. Literary and verbal in conception rather than

pictorial, it is a quick-fire and imaginative patchwork of devices which make another film political cartoon. As to whether this dazzling display would persuade or convince an ordinary audience or merely annoy them, that is another matter. But it was fast and emphatic and explicitly recommended positive action.

By this time Kino had set up the Progressive Film Institute, run by Montagu's wife, to handle 35 mm distribution. It had also gone into production itself. The P.F.I. was backed by the communists Dorothy Woodman, D. N. Pritt and Geoffrey Vevers as well as the Montagus. Like Ralph Bond, Ivor Montagu was a professional film maker as well as a dedicated communist, and was an editor, writer and associate producer of outstanding talent. Something more effective than the usual rather amateurish films of the League was to be expected. His first under the new regime was *Free Thaelmann!* in 1935. He had already realised, it seems, that the rise of fascism was going to be the vital issue of the time, differing in this not only from the Grierson group but also from both his working-class colleagues with their agonising unemployment problem and the pacifist socialists. Thaelmann, the German communist leader, had been held for two years in jail by the Nazis without being charged or brought to trial, one of the many things which our newsreels preferred not to mention. Using clips of film which had been brought out of Germany by refugees such as shots of Thaelmann making speeches, the May Day marches of 1930 and 1931 with police brutality in the streets, shots of book burning with the title "Culture Enrages the Nazis", the Reichstag fire and insets of pamphlets, cuttings about torture and murder, he used a great many titles, some of them dynamic and some stationary :

> Long Live the German Working Class
> Workers pledge struggle against Fascism
> "TRUTH WILL OUT".

Adding a few specially filmed shots, like a pair of wrists bound by wire, and ending with bars superimposed over a picture of Thaelmann, Montagu made a vigorous compilation film for use as part of a campaign to secure his release. Naturally the film was not granted a B.B.F.C. certificate, but it was shown at many special fund-raising gatherings.

In July 1936 the Spanish Civil War broke out, and from then on the P.F.I. and Kino, as well as distributing films from Russia and latterly from China as well, handled material from Spain which was partly shot or edited by them and partly of Spanish origin.

The great Spanish film maker Luis Buñuel, who had produced nothing in Spain since his outspoken film *Land Without Bread* in 1932, was "mobilized to the service of the cinema" on the outbreak of war by the government, according to his biographer Francisco Aranda.[28] Before 1936 was over he was sent to Paris, to make a full-length film of "news footage of the war" from material shot partly by himself and partly by others. Aranda goes on : ". . . he completed a four-reel compilation (he himself remembers it as being in eight reels; so perhaps it was subsequently shortened): *España 1936* or *España leal, en armas!*, a co-production with the French Communist Party." This, according to Aranda, was thought to be lost until found in 1966 by Jay Leyda in East Berlin, where it turned out to be forty minutes long and in French and Spanish versions. But Aranda also mentions a nine-reel version in the Filmoteca Nacional Española. In the fuller version it seems to have dealt with the history of the Republic before the rebellion, dropping most of this in the shorter version. There is also some disagreement as to how much Buñuel was personally responsible for the propaganda material which was now forthcoming, and particularly for this important film. At all events he went to Hollywood in 1938 to keep an eye, on the government's behalf, on two films which were being made about the Spanish war.

Meanwhile the P.F.I. in Britain had also been quick off the mark and by the autumn of 1936 Montagu and Norman McLaren, as cameraman, were in Spain. Early in 1937 they put out *In Defence of Madrid*. A catalogue of documentary films published by the British Film Institute in 1938, which included a number of films on the Spanish war, described this as a Spanish film produced by Ivor Montagu, a fact which suggests that some at least of the material may not actually have been shot by the Kino team. The catalogue says it shows the situation before the revolt, preparations for defending and evacuating Madrid, and the arrival of food ships; and they add that it included film of Ludwig Renn, Eleanor Rathbone, Dr Addison and Hans Beimler, the latter an early leader of the International Brigade. This version was 45 minutes long and silent. Hogenkamp, however, who has studied the Spanish war films through accounts in the English left-wing papers and journals of the thirties as well as from film viewing, refers in the article cited above to a film called *Defence of Madrid*, and says that Montagu and McLaren got footage of the bombing of Madrid and of the International Brigade, but that the surviving copy of the film shows the prehistory of the revolution, the intervention of Germany and Italy and the consequences of the bombing of Madrid with the section on the International Brigade missing.[29]

In view of the obscurity surrounding Buñuel's own activities, it is perhaps not surprising that there are discrepancies in the various accounts of the films available here about the Spanish Civil War. The aim of the British Film Institute was simply to record what was in the films and where to get them, and although its political views were certainly very different from those of the Progressive Film Institute the variations are almost certainly due to the fact that the same material was sometimes used several times in slightly different forms, rather than to any deliberate misinformation in the B.F.I. documentary list. The next P.F.I. film, early in 1937, was called in this list *News from Spain*, and described as showing events leading to the Civil War traced from 1934, as well as the war itself; it was clearly stated to be documentary material edited for the Spanish government by Buñuel himself, with an English commentary added by Isabel Brown for the P.F.I. But the copy now in the National Film Archive, of 3,320 feet and with the English commentary, starts with the outbreak of war and does not mention Buñuel.

The P.F.I. continued to put out films described by different sources variously as British or Spanish productions, but it would seem that most of them consisted of Spanish footage, sometimes re-edited here. There is a short film called *Madrid Today* in the N.F.A., which dates it 1937, and as it has no credits it would appear, in part at least, to be acquired footage edited by the P.F.I. It begins with lovely Spanish music, scenes of Madrid and a close up of a pretty, laughing girl, then a shock cut to a few frames of an explosion, the scene tilting right round the 360° of the frame, overhead views of a square with running people, and a few more quick cuts. This "bomb" sequence is used more than once in the film, and reappears in other films of Spain such as the charity production *Modern Orphans of the Storm*, which suggests that, at this time, anyway, there was something of a shortage of action pictures. Intermittent commentary is quiet and understated. "This is what a bombed house looks like, cut in half like a bit of cheese." And both it and the material, so unfamiliar in 1937, is an effective introduction to what bombing really meant. An animated flame advancing up the screen is used as a wipe. A shot of bombers over-head, like the explosion, is used more than once. The commentary ends on the required positive propaganda note that the defence of Madrid would go on. Scenes of fighting and devastation appeared in later films, and a number consisted of the interrogation of Italian and German prisoners, stressing the involvement of the dictatorships, although as we have seen this was in fact already acknowledged in the ordinary newsreels.

The two major contributions of the P.F.I. were those shot in Spain by their own unit, *Spanish A.B.C.* and *Behind the Spanish Lines*. Both were produced by Ivor Montagu, and according to the credits on the films themselves they were directed and edited by Thorold Dickinson and Sidney Cole, both feature film makers, and shot by Arthur Graham and Alan Lawson. Thorold Dickinson, although left-wing in sympathies, is emphatic that he went with this unit because employment was hard to get in the British film industry at that time and was not a communist as most of the team were. They were in Spain for a few months early in 1938, and the films were post-synchronised at Imperial Sound Studios. *Spanish A.B.C.* was commercially registered in July 1938, the only one of the Spanish films of the P.F.I. to be registered, and received a U certificate from the Censors. A two-reeler, it is called a "Film Report on the work of the Spanish Ministry of Public Instruction". It uses a sound-track composed of narration, written by Montagu and spoken by the communist G. C. T. Giles, backed by the singing of the refugee Basque children living in England. It is strong if unsubtle propaganda to the effect that the government's determination to remedy the previous apathy towards education was being continued despite the war. School scenes, various institutes and lunch-hour lessons for adult workers given with the blessing of the trade unions are shown as building a new Spain in the middle of wartime. The happy, enlightened workers learn trigonometry in the trenches, benefiting from the teaching of "Militiamen of Culture". It was shown at the Film Society in January 1939.

Behind the Spanish Lines was another two-reeler made by the same team from material shot at the same time, but not registered for theatrical showing. Again, it used the singing of the refugee children as musical backing. It was described as a survey of how Spain was governed, with evidence of bombing, especially of British ships in Spanish ports, and it used short interviews with captured German and Italian pilots. It was felt by *Sight and Sound*[30] to be even more propagandist than the other. In fact, whereas the first film had sought to show the admirable social purposes of the government, the second sought to involve British public opinion by drawing attention to the threat to British shipping brought about by fascist intervention. Reassuringly dignified shots of Barcelona and other places, the Cortes, the President and the legally elected leaders stress the safe, almost "Conservative" nature of the Republicans. A lovely, clean, unenclosed camp for enemy prisoners appears to be deserted, but we see happy prisoners lunching with their guards. All is normality – mothers with babies, nurses at their training, people dancing in a trade union hall – and it is pointed out that workers are stepping up their production voluntarily. We are told about air raids and how a German crew admit to bombing British ships, but apart from a wrecked German plane, some ruins, and relief work after bombing we see no action. The British Prime Minister's statement that there is no information on the nationality of the bombers is followed by a title "Two Captured Airmen" and an Italian, Gino Poggi, and a German, Rudolf Fuecker, are briefly interrogated. Foreign intervention itself was no secret, of course, as we have seen in the British Movietone issue of 1937 which we examined in detail, but the film clearly wished to arouse British indignation at the bombing of their own shipping. "And so Spaniards rush to support their Government", and in a brief shot La Pasionaria, unfortunately for posterity filmed mute, is seen exhorting her fellow citizens.

Britain Expects, a two-reeler shot slightly later by Alan Lawson about the blockade runner, the British Captain "Potato" Jones, and

Non-Intervention, a longer production in which Montagu used footage of fascist servicemen to stress the foreign intervention, were other specifically British contributions. But apart from *Spanish A.B.C.* and *Britain Expects* these British films were for non-theatrical audiences only. Not comparable in artistic eminence with the Dutch film maker Joris Ivens's *Spanish Earth*, they were presumably seen more often at Labour and Communist Party groups and workers' film societies than at the many film societies whose interests were aesthetic rather than political. As propaganda, therefore, they suffered the usual disadvantage of preaching to the converted. As films, it is very noticeable that they emphasise the normality of life and the valuable social policies of the Spanish Government, but show comparatively little action, whether ground fighting or air raids, few refugees, little of the bitterness and suffering endured by a country split by civil war. Nor is there much effort to examine or explain the nature and reasons for the tragedy, or the real issue of democracy and fascism. They form a curiously antiseptic, and presumably ineffective, exercise in the art of persuasion.

Whilst the communists were turning to film propaganda through the P.F.I. and the Conservative and National Government had used electioneering films at the 1935 general election, the Labour Party had so far shown little interest in films. In conjunction with the Labour Party Conference of 1936, however, a Special Labour Party Conference on Film Propaganda was held on 3 October in Edinburgh.[31] Here Paul Rotha addressed the meeting and expounded his basic belief that as far as professional film making was concerned "no film dealing with any contemporary subject from a working-class point of view can be made under the existing conditions of commercial film production".[32] Rotha's forthright political views were as important a point of difference between him and Grierson as his film style. He was thinking not in terms of Grierson's socially useful factual films, nor of the Photo League's corrective "newsreels", nor of communist special pleading, but of a world in which the ordinary cinemagoer could see films which were not permeated by the philosophy of the capitalist system. He foresaw the eventual left-wing feature film, "without stars or spectacle, films showing the people and life for which the Labour Movement stands, and films of what this country might be like under different circumstances".[33] Obviously large financial resources would have been necessary to put this dream into effect. The question of distribution, itself, would probably have been a stumbling block. But it also has to be admitted that the cinema-going public, which was largely working-class and which was growing all the time, showed no dissatisfaction at all with the capitalist dream world presented to it. People enjoyed watching the imaginary life of the rich and successful which was put before them, they laughed until they cried at the comically incompetent working-class character played by George Formby, and Andy Hardy's idealised American bourgeois family was what *Kine Weekly* used to call cast-iron box office. Hogenkamp quotes "Benn" in a contemporary left-wing periodical as saying "When once they have seen working class films they will never again be satisfied with the hollow mockeries of Elstree, or Hollywood and of Neubabelsberg."[34]

Surely this is open to doubt. What they would have thought of the kind of story film envisaged by Rotha is hard to guess, but stars and spectacle were very popular, and later generations have come to think that they were deservedly so. Educated left-wing supporters and the politically conscious left-wing minority of the working class would doubtless have welcomed such films, but the vast majority of the cinema public might have hankered for the old escapism. At all events, realising that such films were out of reach until a socialist film movement had created and extended a market and acquired considerable resources, for the time being Rotha recommended only the production of inexpensive documentaries. A joint committee of the Labour Party and the T.U.C. was set up, with the meagre result of a recommendation to work together with the Co-operative Film Committee.

The Co-operative movement was accustomed to the idea of films, the C.W.S. having long used them for publicity and according to Hogenkamp, to whom the reader is referred, the movement had already made several 16 mm films with political themes. Ralph Bond, an underrated but key figure, was again to be one of the prime movers in left-wing film making. An active trade unionist, he made films with a generalised left-wing message for producers as varied as Paul Rotha, in *Today we Live*, the Co-operative Film Committee, and the Workers' Travel Association. Realist Film Unit, for which Bond now worked, made a film in 1939 for four London Co-operative Societies called *Advance Democracy*, as well as *People with a Purpose* and a Workers' Travel Association film called *Passport to Europe*, all of them within the mainstream of documentary and described elsewhere in that context, although partially left-wing propaganda.

Meanwhile the last of the commercial mammoths to deal with international politics with even a pretence of seriousness was *The World in Revolt* of 1937, a distorted five-reel film purporting to contrast unrest abroad with calm in Britain. It was put out as a "Mentone" production edited by Arthur Dent and Howard Gaye, but it was handled by A.B.P.C., the firm whose director of productions was the same Walter Mycroft previously responsible for *Forgotten Men*. Dent was a financial producer rather than an actual film maker, while Gaye was variously an actor and a commentator. All the sequences except those dealing with Spain and Britain have American narrators, and it was suggested in the *Monthly Film Bulletin*[35] that much of it was of American origin.

The whole structure of the film was designed to show the superiority of Britain. Another compilation, it describes itself as a "screen review of the national, political and industrial rebellions in varying countries" and takes us through pre-1914 news shots of royalty, armies, then war and post-war scenes of rioting and the masses on the march. The material is impressive. But it is put together in such a way as to suggest that country after country is either in the throes or .on the verge of revolution : Russia; Austria; Cuba; Italy, with nothing but praise here for Mussolini; Germany, where although the film was made as late as 1937 the Jews are mentioned only once, as being among the few who "disagreed" with Nazism; China; the U.S.A., where labour troubles and the leadership of John L. Lewis are made to appear as a revolutionary threat; and Spain, where foreign intervention is never mentioned. Throughout all this, loud theatrical declamatory voices narrate at such remorseless pressure that they stun the mind into self-protective indifference. It is almost a caricature of the *March of Time* shouter, accompanied continuously by music which is oddly jolly some of the time. The film is a superb collection of actuality shots, fascinating in themselves but selected and put together strictly to show a picture of unredeemed popular violence and rebellion all over the world, giving a cumulative effect which is ruthlessly and deliberately misleading. All the countries except Britain seem to be experiencing revolutions which require to be put down by the armed forces of law and order. Finally Great Britain, as the film says, "the envy of less happier [*sic*] lands, resolute and calm, goes forward to her destiny, a power for peace in a disordered world".

True, a few shots are shown of the unemployed, and of Molly and her brothers in their rat-infested room from *The Great Crusade*, but "RECOVERY IS ON ITS WAY". Parliament is shown, the government is praised and shots of rearmament are seen. In fact, since international relations are never mentioned, military exercises in every country seem by implication to be for the re-establishment of law and order over all those rebellious masses. We end with shots of battleships, for it is not good enough for us to be secure here in Britain, but "The basis of a new world order must be peace and contentment." There is more than a hint that this will be attained by Britain, "resolute and calm", patrolling the seas.

From his strangely inadequate review in *World Film News*[36] it seems that Grierson was so delighted by the unique and fascinating assemblage of authentic film material, and the sweeping portrayal of mass movements almost in the Russian manner, that he criticised it not for its dishonesty so much as for its amateurish lack of shape and balance and its excessive length. His genuine lack of real political interest or instinct is nowhere more clearly shown than here. Even the anonymous reviewer in the Film Institute's *Monthly Film Bulletin* was more perceptive, mentioning the hysterical commentary, the omissions, and the inadequate interpretation of recent history. Fast, loud and violent, this dangerously persuasive film whips up feeling for no clear purpose and with no real understanding of the meaning of the mass movements shown. Perhaps, after all, it is just as well that the big production companies stuck to their dream world.

But from early 1937 when serious rearmament began the industry, like the newsreel, turned to the task of helping the government, and a number of "patriotics" followed. The public's emotional reaction against the last world war was sufficiently faded for some enthusiasm for the British armed forces to be acceptable once more in the short interest film. John Betts, who had made a film about the Navy back in 1933, had ventured a crude recruiting film for the air force, called *R.A.F.*, for Gaumont-British in 1935. In 1937 Bruce Woolfe had made his recruiting film *The Gap*, described in the companion volume to this book. In 1937, also, Commander J. L. F. Hunt, who had been dabbling in films for several years, made *Our Island Nation*, a five-reeler about life in the Navy made with the co-operation of the Admiralty. Other Naval films by Hunt followed. Early in 1938 a film to encourage recruitment to the Territorials, *Territorial Cavalcade*, was personally sponsored by the exhibitor Oscar Deutsch, who as a Jew himself had special reason to feel strongly about the Nazis. Later, in August 1938, two films called *Rule, Britannia* were put on the market in the same month. Hunt's was a short film compiled for the Director of Naval Recruiting. The other, independently made and directed by Bud Pollard, was a full-length anti-war semi-dramatic film which tried to cover a very wide scope, including a compilation of actuality material and interviews with ex-servicemen of both sides. Alas for good intentions, *Kine Weekly* regretted its "overstatement . . . reckless and redundant as its rhetoric sometimes is".[37]

The Warning, a three-reel film produced by Aubrey Baring for British National and distributed to the cinemas in 1939 by A.B.P.C., was made with official co-operation, although without a subsidy. It was intended to encourage recruitment to the Civil Defence Services by showing a dramatised version of an air raid, and begins with foreboding music, specially composed by Ronnie Munro, and a siren; this is followed by bright busy scenes in crowded streets, parks, beaches and sports grounds. Attention shifts to newspaper placards and headlines as a call-up is announced, with shots of the B.B.C. and a pub where people are listening to the radio news.

"MOBILISATION". The word appears diagonally across the screen. A map of Britain is followed by suitable shots of the Navy, anti-aircraft batteries and so on accompanied by "important" music, all conveying an impression of efficiency, power and alertness slightly betrayed by the panicky tone of phrases like "No time now ! The hour of trial is upon us !" Much was made of the fact that a real air raid was to be shown. But the one which follows appears more like a practice with a few real explosions thrown in, and is

not very convincing. The same applies to an aerial dogfight in which
the British pilot shoots down a modern raider despite his apparently
superior aircraft. "Let us be glad there is still time for us to train!"
This is followed by yet another desk chat, this time from Sir John
Anderson, Lord Privy Seal.

Rotha describes this as a "grotesque" film, which had to be
finished by the G.P.O. unit under Cavalcanti to save it from utter
disaster. It ends with shots of heads looking skywards (according
to Rotha they were the heads of members of the G.P.O. Film Unit)
and a clouds-and-trumpet ending.[38] Certainly the general tone, "It
will be alright if we all pull together", does not inspire confidence
and hardly seems to have been justified by the facts at the time.
But as a film it was greatly improved by the music and the good
brisk cutting of the G.P.O.'s Richard McNaughton, and it seems
considerably less grotesque than some other films made for the same
purpose of preparing the nation for war, films such as Bruce
Woolfe's *The Gap* and even Korda's feature film *The Lion has
Wings*. Tame and conventional would seem a more appropriate
description, but as it had an assured distribution through A.B.P.C.
it was estimated by the autumn that it had been shown in 2,000
cinemas in the United Kingdom.[39]

Finally, in 1939 Ivor Montagu's *Peace and Plenty* was the last,
and best, left-wing film. It must have been obvious that the limited
distribution and usually rather amateurish nature of these films
had done little to counterbalance the pervasive values of the commercial cinema. If a propaganda film was to have any effect it must
hit hard and for a specific purpose. Asked by the Communist Party
of Great Britain to make a film to help defeat the National Government in the election which was expected in 1939, Ivor Montagu
at the P.F.I. made a film which, like Rotha's Peace Film, asked the
audience to take a clear, limited action, in this case to vote against
the National Government candidates. A two-reel sound film
designed for non-theatrical distribution, it was shown to the press
and to M.P.s in May 1939, and proved to be a sharp, stinging
attack on the Government's home and foreign policy. Subtitled
"A Portrait of Our Times", it used compilation, excellent graphics,
a little animation, some still material, a puppet of Chamberlain and
the odd quirky shot like one of an umbrella, which was already an

easily identified symbol for Chamberlain. With a sparse, calm and factual narration and no titles, the film has a rather overpowering musical backing and is, in fact, practical rather than elegant in style. The general effect, however, is one of irony, pace and impact. Rural and industrial scenes are shown, the slums, some appalling statistics of poverty brought to life by shots of the real people and occupations to which they refer, together with portraits of government Ministers and information about their wealth and landowning background, and the simple, telling sentence "This Government is a Government of rich men". "They give us this", with images of gas masks and air raid shelters, "to send us against this", and we see shots of war devastation. This leads to the punch line "This Government has done enough – how can we get rid of them?"

The film ends after Harry Pollitt, in close mid-shot, delivers an outright exhortation to defeat the National Government in the next election. And unlike the actors of the National Government films or the well-meaning amateurs of the Socialist Film Council, or even the condescending politicians, he speaks as if he means what he says. The election did not take place, because of the outbreak of war. But the film proves, like the Peace Film, that propaganda is only as good as the people making it. Montagu was an exceptional man in many ways and a brilliant film maker, and it is not surprising that *Peace and Plenty* is outstanding among the political films of the time.

7

Film as a Historical Document

We have seen that in the thirties the film was rapidly shaking itself free from its exclusively theatrical role and developing as a real medium of communication, with a vast outpouring of films being produced outside the large story-feature studios. Both in this book, dealing with travel and expeditions, news, good cause films, political propaganda, interest films and the unclassifiable productions of independents and amateurs of every description, and in the companion volume describing the educational and documentary film movements, we have sought an overall view which would give us some sort of perspective on this development. In both books it is clear from the text, I hope, which films are described from personal viewing and which from hearsay. In the enormous quantity of film of every type we find a treasure trove of a new form of historical document. A few pioneering historians have been quick to discover this.

The terms of reference under which the British Film Institute was incorporated in 1933 include the instruction "to encourage the development of the art of the film, to promote its use as a record of contemporary life and manners". There is a slight ambiguity here, which has been largely ignored. Did it mean encouraging the production of commercial feature films which would more truly reflect the contemporary world than the shoddy falseness of many of those made at the time, or encouraging people to make and show factual and documentary films? The original aims of many of those who initiated the B.F.I. was certainly the former. But owing to the stranglehold which the film trade had on the Institute this was conveniently overlooked and its activities largely confined, although somewhat ineffectively, to the latter. Among those activities was the creation of a large film archive which, together with those of the newsreel companies, the Imperial War Museum and other collections, was later to be of interest to historians.

It was not until the fifties that the potential value of films as a source of historical information attracted much attention outside the film archives themselves. Sir Arthur Elton's important address at the Aslib Annual Conference in September 1955, 'The Film as Source Material for History',[1] enthusiastically described film as "a new and critical method of dealing with the politics and policies and events, of times that have passed".

The films of comment and persuasion discussed here are waiting to provide fascinated researchers with a rich store of information and nostalgia, a way of conjuring up the past which has not previously been available except, to a limited degree, through archaeology and museums. I exclude the fiction films of the feature studios, which have their own way of speaking of the past but which do not concern us here. In the companion volume we have already discovered some of the pitfalls in the relation of film to reality and, since historians are sure to use this magnificent tool more and more, perhaps we should consider what exactly is the nature, and what are the limitations, of the material with which they will be dealing. It is pertinent to consider what we can learn of the past, and teach of the past, from the films of the past.

A historian can look at film in two ways, as a historical document and as a teaching medium. As a historical document there are three things to be considered, first the facts of the film's existence; second the message or content intended to be conveyed by the film; and third the message and content given by the film other than that intended by its maker, including what we can read from it of contemporary attitudes. As a teaching medium, on the other hand, we must consider the validity of using old film in the teaching of history either in its original state or made into compilations by the historian.

First, a film or fragment of film as a historical document. The historian of films, as distinct from the historian of the things studied by means of the film, is acutely aware of the difficulties involved in the authentication and attribution which will alone enable other historians to use it safely as a source of information. When it was made, where and by whom as well as why, whether it was all newly shot or included library shots or even faked and misattributed material, and what has been done in the way of cutting, re-editing and altering the meaning since it was made are all matters which can be difficult to discover, and are the subject of many a lively argument among film historians. The conventional sources of historical information have to be used for corroboration. But there is also a whole new branch of archival detective work concerning the intricacies of dating or identifying different film stocks, types of lighting, certain firms' or individuals' characteristic use of punches, marks and so on, the evidence or tracing of offcuts and discarded material and in the case of news films, in particular, the tracking down of what was cut out, and commentaries delivered or removed. The question of who saw the films and what they thought of them is even more difficult. Box office takings may indicate the popularity of a feature film, although in fact they are rarely ascertainable, but they do not indicate the popularity of the films in their supporting programmes. The circulation of newsreels is more easily calculable, although with the same limitation, but as for the non-theatrical distribution of most of these films, it must be largely a matter of guesswork. And if it is impossible even to assess how many people saw a film there is little hope of forming an accurate opinion of its effect, if any. Some contemporary reviewers' opinions are of interest, but the taped memoirs of the film makers themselves should be treated with great reserve.

If the authentication and attribution are satisfactory the overt content of the film may be considered. But if the film is to be regarded as historical evidence this term itself requires definition. Reluctantly, one must conclude that evidence in this context means illustration, rather than proof. A news item "Mr Eden on his way to the Geneva talks" may be Mr Eden but filmed some other time and kept on hand for just such an occasion; he may well have gone to the Geneva talks, but that is a fact we must ascertain in other ways. In discussing the relation of film to reality in Chapter 4 of the companion volume to this book, reference is made to Pudovkin's famous example of how the identical shot of an actor's face can appear to convey different emotions if the adjacent shots of what he is apparently watching are changed. The film's capacity to deceive being what it is, "Remember Pudovkin!" should be the motto of every historian using it. Dr Rolf Schuursma of the Foundation for Film and Science in Utrecht, and himself the maker of a historical compilation film, said in December 1972 that film by itself is not likely to prove anything not already known from other sources,[2] and this would seem to be true. Christopher Roads, Deputy Director and Keeper of the Department of Records at the Imperial War Museum, more trusting, had written in 1966 of its value in such military evidence as the topographical details of a battlefield, what and who was present, the difficulty of appreciating how a battle is going when you are involved in it, and what the terrain is like. But all this can be faked, and indeed what he writes could apply equally well to Peter Watkins's 1964 reconstruction of *Culloden* for the B.B.C. He wrote that the film could prove, for example, the existence of Belsen. But even here, although the film gives visual proof that such a place existed and was populated by the ghastly figures we see on the screen, the time and place, the reasons and the people behind it can be, and strangely enough actually have been, questioned. Proof lies elsewhere.[3]

But if we have a shot of Hitler addressing a rally, or for example the Beaverbrook film wooing us on Imperial Preference, and we know it to be what it seems to be, it has a value of a different sort. The film has a unique capacity to record and illuminate. Roads, like Elton, was impressed with its power to convey the bearing of both individuals and crowds. Portraits have always been of immense interest in history, and films are moving portraits of the person in action, subject like other portraits to the selection and emphasis of another person's interpretation. In the case of interviews, especially in the thirties when equipment was cumbersome and obvious, what I have called elsewhere the intrusion factor should not be overlooked. Beaverbrook was a great performer, but most thirties interviews were stiff desk chats, the presence of the camera freezing even seasoned politicians into character-hiding conventionality. But it is intriguing to see, in our two Movietone sections of 1932 and 1937, the Mussolini of the first, uniformed and with theatrically heroic jaw, become the coarsened and ornately accoutred figure of 1937. It is not new knowledge, merely visual confirmation of a particularly vivid and attention-catching kind. When it comes to the demeanour of crowds, the perfunctory and good-natured fist clenching of the busmen's strike, the fiercer mien of other demonstrations, we are faced once more with the importance of knowing who took the film and why, what they chose to show and what to conceal. We must not be misled, in fact, into imagining that we are able to form a first-hand impression of our subject.

Elton, the supreme master of films about technology, mentioned their great capacity to show the routines and procedures of technical processes. Films of dying crafts, for example, are among the most perfect examples of film as record that we have. To take a small and insignificant example, the packaging company Metal Box has a film of two very old craftsmen demonstrating the hand manufacture, which they had practised through their long working lives, of the tin wig-boxes traditionally used by the legal profession. No written record could have given such a clear idea of the process, long since mechanised, or the skill and pride with which they exercised it.

Many such films must exist. But as historical documents they lack glamour and importance. At the other extreme, films setting out to portray an unfamiliar life-style are a different matter, and although of great fascination require much more corroboration and detail. The chapter on travel and expedition films provides many examples, including Mrs Chapman's amateurish films of Lapland and the interesting but unacademic sequences on Australian aborigines by Hurley, the more knowledgeable filming of Dr Lindgren and her colleagues in north-west Manchuria, Ralph Cutler in his East African villages and the rare and beautiful films of the Lhasa expedition of 1936. There are many, many others, including the home movies of British families all over the then flourishing Empire. As visual records of societies which were soon to change they are interesting, but less like a record than like archaeological fragments upon which to build hypotheses. These fragments survive, sifted first by the selection exercised by the original film maker, and secondly by the haphazard selection of time, which has destroyed or preserved largely by chance. However stimulating to the imagination, they are both subjective and partial.

The more sophisticated the film maker, the greater his skill and conscious intentions, the more subjective the content. *These Children are Safe*, an excellent documentary of 1939 described in the companion volume, uses film of the wartime evacuation of children from the big cities to the country and a narration which implied with some subtlety that the operation had been far more satisfactory than we know, from other sources, was the case. And, once you get to the film compilations about current affairs made during the thirties, you are in an area where actuality film is used in the service of distortion. *Crown and Glory*, for example, was a superficial historical perspective of the years from 1895 made by Paramount to mark the 1937 Coronation. It slipped in some horrifying actuality shots of a sinking battleship with the implication that it was a German ship at Jutland, which was untrue. *World in Revolt* is an even more alarming case, praised by Grierson himself at the time, so bowled over was he by the massive assembly of authentic footage of world events that he was apparently indifferent to the fact that they were put together as a historical misrepresentation on a staggering scale. Once again, however vividly and dramatically such films bring the past to life, their use is limited. They do not enable us to form first-hand impressions of the subject of the film.

But this is not the whole story. A mass of information can be conveyed by the film over and above its intended subject. As Elton remarked in his Aslib lecture, the film records everything in front of it, whether of interest to the film maker or not, and he might have added that it also implies a great deal about the attitudes of the film maker, those filmed, and the audience to which it is addressed.

The evocation of atmosphere, as Dr Schuursma has stressed, though stimulating, is as selective and as much in need of confirmation as everything else. The most highly developed films are not always the most informative from this point of view. The mainstream documentaries *Housing Problems* and *Children at School*, designed to awaken the consciences of the thirties to some of the social conditions and needs of the time, deliberately gave a carefully ordered account to support their view, and the impact in the case

of these two unusually fine films is very great. But the facts themselves are known from other sources and the atmosphere conjured
up, strangely enough, can be equalled by far less skilful films, or
by films which were made for some completely different cause.

The work of some of the leading film makers did, of course,
sometimes consciously aim at evoking atmosphere, for example the
G.P.O. documentary *B.B.C. – the Voice of Britain* and Jennings's
Spare Time. But as the film makers could not tell what was going
to appear strange to viewers in years to come, the very complete-
ness of their control of the material impeded the casual inclusion of
incidentals, and it is often other films, made for other purposes,
which unexpectedly bring to life the time and place. Some are the
work of the most talented film makers. Rotha's filming of the
British countryside, with its shire horses, its traditional ways of
harvesting and stacking grain, even the physical look of the fields,
the hedges and the paling fences, together with Jennings's beautiful
Spring Offensive and even Cavalcanti's *Midsummer Day's Work*
are all convincing pictures of rural England in the thirties, matched
by the Boulting brothers' *Ripe Earth*. These were the professionals,
able to interpose their personal viewpoint between their raw
materials and their audience. Newsreels and the *March of Time*,
and many other lesser documentaries, observed less and interpreted
less. But it was not necessary to be a great film maker to pass on
to the future many delightful and sometimes surprising insights. The
honest and unimaginative filming of the less sophisticated has its
place here. *Power Farming by Fordson*, for example, although
simply an advertising film, was also a fascinating and convincing
picture of the English countryside and farming methods. The
kitchen equipment shown in two modest films featuring the French
chef M. Boulestin, and in the old-fashioned and otherwise negligible
electricity advertising film *Country Currents*, are as illuminating
about women's work in the kitchen as any documentary or feature
of the thirties. *Roadways* and *Telephone Workers*, both mainstream
documentaries with limited aims of their own unconnected with the
evocation of atmosphere, incidentally give a very powerful sense
of the suburban surroundings of the thirties. But so, to an even
greater extent, does *The Highway Code*, made by a minor and
undistinguished company, and so do the unselfconscious little films

of our friends Mr Bush and Mr Lumley of the Bermondsey Borough Council, which conjure up the very feel of the modest pavements, the comparative emptiness of the roads, the clean, respectable and shabby, but tree-lined, streets. In their sheer inability to select and emphasise, to interpret and pre-digest the truth, the worst of these films from the artistic point of view have a strength for the historian as documents. And there were others, minor gems like *Out to Play* which today would be called a fringe production, with its children playing in the streets, which was not surpassed in its portrayal of that one small corner of life even by Ruby Grierson's *Give the Kids a Break* or Basil Wright's *Children at School*, fine as these films were.

Insights into attitudes, as well as atmosphere, can be illuminating too. Amy Johnson's boy passenger who asks her if he can tell the fellows at school that it was a man who took him flying does not surprise us, as it shows an attitude to women which has been much discussed, but it is a wry pleasure to find such a perfect example tucked away in the archives. The lady drivers at Brooklands who are glad that they have won an important race because no other woman has done so are a sign of the times. More unexpected is the physical appearance of women of all social classes in the bulk of the films which clearly suggest that, still untouched by the high intensity of television advertising, they were much more relaxed in their attitude to weight, waistlines, hair styles and "grooming" than post-war generations, even though the film star example was supposed to have made an impact already. The patronising "kindly" attitude to coloured people which is apparent in *Plantation People* and which Paul Robeson politely seeks to rebut in *Song of Africa* is still evident even in the more enlightened G.P.O. *Men of Africa* of 1939–40, while the travellers'-tale type of film usually ignored the very existence of native Africans and concentrated on the animals. Class attitudes are equally easy to foresee, from the upper-class tones of the unseen conversationalists of the Orient cruise film *People and Places* to the more chummy atmosphere of Ralph Bond's Workers' Travel Association film *Passport to Europe*, and the appearance of the striking busmen's chilly day by the sea in the Labour movement's *The Busmen's Holiday*. More noteworthy still is *Job in a Million*, a documentary about an undersized working-class boy of 14 who is lucky enough to be accepted by the Post Office for training as a G.P.O. messenger; his anxious humility, the stress laid on his good fortune and the greatness of the service for which he works and for whose good name he is now responsible all seem strange forty years later. The ladies bountiful of the Welfare explaining the system to an ignorant and grateful mother in *Health for the Nation*, the peremptory and even insulting tone of authority in the training film for railwaymen, *Engine Shed*, and the dismaying sight of shabby boys being prepared for lonely emigration to Canada in *Farming for Boys* may add little to written knowledge but they sharpen our awareness of what poverty and the class system were like in the thirties. Again and again, the little that was expected from life by the less fortunate is brought home by films intended at the time to cheer rather than to depress, and to bring a message of hope. The delighted woman who has been rehoused in *Kensal House* and actually has a bathroom, the sad and humiliating plight of old people, men and women in separate institutions, presented with such pride in *Health for the Nation*, and a jolly Pathé item about what a good time the unemployed were having at their week's "holiday camp" are further examples. These unintentional glimpses of low expectations in films which are meant to please and encourage can sometimes provoke thought which even the best outright exposé of bad conditions does not. Political propaganda, too, can be interesting, like the British films on the Spanish war. *Spanish A.B.C.* shows the communist-backed Progressive Film Institute stressing the excellent social programme of the Republican Government, and *Behind the Lines* appealed to British opposition to fascist intervention in Spain by drawing attention to the fact that British shipping and property were at risk. Surprising, too, among a mass of crude political speeches and feeble cartoons made for the Conservative and Unionist Party, is the find of a few small films which paid their audience the compliment of presenting not emotional manipulation, but a simple economic argument. The widespread feeling that arms manufacturers were wicked men, personally responsible for war, is a thread which appears again and again.

Thus both the intentional and unintentional messages of our films can illustrate and bring to life the people and places, the atmosphere and attitudes, of the 1930s. Little wonder that, despite the subjective nature of the films and the chancy selection of them which has survived, the historian is intrigued, and inspired to use it not only as a source but as a teaching medium, in other words as excerpts or compilation films chosen and arranged by historians themselves. In a way, this is like presenting a facsimile of written documentation, with or without commentary and interpretation, rather than using it simply as the basis of a historical assessment. Because of its association with entertainment this is a most attractive idea, and historians who deplored Dr Schuursma's cautious attitude in 1972 wanted to "make films which in an imaginative way would enable students or other viewers to penetrate beneath the surface and gain a deeper understanding of the subject".[4] A number of excellent compilations, dealing necessarily with more recent events and relying heavily on news film, have already been made. The lure of being your own film maker is almost too great to resist, and in time taped voices will certainly be used also, as they already are in many books of taped interviews. As fingers itch to hold those strips of celluloid, it is more than ever necessary to remember the treacherous nature of the medium.

For film can illustrate, and as evidence it can tend to confirm something at two removes, but it is not proof itself. Despite its innocent air of truthfulness a historian's film, like a historian's book, is simply his own presentation of the material at his disposal. The material to date, and especially up to 1939, may be a bit more scarce and a lot more subjective than the conventional written sources of information, and in some cases its authenticity is more difficult to establish, but provided the usual integrity is shown in its use this is legitimate and stimulating. But it is important that the public should be as aware of the true nature of film evidence as they are of the nature of other sources of evidence. In our study of the documentary movement to which reference has been made we found much confusion as to the relation of documentary to reality. The recent development of a high degree of realism in the filmed documentary drama can lead the naïve to mistake it for something they vaguely think of as "fact". But the dramatist himself, short of deliberate deception, is not responsible for this naïvety, and the use of any technical resources available to him to convey his dramatic truth is perfectly valid. The realistic documentary drama and the historical compilation film have something in common in this respect. Both are modern extensions of old forms, using modern technology to present interpretations of truth, in the one case that of the dramatist and in the other that of the historian. The danger to both lies in a lack of understanding on the part of their public. They both depend on an audience sufficiently educated to appreciate the film as a medium of expression, and remember that what they see is not life at first hand but, in their different ways, accounts of it through other people's eyes.

Notes

CHAPTER 2 NEWS FILMS

1   *Sight and Sound*, No. 7, autumn 1933, p. 89.
2   ibid.
3   *Kine Weekly*, 6 Feb 1936, p. 23.
4   *Kine Weekly*, 8 March 1934, p. 4.
5   *Kine Weekly*, 25 Oct 1934, Newsreels and Shorts Supplement, p. 8.
6   *Kine Weekly*, 8 Nov 1934.
7   *Kine Weekly*, 23 July 1936, pp. 5 & 27; *Kine Weekly*, 15 Oct 1936, p. 43.
    and *Kine Year Book*, 1937, pp. 208–9.
8   Harry Wynder, talking about Pathé.
9   *Kine Weekly*, 18 March 1937, p. 29.
10 *Kine Weekly*, May and July 1937.
11 Naval source quoted at the N.F.A.
12 *Kine Weekly*, 3 Aug 1939, p. 5.
13 *British Newsreels in the 1930s* – 1. *Audience and Producers* and 2. *Their Policies and Impact*, in *History*, Volume 56, No. 188, October 1971 and Volume 57, No. 189, February 1972; and *The Newsreels: the Illusion of Actuality* in *The Historian and the Film* edited by Paul Smith, 1976.
14 Quoted by Nicholas Pronay from D. H. E. Butler and S. Freeman, *British Political Facts 1900–1960*.
15 *Kine Weekly*, 11 Sept 1930, p. 22.
16 *Kine Weekly*, 30 March 1933, p. 5.
17 *Kine Weekly*, 14 March 1933, p. 43.
18 *Kine Weekly*, 26 Oct 1933, p. 3.
19 ibid.
20 *Sight and Sound*, No. 18, summer 1936, p. 21.
21 *Kine Weekly*, 7 Oct 1937, p. 4.
22 *Kine Weekly*, 3 March 1938, p. 4. The item refers only to a "prominent anti-Government person" but research by Jonathan Lewis reveals this to have been Clement Atlee.
23 David Low, *Years of Wrath*, p. 58.
24 *Sight and Sound*, spring 1977, pp. 68–73.
25 *Kine Weekly*, 1 Jan 1931, p. 14.
26 Harry Wynder, interviewed in 1977. Film sources taken from bound volumes of post-production commentary sheets, in which each item is accompanied by its source; these are not named after about June 1938.
27 *Sight and Sound*, spring 1977, pp. 68–73.
28 *Kine Weekly*, 31 Aug 1933, p. 4.
29 Charles Grinley, 'Notes on the Newsreel', in *Life and Letters Today*, winter 1937, pp. 122–8.
30 Paul Smith (ed.), *The Historian and the Film*, p. 113.
31 *Sight and Sound*, summer 1977, p. 154.
32 *Kine Weekly*, 27 Aug 1936, p. 35.

33 Harry Watt, *Don't Look at the Camera*, p. 75.
34 Jay Leyda, *Films Beget Films*, p. 43.
35 Elizabeth Sussex, *The Rise and Fall of British Documentary*, pp. 88 and 103.
36 Jay Leyda, *Films Beget Films*, p. 43.
37 *Spectator* 8 Nov 1935.
38 *Life and Letters Today*, winter 1935/6, p. 192.
39 *Sight and Sound*, No. 15, autumn 1935, p. 123.
40 *Kine Weekly*, 18 March 1937, p. 10.
41 Trade Show 1. in May 1939, issues 1, 2 and 3; Trade Show 2. in November 1939 with issues 4 and 5; Trade Show 3. in December 1939 with issue 6. All about 1,500 feet long.
42 *Sight and Sound*, No. 30, summer 1939, pp. 60–1.
43 Forsyth Hardy (ed.) *Grierson on Documentary*, pp. 134–5.
44 B.B.C. television programme in November 1976, *John Logie Baird and the Beginning of TV*.
45 *Life and Letters Today*, winter 1936.
46 *Kine Year Book*, 1931, p. 221.
47 B.B.C. television programme.
48 ibid.
49 *Kine Weekly*, 2 Nov 1937, p. 3.
50 *Kine Year Book*, 1937.
51 *Kine Weekly*, 13 April 1939, p. 3.
52 *Sight and Sound*, Volume 7, No. 27, autumn 1938, p. 140.
53 *Kine Weekly*, 20 Aug 1936, p. 4.
54 This was *The Student of Prague*.
55 *Kine Weekly*, 20 Aug 1936, p. 4.
56 *Sight and Sound*, Volume 8, No. 31, autumn 1939, pp. 114–15.
57 5 x 4 feet, according to *Kine Weekly*, 31 Dec 1936.
58 16 x 12 feet, according to *Kine Weekly*, 15 July 1937.
59 *Kine Weekly*, 29 March 1939, p. 21.
60 *Kine Weekly*, 6 April 1935, p. 3.
61 *Kine Weekly*, 25 May 1935, p. 3.

CHAPTER 3   FILMS OF TRAVEL AND EXPLORATION

1 *Kine Weekly*, 1 March 1934, p. 33.
2 *Rome Hunt, Rome Symphony* and *The Eternal Fire*
3 It kept the same length and E registration number; in 1938 it was reissued in its original length and title, but with a shorter version as well called *Africa Sings*.
4 Adrian Brunel, *Film Production*, p. 17.
5 Stella Court Treatt, *Cape to Cairo*, p. 26.
6 Stella Court Treatt, *Sudan Sand*, p. 30.
7 ibid. p. 3.
8 *Close Up*, Volume v, No. 6, Dec 1929.
9 *Close Up*, Volume vi, No. 1, Jan 1930, p. 84.
10 *Sight and Sound*, No. 27, autumn 1938, pp. 130–31.
11 Julian Duguid, *Green Hell*, pp. 75–6.
12 ibid. p. 54.
13 ibid. p. 54.

210 Films of Comment and Persuasion of the 1930s

14 See Ralph Barker, *One Man's Jungle*, p. 83.
15 In *Northern Lights* by F. Spencer Chapman, pp. 180–9.
16 F. Spencer Chapman, *Watkins' Last Expedition*, p. xiii.
17 *Sight and Sound*, No. 23, autumn 1937, pp. 122–5.
18 See H. J. P. Arnold, *Photographer of the World*.
19 26,250 feet, according to Dr Paul Bauer in *Himalayan Campaign*.
20 Again according to Dr Bauer.
21 Capt. J. B. L. Noel, *Through Tibet to Everest*, pp. 212–13.
22 *Cinema Quarterly*, autumn 1932, p. 33.
23 Audrey Field, *Picture Palace*, p. 112.
24 *Cinema Quarterly*, autumn 1932.
25 Capt. F. S. Smythe, *Kamet Conquered*.
26 According to books by H. Ruttledge and F. Young-Husband.
27 *Sight and Sound*, No. 8, winter 1933/4.
28 *Life and Letters Today*, spring 1937, p. 140.
29 *Cinema Quarterly*, Volume 1, No. 1, autumn 1932, pp. 28–9.
30 *Sight and Sound*, No. 10, summer 1934.
31 *Cinema Quarterly*, Volume 2, No. 4, summer 1934, p. 252.
32 *Cinema Quarterly*.
33 F. Spencer Chapman, *Watkins' Last Expedition*, p. xi.

CHAPTER 4 INTEREST FILMS AND THE INDEPENDENT FILM MAKER

1 *Kine Weekly*, 21 July 1938, p. 28.
2 Ian Coster, *Friends in Aspic*, pp. 245–6.
3 *Film Art*, No. 6, autumn 1935, pp. 64–7.
4 *Film Art*, No. 4, summer 1934, p. 70.
5 *Film Art*, No. 6, autumn 1935, pp. 64–7.
6 *Sight and Sound*, Vol. 8, No. 30, summer 1939, pp. 60–1.
7 According to John Huntley, *British Technicolor Films*, p. 128, they secured registration after the outbreak of war.
8 21,280 children aged from 3 to 14 years in 29 schools were studied.
9 Cinemas in Enfield, Leytonstone, Willesden and Edmonton.
10 Paper read by S. Bernstein at the 1936 B.F.I. Conference on Films for Children.
11 *Sight and Sound*, No. 23, autumn 1937.
12 *Sight and Sound*, No. 21, spring 1937.
13 See Oleg Kerensky, *Anna Pavlova*.
14 *Museum of Modern Art Film Index*, p. 642.
15 *Film Art*, No. 9, autumn 1936, p. 31.
16 *Close Up*, Vol. VII, No. 5, November 1930.
17 *Cinema Quarterly*, Volume 1, No. 1, autumn 1932, p. 40.
18 Dorothy Knowles, *The Censor, the Drama and the Film, 1900–1934*, p. 237.
19 *Sight and Sound*, No. 12, winter 1934.
20 *Museum of Modern Art Film Index*, p. 644; *Close Up*, Volume VII, No. 4, December 1931.
21 *Turning her Round* was later acquired by the G.P.O. and is sometimes referred to, erroneously, as a G.P.O. Film Unit production.
22 *Kine Weekly*, 1 Feb 1934, p. 36.
23 *Memorial to Richard Massingham*, and *World Film News*, April 1937, p. 29.

24 ibid.
25 *World Film News*, April 1937, p. 29.
26 *Kine Weekly*, 5 Nov 1936, p. 30A.
27 Richard Kostelanetz, *Moholy-Nagy*, pp. 159–60.
28 ibid. p. xvii. According to John Russell Taylor in *Sight and Sound*, autumn 1975, the sequence still exists. Karol Kulik states on p. 149 of her biography of Korda that Moholy-Nagy designed sets for the film, which were not used.
29 Called *Life of the Lobster* in the book by Kostelanetz.
30 Two earlier substandard silent films, *Gypsies* of 1934 and *Marseilles* of 1929, were not made in Britain.
31 Moholy-Nagy quoted in Kostelanetz's book, p. 133.
32 *Cinema Quarterly*, Volume 2, No. 3, spring 1934.
33 Interview, May 1976.
34 John Grierson is credited as joint cameraman in Karol Kulik's biography of Korda, but this seems unlikely.
35 *Cinema Quarterly*, Volume 3, No. 3, spring 1935.
36 *Sight and Sound*, No. 12, winter 1934/5.
37 *Cinema Quarterly*, Volume 3, No. 3, spring 1935.
38 The saga was not finished. A final version was trade shown in May 1940.
39 1928: *Dark-Ground Illumination: Showing the Internal Structure of the Cell* (324 ft); 1929–31: *The Cultivation of Skeletal Tissues: The Development in Vitro of the Lower Limb of the Embryonic Fowl* (896 ft) with Dr Honor Fell; 1930: *The Cultivation in Vitro of the Chick Embryo* (749 ft) with Dr C. H. Waddington; 1931: work on rabbit ovum *in vitro* with Dr G. Pincus, but in the opinion of Professor G. E. H. Foxon no film resulted; 1933: *The Cultivation of Living Tissue* (2,459 ft), a compilation of earlier films of Canti, Fell and some by Pincus on rabbit ovum. Made for the British Empire Cancer Campaign, for a lay audience; 1935: *Psittacocis Virus* (737 ft) with Dr J. O. W. Bland for the British Empire Cancer Campaign; 1935: *Tissue Culture of Gliomata* (532 ft) with Dr J. O. W. Bland and Dr D. S. Russell for British Empire Cancer Campaign.
40 *Film Art*, No. 5, winter 1934, p. 22.
41 *Sight and Sound*, Volume 5, No. 20, winter 1936/7, p. 119; *Film Art*, Vol. III, No. 9, autumn 1936, p. 31.
42 W. H. George, *The Cinema in School*, pp. 93–4.

CHAPTER 5 COMMERCIAL, MORAL AND SOCIAL PERSUASION

1 Sydney Box, *Film Publicity*, pp. 16–17.
2 Other films included Smart's *Here's Health* for Beecham's: *Generation after Generation* to celebrate the centenary of Bird's Custard; *Land of the Four Kings* about Somerset, for Cow and Gate; *Black Diamonds* about the production of motor spirit; *Gallons of Goodness* about milk; *The Material of Infinite Uses* about Bakelite; *Meat for the Millions* about the meat trade; *Merry Mondays* on soap making; *A Visit to Intertype* about type-setting; and *Wagon Wheels* about tyres.
3 *Sight and Sound*, No. 8, winter 1933/4, p. 148.
4 Harry Watt, *Don't Look at the Camera*, p. 79.
5 Sometimes known as *No: 62007 – A Study in Steel*.
6 e.g. *Philip's Big Broadcast*, 1937.

7 *Kine Weekly*, 14 Oct 1937, p. 43.
8 Not to be confused with the Visual Education film *The Highway* of autumn 1933 made by Eric Spear and Christopher Radley, which followed a walking tour of Kent.
9 National Film Library 1938 Catalogue, p. 162.
10 *Life and Letters Today*, winter 1935, p. 189.
11 ibid.
12 *The Artist*, Volume XIII, March–August 1937, pp. 11, 43, 75, 105, 150 and 182.
13 This film is dated 1937 by the National Film Archive.
14 Lally, p. 154.
15 R. G. Burnett, *The Cinema for Christ*, Appendix I, pp. 126–7.
16 Alan Wood, *Mr. Rank*, p. 69.
17 *Sight and Sound*, No. 7, autumn 1933, p. 107.
18 *Monthly Film Bulletin*, Vol. 1, No. 2, March 1934.
19 Alan Wood, *Mr. Rank*, p. 70.
20 Lally, p. 137.
21 *Sight and Sound*, No. 12, winter 1934/5.
22 Lally, p. 137.
23 *Educational Film Review*, Volume I, No. 4, p. 82.
24 Lally, p. 203.
25 Lally, p. 199.
26 The large number of health and medical films in the Kodak and Red Cross collections were mostly American and French.
27 *The Story of Papworth*, a two-reeler of 1936 made by Jeapes of British Pictorial Productions, was a different film.
28 *Kine Weekly*, 29 Dec 1938, p. 17. Completion untraced.
29 Lally, p. 285.
30 *Kine Weekly*, 2 June 1938, p. 21.

CHAPTER 6   POLITICAL PROPAGANDA

1 Paul Rotha, *Films and the Labour Party*.
2 *Close Up*, Vol. VII, No. 5, November 1930, pp. 347–8.
3 *Experimental Cinema*, No. 4; and National Film Archive Catalogue, Part II, p. 111.
4 *Experimental Cinema*, No. 4; and *Film Index*, p. 576.
5 Bert Hogenkamp's interesting interpretation of the use of film by the labour movement in Britain during this period appeared in *Sight and Sound* in Spring 1976, pp. 68–76.
6 Victoria Wegg-Prosser's account of two collections of films found by Jonathan Lewis and Elizabeth Taylor-Mead appears in *Sight and Sound*, autumn 1977, pp. 245–7.
7 Peter Baechlin and Maurice Muller-Straus, *Newsreels Across the World*.
8 *Kine Weekly*, 21 Dec 1933, p. 19.
9 *Sight and Sound*, No. 9, spring 1934.
10 *Kine Weekly*, 14 Feb 1933, p. 23.
11 *Sight and Sound*, No. 5, spring 1933.
12 *Cinema Quarterly*, Vol. 2, No. 1, autumn 1933, pp. 65–6.
13 Paul Rotha, *Documentary Diary*, p. 110.
14 *Kine Weekly*, 16 April 1936, p. 27.

15 *Sight and Sound*, No. 11, autumn 1934, pp. 110–12.
16 Previously called *The Night Patrol*.
17 *Sight and Sound*, Vol. 3, No. 2, winter 1935, p. 119.
18 *Cinema Quarterly*, Vol. 2, No. 4, summer 1934, p. 262.
19 *Cinema Quarterly*, Vol. 3, No. 2, winter 1934, pp. 127–8.
20 *International Review of Educational Cinematography*, Year II, No. 6, June 1930, pp. 717–28. Nieter is also usually credited with another L.N.U. film, *Lest We Forget*.
21 *Kine Weekly*, 29 Sept 1936, p. 12.
22 *Kine Weekly*, 7 Nov 1935, p. 27.
23 *Sight and Sound*, Vol. 4, No. 14, summer 1935.
24 "Omnibus" Programme, B.B.C. 1, 25 Feb 1973.
25 *Cinema Quarterly*, Vol. 3, No. 2, winter 1935.
26 *World Film News*, No. 2, May 1936, p. 24.
27 *Sight and Sound*, No. 21, spring 1937, p. 44.
28 Francisco Aranda, *Luis Buñuel*, pp. 118–21.
29 Bert Hogenkamp in *Sight and Sound*, spring 1976.
30 *Sight and Sound*, Vol. 7, No. 26, summer 1938, which calls it *Behind the Lines*.
31 The date is that given in the reprint of a speech made by Paul Rotha at that meeting, called *Films and the Labour Party* on the cover, and *Films and the Labour Movement* inside.
32 ibid. p. 11.
33 ibid. p. 14.
34 *Sight and Sound*, spring 1976.
35 *Monthly Film Bulletin*, Vol. 2, No. 8, November 1937, p. 18.
36 *World Film News*, Vol. 2, No. 8, November 1937, p. 18.
37 *Kine Weekly*, 17 Aug 1939.
38 Paul Rotha, *Documentary Diary*, p. 230.
39 *Kine Weekly*, 23 Nov 1939, p. 26.

CHAPTER 7   FILMS AS A HISTORICAL DOCUMENT

1 Aslib *Proceedings*, Volume 7, No. 4, November 1955, pp. 207–39.
2 *University Vision*, No. 10, June 1973, pp. 48–50.
3 *Journal of the Society of Archivists*, Vol. III, No. 4, October 1966, pp. 183–91.
4 *University Vision*, No. 10, June 1973, pp. 48–50.

Bibliography

Aldgate, Dr Tony, '1930s Newsreels: Censorship and Controversy', in *Sight and Sound*, summer 1977, p. 154–7.

Aldgate, Dr Tony, 'The Production of "Spanish Civil War" Part 1: The Archives and the Newsreels', in *University Vision*, No. 11, April 1974, p. 16.

Aldgate, Dr Tony, 'The Production of "Spanish Civil War" Part 2: a Film in the Making', in *University Vision*, No. 12, December 1974, p. 42.

Aranda, Francisco, *Luis Buñuel* (English translation, Secker and Warburg, 1975).

Arnold, H. J. P., 'Herbert Ponting as Cinematographer', in *Cinema Studies*, Vol. 2, No. 3, March 1967.

Arnold, H. J. P., *Photographer of the World* (Hutchinson, 1969).

The Artist, Vol. XIII, March–August 1937.

Arts Enquiry, The, *The Factual Film* (Geoffrey Cumberlege, Oxford University Press, 1947).

Baechlin, Peter and Muller-Straus, Maurice, *Newsreels Across the World* (UNESCO, 1952).

Barker, Ralph, *One Man's Jungle: a Biography of F. Spencer Chapman* (Chatto & Windus, 1975).

Bauer, Paul, *Himalayan Campaign* (Basil Blackwell, 1937).

Box, Sydney, *Film Publicity* (Lovat Dickson, 1937).

British Film Institute, *Report of the Conference on Films for Children, November 1937* (1937).

Brunel, Adrian, *Film Production* (Newnes, 1936).

Burbidge, Claude, *Scruffy, the Adventures of a Mongrel in Movieland* (Hurst and Blackett, 1937).

Burnett, R. G., *The Cinema for Christ* (The Religious Tract Society, 1934).

Burnett, R. G. and Martell, E. D., *The Devil's Camera: Menace of a Film-ridden World* (The Epworth Press, 1932).

Carl Mayer memorial programme, *A Tribute to Carl Mayer* (1947).

Chapman, F. Spencer, *Lhasa: the Holy City* (Chatto & Windus, 1938).

Chapman, F. Spencer, *Northern Lights* (Chatto & Windus, 1932).

Chapman, F. Spencer, *Watkins' Last Expedition* (Chatto & Windus, 1934).

Chapman, Olive Murray, *Across Lapland* (John Lane the Bodley Head, 1932).

Cinema Quarterly 1932–5.

Cinematograph Films Acts, 1929 and 1938.

Close Up, 1928–33.

Commission on Educational and Cultural Films, The, *The Film in National Life* (Allen and Unwin, 1932).

Cons, G. J., *The Challenge of Everest* (University of London Press, 1934).
Coster, Ian, *Friends in Aspic* (John Miles, 1939).
Duguid, Julian, *Green Hell* (Jonathan Cape, 1931).
Educational Film Review from April 1935 to October 1935.
Elton, Sir Arthur, 'The Film as Source Material for History', in *Aslib Proceedings*, Vol. 7, No. 4, November 1955 (Association for Special Libraries and Information Bureaux).
Experimental Cinema 1930–4.
Field, Audrey, *Picture Palace* (Gentry Books, 1974).
Film Art, 1933–7.
Film Index Vol: 1 The Film as Art (Museum of Modern Art Film Library, 1941).
Film Producers' Group of the Federation of British Industries, *Cinematograph Films Bill. A summary of the Present Position showing the Defects of the Measure from the Point of View of the British Film Producers* (1938).
Film Quarterly, The, spring and summer 1937.
Film Society, The, programmes for Seasons 5 (1929/30) to 14 (1938/39).
Foxon, Professor G. E. H., *The Strangeways Collection* (British Film Institute, 1976).
George, W. H., *The Cinema in School* (Isaac Pitman, 1935).
Greene, Graham, *The Pleasure Dome* (Secker & Warburg, 1972).
Greville, J. A. S., *Film as History* (University of Birmingham, 1930).
Grierson, John, 'The Cinema', in Geoffrey Grigson (ed.), *The Arts Today* (1935).
Hardy, Forsyth, *Grierson on Documentary* (Collins, 1946).
Hogenkamp, Bert, 'Film and the Workers' Movement in Britain 1929–39', in *Sight and Sound*, Vol. 45, No. 2, spring 1976, pp. 68–76.
Kearton, Cherry, *Cherry Kearton's Travels* (Robert Hale, 1941).
Kerensky, Oleg, *Anna Pavlova* (Hamish Hamilton, 1973).
Kine Weekly, 1929–39.
Kine Year Book 1929–40.
Kipling, Rudyard, *Thy Servant a Dog* (Macmillan, 1930).
Knowles, Dorothy, *The Censor, the Drama and the Film, 1900–1934* (Allen & Unwin, 1934).
Kostelanetz, Richard, *Moholy-Nagy* (Allen Lane The Penguin Press, 1971).
Kulik, Karol, *Alexander Korda – The Man Who Could Work Miracles* (W. H. Allen, 1975).
Lally, William L. (ed.), *A National Encyclopaedia of Educational Films and 16 mm. Apparatus* (Central Information Bureau for Educational Films, 1937).
Lewis, Jonathan, 'Before Hindsight' in *Sight and Sound*, spring 1977, pp. 68–73.
Leyda, Jay, *Films Beget Films* (Allen & Unwin, 1964).
Life and Letters, 1928–35.
Life and Letters Today, 1935–9.

Lindgren, Dr E. J., 'North Western Manchuria and the Reindeer-Tungus' in *Geographical Journal*, Vol. LXXV, No. 6, June 1930.

Lindgren, Dr E. J., *The Reindeer-Tungus of Manchuria* in *Journal of the Royal Central Asiatic Society*, Vol. XXII, Part II, April 1935, p. 221–31.

Low, David, *Years of Wrath* (Victor Gollancz, 1949).

MacGregor, Alasdair Alpin, *A Last Voyage to St. Kilda* (Cassell, 1931).

Memorial booklet on Richard Massingham, 1955.

Monthly Film Bulletin, 1934–9, (British Film Institute).

Moyne Committee, *Cinematograph Films Act 1927: Report of a Committee appointed by the Board of Trade* (1937).

National Film Archive, *Catalogue of Viewing Copies* (1971).

National Film Archive, *Catalogue of Viewing Copies Supplement* (1974).

National Film Archive Catalogue Part II, Silent Non-Fiction Films 1895–1934 (1960).

National Film Library Catalogue, 2nd edition (1938).

Noel, Capt. J. B. L., *Through Tibet to Everest* (Edward Arnold, 1927).

Political and Economic Planning, *The British Film Industry* (1952).

Powell, Michael, *200,000 Feet on Foula* (Faber and Faber, 1938).

Pronay, Nicholas, 'British Newsreels in the 1930s, 1. Audience and Producers', in *History*, Vol. 56, No. 188, October 1971, pp. 411–18.

Pronay, Nicholas, 'British Newsreels in the 1930s, 2. Their Policies and Impact', in *History*, Vol. 57, No. 189, February 1972, pp. 63–72.

Pronay, Nicholas, 'The Newsreels: the Illusion of Actuality', in Paul Smith (ed.), *The Historian and the Film* (Cambridge University Press, 1976).

Roads, Christopher, 'Film as Historical Evidence' in *Journal of the Society of Archivists*, Vol. III, No. 4, October 1966, pp. 183–91.

Robeson, Eslanda C., *Paul Robeson, Negro* (Victor Gollancz, 1930).

Rotha, Paul, *Documentary Diary* (Secker & Warburg, 1973).

Rotha, Paul, *Films and the Labour Party* (1936).

Ruttledge, Hugh, *Everest 1933* (Hodder & Stoughton, 1934).

Sewell, George H., *Commercial Cinematography* (Isaac Pitman, 1933).

Sight and Sound, 1932–9.

Smith, Paul (ed.), *The Historian and the Film* (Cambridge University Press, 1976).

Smythe, Capt. F. S., *Kamet Conquered* (Victor Gollancz, 1932).

Smythe, F. S., *The Kanchenjunga Adventure* (Victor Gollancz, 1930).

Some British and Foreign Documentary and Other Short Films, (British Film Institute, January 1939).

Sussex, Elizabeth, *The Rise and Fall of British Documentary* (University of California Press, 1975).

Treatt, Stella Court, *Cape to Cairo* (George G. Harrap, 1927).

Treatt, Stella Court, *Stampede* (Hutchinson, 1930).

Treatt, Stella Court, *Sudan Sand* (George G. Harrap, 1930).

University Vision 1968–76 (British Universities Film Council).

various authors, *First Over Everest*, 1933 edition (John Lane The Bodley Head).

Vesselo, Arthur, *Early Films, a Selected Catalogue* (British Film Institute, 1939).

Watt, Harry, *Don't Look at the Camera* (Paul Elek, 1974).

Wegg-Prosser, Victoria, 'The Archive of the Film and Photo League', in *Sight and Sound*, autumn 1977, pp. 245–7.

Wood, Alan, *Mr. Rank* (Hodder & Stoughton, 1952).

World Film News 1936–8.

Wyand, Paul, *Useless if Delayed* (George G. Harrap, 1959).

Young-Husband, Francis, *Everest: the Challenge* (Thomas Nelson, 1936).

Film List

A complete list of the thousands of films made outside the feature studios in Britain between 1929 and 1939 is hardly possible. I have made up a preliminary list, which I hope will be used as a basis for further study by other people. It should be remembered that many such films were not registered with the Board of Trade, that standard and substandard versions, as well as sound and silent versions, of the same subject might be produced and even given different titles, and that they might be cut up and re-used. Another book by the present author, *Documentary and Educational Films of the 1930s*, includes most films made by the mainstream documentary film producers and the more interesting educational films. In the following list the films mentioned in the text of the present volume are included, and any others which seem interesting enough individually, as typical of some form of film making, or as likely to require identification. It is not possible to list individually all the titles in long series. It is thus not intended to be a comprehensive list. I have included such production details as to date, length, company and personnel as are available and reasonably reliable. In cases where disagreement is known to exist I have tried, wherever possible, to use the credits as given on the film itself, but some other possibilities have been noted in the main text of the book. The use of abbreviations in the Film List is in the interests of economy.

KEY TO ABBREVIATIONS OF PRODUCTION DETAILS USED IN FILM LIST

	distributing company
alt.	alternative or working title
anim.	animated drawing or puppet film
assoc.	associate (producer or director, according to position in list)
asst.	assistant (the same)
c.	cameraman
comp.	compilation
cr.	commentator
cy.	writer of commentary
d.	director
des.	design or art direction
diag.	diagrams, usually animated
Dun.	Dunning colour
Dufay	Dufaycolor
ed.	editor
ft.	length in feet
f.	featuring
Gasp.	Gasparcolor

Koda.	Kodachrome
m.	music
m.d.	musical director
mins.	length in minutes
p.	producer
p.c.	production company or unit
p.m.	production manager
reels	length in reels
reg.	registered with Board of Trade (applies to length and date)
sc.	writing
sd.	sound recording
Spicer.	Spicer colour
st.	silent film
sup.	supervision or consultation
synch.	synchronisation
tech.	technical
Tech.	Technicolor
T.S.	date of trade show

Films are 35 mm unless otherwise indicated, and are sound films unless otherwise indicated. If substandard and silent versions existed as well as standard and sound versions, this is not necessarily indicated.

ALPHABETICAL LIST OF ABBREVIATIONS OF PRODUCERS, DISTRIBUTORS, SPONSORS, ETC., USED IN FILM LIST

A.B.F.D.	Associated British Film Distributors
A.B.P.C.	Associated British Picture Corporation
Ace	Ace Films
A.I.P.D.	Associated Independent Producers and Distributors
Alba	Alba Films
Albion	Albion Film Syndicate
Anglia	Anglia Films
A.P. & D.	Associated Producers and Distributors
A.P.D.C.	Associated Producing and Distribution Company
Assoc.	Association
Austin	Austin Motor Co.
B.B.C.	British Broadcasting Corporation
B.E.D.A.	British Electricity Development Association
Berm. B.C.	Bermondsey Borough Council
B.I.F.	British Instructional Films
B.O.C.	British Oxygen Company
B.I.P.	British International Pictures
Brd.	Board
Brit.	British
Brit. M.N.	British Movietone News

Brit. Nat.	British National
Brit. Th-H	British Thompson-Houston
Brit. Ut.	British Utility Films
B.R.T.A.	British Road Tar Association
B.S.H.C.	British Social Hygiene Council
B.S.S.	British Screen Service
Bury	Bury Productions
Butch.	Butcher's Film Service
Cad.	Cadbury Bros.
C.C.H.E.	Central Council for Health Education
Com.	Committee
Den.	Denning Films
Dev.	Development
E-B	Equity-British Films
Ed.	Educational
E.G.S.	Educational and General Services
Excl.	Exclusive Films
Exped.	Expedition
F.	Films
Famous	Famous Films
F.B.O.	Film Booking Offices
F-L	Famous-Lasky Film Service
Fidelity	Fidelity Films
F-N	First National Film Distributors
Ford	Ford Motor Co.
Freenat	Freenat Film Productions
G-B	Gaumont-British
G-BE	Gaumont-British Equipments
G-BI	Gaumont-British Instructional
G.B.P.C.	Gaumont British Picture Corporation
Gee	Gee Films
G.F.D.	General Film Distributors
Govt.	Government
G.W.R.	Great Western Railway
H. & C.C.	Health & Cleanliness Council
Ideal	Ideal Films
Imp. Air.	Imperial Airways
Insp.	Inspiration Films
Internat.	International Films
J.W.T.	J. Walter Thompson
King. Ed. H.F.L.	King Edward's Hospital Fund for London
Kino	Kino Films (1935) Ltd.
Kinog.	Kinograph Distributors
L.F.P.	London Film Productions
L.M.B.	L.M.B. Films
L.M.S.	London Midland & Scottish Railway

L.N.U.	League of Nations Union
Mackane	David Mackane Productions
Merton	Merton Park Studios
M.F.S.	Manchester Film Society
M-G-M	Metro-Goldwyn-Mayer Pictures
Min.	Ministry
Nat.	National
Nat. Prog.	National Progress Film Co.
N.F.L.	National Film Library
Para.	Paramount Pictures
Pathé	Pathé Pictures
P.D.C.	P.D.C. Ltd. (producers and renters)
Pearl	Pearl Assurance Co.
P.F.I.	Progressive Film Institute
Pres.	Preservation
Prods.	Productions
Pub. F.	Publicity Films
Pub. P.P.	Publicity Picture Productions
Rev.	Revelation Films
R.F.S.	Religious Film Society
R.G.S.	Royal Geographical Society
R.K.O. – Radio	R.K.O. – Radio Pictures
Sc. F.P.	Scottish Films Productions
Sd. City	Sound City Distributors
S.F.C.	Socialist Film Council
Short	Short Film Productions
Soc.	Society
Spect.	Spectator Short Films
Techq.	Technique Distributors
T.I.D.A.	Travel and Industrial Development Association
Topical	Topical Press Agency
U.	University
U.A.	United Artists
Unity	Unity Films
Universal	Universal Pictures
Vis. Ed.	Visual Education
W & F	W & F Film Service
W.B.	Warner Brothers
W-E	Western Electric
W. R. Holmes	W. Ratcliffe Holmes
Y.H.A.	Youth Hostels Association
Y.M.C.A.	Young Men's Christian Association
Zeni	Zenifilms

FILM LIST

Across Bolivia *p*. Julian Duguid for Bolivian Govt./Condor Films 10,000 *ft. unedited* 1930 *st. p.* Julian Duguid *d.ed.* Mamerto Urriolagoita *c.* J. C. Bee-Mason.

Across Lapland *p*. Olive Murray Chapman/Zeni 1154 *ft. reg.* 10.33 *st. c.ed. and described* Olive Murray Chapman.

Across the Sahara *p.c.* B.I.P./ Wardour 1774 *ft.* 1933 *d.cy.* Capt. Walter Summers.

Africa Looks Up See **My Song Goes Forth.**

African Adventure Internat. Com. for Bird Preservation 8 *reels* 1937 *st. c. lecture by* Capt. C. W. R. Knight.

Africa Sings See **My Song Goes Forth.**

Air Ways to Cape Town *p*. Richard Wainwright with Imp. Air. 3 *reels 16 mm.* 1934 *st.*

Albania *p.c.* Vis.Ed. 2 *reels* 1934 *d.sc.* L. G. Barbrook.

Alert Today, Alive Tomorrow *p.c.* Nat. Safety First Assoc. 46 *mins.* or 2 *reels* 1933.

All Living Things *p.c.* G-BI/Excl. 1797 *ft. reg.* 2.39 *d.sc.* Andrew Buchanan *from story by* Nell St. John Montagu, "The Hallmark of Cain" *f.* G. H. Mulcaster.

All the Fun of the 'Air *p.c.* Anson Dyer for Bush Radios 272 *ft.* about 1931 Dun *anim. p.* Anson Dyer *m.d.* J. Norman.

'Alt, Oo Goes Theer? *p.c.* Anglia/ Reunion 868 *ft. reg.* 4.36 *colour anim. d.* Anson Dyer.

And Now They Rest *p.c.* J. V. Durden and Brian Salt/Excl. 1625 *ft. reg.* 7.39 *c.* J. V. Durden,

Brian Salt *tech. sup.* Rex Wailes *cy.* Ruth Walder *cr.* Carleton Hobbs.

And So To Work *p.c.* Richard Massingham/Kinog. 1654 *ft. reg.* 10.36 *p.d.sc.ed.* Richard Massingham *c.* Karl Urbahn *sd.* H. L. Sheridan *m.* H. Murrill, South London Orchestra *f.* Russell Waters, Alan Fosse.

Animal Friends *p*. A. F. H. Baldry 1875 *ft. reg.* 5.30.

Arctic: Haigh Thomas *p*. Haigh Thomas 2 *reels* 1938 *st.*

Arise and Walk *p.c.* Oxford Films for Central Council for the Care of Cripples 2715 *ft.* 1929 *st. d.* John Greenidge *c.* Randall Terraneau, Frank Canham *sc.* John and Terence Greenidge.

Athlete, The *p.c.* John Betts/Butch. 3100 *ft. sd.* 3115 *ft. st. reg.* 4.30 *p.* John Betts.

At School in Tanganyika *p*. Ralph Cutler 250 *ft.* 16 *mm. st.* 1936.

Be a Sport *p.c.* John Betts/Butch. 3013 *ft. reg.* 1.32 *p.* John Betts.

Beat the Retreat *p.c.* Anglia/A.P. & D. 810 *ft. reg.* 11.36 *colour anim. d.* Anson Dyer.

Behind the Silver Screen *p.c.* Ace 1933 *ft. reg.* 9.35 *d.* Frank Green.

Behind the Spanish Lines *p.c.* P.F.I. 1797 *ft.* 1938 *p.* Ivor Montagu *d.ed.* Thorold Dickinson, Sidney Cole *c.* Arthur Graham, Alan Lawson *asst.ed.* Philip Leacock, *cy.* Ivor Montagu *cr.* G. C. T. Giles.

Betwixt Land and Sea See **Shrimp Fishers of Gravesend, The** and **Turning Her Round.**

Beyond This Open Road *p.c.*

Film Art Group 1000 *ft.* 1934 *st.*
d.c. B. Vivian Braun, Irene
Nicholson.

Biblical Palestine *p.c.* G-B 2506 *ft.*
1934 *sup.cy.* Lord Lee of Fareham
c. Edward Cooper *ed.* Andrew
Buchanan.

Big Game of Life *p.* Cherry and
Ada Kearton 6300 *ft. reg.* 4.35
reg. 7.35 by Columbia Pictures.

"Bingo" Cartoons *p.c.* Horace
Shepherd/M-G-M 4 *one-reel anim.*
reg. 12.30 – 1.31.

Birds *p.c.* Bury/Techq. 700 *ft. reg.*
7.38.

Birthplace of America, The *p.* A.
Moncrieff Davidson/M-G-M 858
ft. reg. 4.36 *p.d.c.* A. Moncrieff
Davidson.

Black Diamonds *p.c.* Hanmer
Prods./Wardour 4816 *ft. T.S.* 6.32
d.sc. Charles Hanmer *f.* Beckett
Bould, Jennie Stevens, Norman
Astridge.

Blind Dogs for Guide Dogs for the
Blind 1938 Dufay *p.* Cecil Blacker
d. Anthony Asquith *f.* Leslie
Banks, Vivien Leigh, Lee Tracey.
Production unconfirmed.

Blow, Bugles, Blow *p.c.* Rudolph
Messel and S.F.C./P.F.I. 6721
ft. reg. 4.36 *Made* 1934 *d.* Rudolph
Messel.

Bob Bowman Calling *p.c.* Ace
1646 *ft. reg.* 5.36.

Bonnie Scotland Calls You *p.c.*
A.B.P.C. and J. C. Elder/A.B.P.C.
3057 *ft. reg.* 5.38 *d.* Howard Gaye.

Border Collie *p.c.* B.S.S. 1720 *ft. reg.*
7.39.

Borderline *p.c.* Pool Films 5700 *ft.*
Made 5.29–6.30 *Shown* 10.30 *st. d.*
Kenneth Macpherson *f.* Paul
Robeson, Eslanda Robeson.

Bournville *p.c.* Pub. F. for Cad. 1

reel 1936.

Breakers Ahead G-BI/G.F.D. 3318
ft. reg. 6.38 *d.* Vernon Sewell *sc.*
from story by Leo Walmsley *f.* Belle
Chrystal, J. Fisher White.

**Bristol, City of a Thousand
Years** *p.c.* F. G. and R. F. Warne
for Bristol Dev. Brd. 32 *mins.*
16 mm. 1937.

Britain Expects *p.c.* P.F.I. 1360
ft. reg. 3.39 *d.* Ivor Montagu *c.*
Alan Lawson.

Britannia Rules the Air *p.c.* Roy
Tuckett/M-G-M 3394 *ft. reg.* 2.35.

British Graham Land Expedition
p. J. R. Rymill Exped. 12778 *ft.*
unedited 1937.

Busmen's Holiday, The *p.c.* S.F.C.
half-reel 16 mm. 1937 *st. p.* H.A.
and R. Green.

Campanions *p.* Herbert Wilcox/
R.K.O.-Radio 850 *ft. reg.* 6.38 *d.*
Frank Bundy *c.* John Lawrence *ed.*
Peggy Henessey *cr.* E. V. H.
Emmett.

Cape to Cairo *p.* T. A. Glover/
Famous 4500 *ft. T.S.* 3.34 reissue
of 1926 film with sd. *d.* Charles
Barnett *f.* Major and Mrs Court
Treatt.

Carmen *p.c.* Anglia/Reunion 850
ft. reg. 4.36 *colour anim.* d. Anson
Dyer.

Castles and Fisherfolk Pub. F.
for Cad. 10 *mins.* 1933 *d.* Walter
Creighton *c.* Jimmy Rogers.

Cavalcade of the Navy *p.c.* Frank
Green-Insp./Ace series, 1 *reel each,*
T.S. 10.39 part Tech. *p.d.* Horace
Shepherd, *c.* E. Hague.

Caves of Perigord, The *p.* C.
Byng Lucas/Unity 1260 *ft. reg.*
10.39 *d.sc.* Caroline Byng Lucas *c.*
Georges Baye *cr.* John Abbot *m.*
Barbara Banner.

224 *Films of Comment and Persuasion of the 1930s*

Century of Hospital Progress, A *p.* for King Ed. H.F.L./H. Saving Assoc. 1 *reel* 1934 *st.*

Christopher Wren Comes to Life *p.c.* Ratcliffe Holmes Prod./M-G-M 3487 *ft. reg.* 3.36 *d.* F. W. Ratcliffe Holmes *f.* Thomas Pounceford, Wilson Coleman, etc.

Cities of the Desert *p.* T. A. Glover/L.M.B. 3750 *ft. TS* 5.34 *d.* T. A. Glover.

City of Shadows, The *p.c.* Harry B. Parkinson/M-G-M 4379 *ft. reg.* 1.31 *Made* 1929 *alt.* **The Night Patrol** *st. d.sc.* Norman Lee *f.* Elizabeth Baxter.

Climbing Mount Everest *p.* R.G.S. 30 *mins.* 16 *mm.* 1933 *sd. or st. c.* Wyn Harris *cy.* Frank Smythe.

Come Back to Erin *p.c.* Brit. Nat./A.B.P.C. 2698 *ft. reg.* 4.39 Dufay.

Come for a Stroll *p.* Richard Massingham 860 *ft.* 1938/9 *d.sc.ed.* Richard Massingham *c.* S. D. Onions *assoc. ed.* R. Johnson *f.* Arthur Brander, Philip Morant.

Come On Steve cartoons *p.c.* Roland Davies Cartoon Films/ Butch. 6 *one-reel b-w cartoons T.S.* 12.36 *and* 4.37 *d.* Roland Davies from cartoons in "Sunday Express" *m.d.* John Reynders. **Steve of the River, Steve Steps Out, Steve's Treasure Hunt, Steve's Cannon Crackers, Steve-Cinderella, Steve in Bohemia.**

Common Round, The *p.c.* Brit. Nat. for R.F.S./R.F.S. 4 *reels* 1935 *d.* Stephen Harrison.

Consumption (Tuberculosis of the Lungs) *p.c.* Berm. B.C. 700 *ft.* 16 *mm. st.* 1932 *p.* H. W. Bush *c.* C. F. Lumley.

Country Currents *p.c.* B.E.D.A. 358 *ft.* 16 *mm.* 1935/6 (?) *p.* Joseph Best *shortened version of* **Rural Electrification.**

Country Fare *p.c.* Pub. F. for Cad. 2000 *ft.* 1937 *d.* Evelyn Spice.

County of the White Rose *p.c.* Alba/T.I.D.A. 967 *ft.* 1934 *d.ed.* Robin J. Carruthers *c.* Jimmy Rogers *cy.* Harry J. Clifford *m.d.* Alfred Filer *Songs* Thorpe Bates.

Crown and Glory *p.c.* Para. 4003 *ft. T.S.* 4.37.

Danger at Sea *p.c.* Short/Fidelity 1437 *ft. reg.* 11.37 *p.d.* Harold Lowenstein, B. Vivian Braun.

Dassan *p.c.* Cherry Kearton 6300 *ft. reg.* 11.30 *p.d.* Cherry and Ada Kearton *ed.* Adrian Brunel.

Day at Oundle School, A amateur 1242 *ft.* 1931.

Day in the Life of a Msukuma Called Kinga Mkona Bara, A *p.* Ralph Cutler 446 *ft.* 16 *mm. st.* 1936/7.

Deeds Men Do, The Betta Films 6200 *ft. T.S.* 8.32 *synch. version of* **The Battles of the Coronel and Falkland Islands** *cr.* R. E. Jeffrey.

Don Bradman in "How I Play Cricket" *p.* James Hurll/M-G-M 892 *ft. reg.* 2.33.

Door in the Wall, The *p.c.* Wytham Country Classrooms Scheme 65 *mins.* 16 *mm.* 1934 *p.* Col. Raymond ffenell *c.* G. L. Hawkins.

Dragon of Wales *p.c.* W. B. Pollard 1501 *ft. reg.* 1.36.

Drawings that Walk and Talk *p.c.* N.F.L. 3060 *ft.* 1938 *comp.* Marie Seton, K. H. Frank *m.d.* Barbara Banner.

Drummed Out *p.c.* Anglia/Sd. City 863 *ft. reg.* 2.37 *colour cartoon d.*

Anson Dyer.
Dual Control *p.c.* B.I.P./Wardour 1800 *ft.* *T.S.* 8.32 *d.sc.* Walter Summers *asst.* Arthur Woods *c.* James Wilson *ed.* Walter Moss *sd.* J. A. Murray *f.* Amy Johnson, Jim Mollison.

Earth Remaineth, The *p.c.* L. G. Jonas/Excl. 3086 *ft.* *reg.* 7.37 *p.d.c.* L. G. Jonas, Sherard Powell.

Electricity *p.c.* B.I.F. for B.E.D.A. 2 *reels* early 1930s *st.*

End of the Day *p.c.* G-BI/G.F.D. 953 *ft.* *reg.* 2.39.

Endurance *p.c.* W & F 5670 *ft.* *reg.* 5.33 *by* Frank Hurley and Sir Hubert Wilkins *cr.* Commdr. Frank A. Worsley.

Engine Shed *p.c.* Commercial and Ed. F. for L.M.S. 1 *reel* 1936 *cy.* F. Morton King.

England's Playground *p.c.* A.B.P.C./Ward. 996 *ft.* 1934 *d.* Vernon Clancey *c.* A. E. Jeakins *m.* Horace Shepherd.

Ephemeral *p.* Irene Nicholson 7 *mins.* 1934 *st.*

Eriskay *p.c.* Zeni 1750 *ft.* 1935 *p.d.* Dr Werner Kissling *ed.* *sup.* John Gifford.

Eternal Fire, The *p.c.* U.A. 11 *mins.* 1938 Tech. *p.* F. W. Keller.

Europe Today Brit. M.N./W-E 2 *reels* 1934 *16 mm.* *ed.* Leslie Landau *f.* Vernon Bartlett.

Facts and Figures *p.c.* Central Film Prod./Zeni 1723 *ft.* 1935 *p.* Eric Humphreys *d.* Vernon Sewell *c.* Frank Bowden *cr.* P. Godfrey *m.d.* John Reynders.

Family Life of the Golden Eagle, The *p.c.* Sc. F.P./Zeni 726 *ft.* *reg.* 8.35 *d.* Seton Gordon *c.* Audrey Gordon.

Farm, The *p.c.* Dufay-Chromex/

G.F.D. 1190 *ft.* *reg.* 8.38 *d.* Capt. Blacker.

Farming for Boys *p.c.* Y.M.C.A. for Liverpool Education Committee 752 *ft.* 1930 *st.*

Fascinating Facts Pub. F. for Cad. 1000 *ft.* 1937 *d.* Meg Bennett.

Father Thames *p.c.* C. P. V. Collin and W. G. Duncalf/Kinog. 1550 *ft.* *reg.* 7.35 *p.* Peter Collin, *c.* Gordon Duncalf *cy.* C. E. Hodges *cr.* Alan Howland *m.d.* John Reynders.

Fire Fighters *p.c.* W. B. Pollard and Peter Collin for London Fire Brigade/Kinog. 1402 *ft.* *reg.* 8.36 *p.* Peter Collin.

Forbidden Frontier, The *distrib.* Kinog. 22 *mins.* 1937 *sup.* Sir Philip Gibb.

Forgotten Men *p.c.* B.I.P./Wardour 7138 *ft.* *T.S.* 12.34 *d.* Norman Lee *asst.* George Black Jnr., David Couseland *c.* *(studio)* Bryan Langley *cr.* *and* *cy.* Sir John Hammerton *introduction* General Sir Ian Hamilton.

Fox Hunt, The *p.c.* L.F.P./Denning, U.A. 716 *ft.* *reg.* 10.36 Tech. *anim.* *Made* *by* Hector Hoppin, Anthony Gross with Laszlo Meitner.

Free Thaelmann! *p.c.* P.F.I./Kino 2 *reels* *16 mm.* *st.* 1935 *Comp.* Ivor Montagu.

From Acorn to Oak *p.c.* Merton for Dunlop Rubber Co. *half-reel* 1937/8 *d.* Montgomery Tully *c.* Jimmy Rogers *cy.* H. V. Purcell *cr.* Oswald Skilbeck *ed.* Catherine Miller *sd,* Charles Poulton.

From Coal-Mine to Road *p.c.* B.R.T.A. 2012 *ft.* 1931.

Frozen Fate *p.* Ben R. Hart and St. John L. Clowes 5080 *ft.* *reg.*

5.29 *st.*

Functional Treatment of Fractures *p.* Dr K. H. Pridie 3 *reels* 1935 *16 mm. st.*

Germs *p.c.* Berm B.C. (Health Dept.) 472 *ft. 16 mm. st.* 1931.

Getting into Hot Water *p.c.* Pub. P.P. for Gas Light and Coke Co. 1 *reel* 1937 *d.* Ralph Smart *c.* Harry Waxman *sc.* H. V. Purcell *m.* John Reynders.

Giro films *p.c.* C.C.H.E. for H.C.C. 4 *one-reelers* 1934 *anim.*

Glasgow, City of Achievement *p.c.* Sc.F.P./A.B.F.D. 900 *ft. reg.* 3.39.

Glimpses of Modern Russia *p.c.* Workers' Film Movement/Atlas 1025 *ft.* 1930 *st. comp.* Ralph Bond.

Gordon Richards *p.c.* Ace 2 *reels* *T.S.* 11.33 *d.* Widgey Newman.

Gray's Elegy *p.c.* Avenue F.P./ Techq. 1520 *ft. reg.* 10.38 *p.* Victor M. Gover *devised, ed.* Harold Simpson *c.* Jimmy Rogers, Peter Sargent *cy.* Morton King *poem recited* Laurence Anderson *m.* W. H. Ewen.

Great Crusade, The *p.c.* Pathé for Min. of Health 1540 *ft. reg.* 3.36 *prod. man.* Freddie Watts *assoc.pr.* W. Gell *sc.* H. Brandon Fleming *tech. sup.* Alister MacDonald *help with sc.* J. B. Priestley.

Grey Seal, The *p.c.* Bury/A.B.F.D. 1787 *ft. reg.* 4.37 *p.d.* Cyril Jenkins, John Mathias *c.* Cyril Jenkins *m.d.* John Reynders *m.* Victor Yates *ed.* John Mathias *scientific sup.* H. R. Hewer *cr.* Alan Howland.

Gunner Sam *p.c.* Anglia/Sd. City 802 *ft. reg.* 5.37 *colour cartoon d.* Anson Dyer.

Happy Hampstead! *p.c.* J. Fairfax-

Jones/Den. 966 *ft. reg.* 11.36 *p.* J. Fairfax-Jones *d.c.* R. B. Pearce *m.d.* John Reynders.

Head Hunters of Papua *p.c.* Frank Hurley/A.P.D.C. 2 *reels p.* Capt. Frank Hurley.

Health of the Nation, The *p.c.* Nat. Prog. for Min. of Health and Brd. of Ed. 990 *ft. reg.* 3.37 *d.* Charles Barnett *cr.* John Watt.

Hell Below Zero *p.c.* Ideal 3500 *ft.* *T.S.* 4.31 *p.* Carveth Wells.

Hell Unlimited amateur/Kino 520 *ft. 16 mm. st.* 1936 *p.* Norman McLaren, Helen Biggar.

Here Comes the Zoo *p.c.* Ace 1700 *ft. reg.* 10.34 *p.* R. W. Lotinga.

Highway, The *p.c.* Brit. Films for B.R.T.A. 12 *mins.* 1933 *p.d.* James Fenton *c.* Leo Rogers *m.d.* Horace Shepherd.

Highway, The *p.c.* Eric Spear and Vis. Ed./Zeni 1688 *ft.* 1933 *p.* Christopher Radley *d.m.* Eric Spear *sd.* Lance Comfort *f.* Lionel Dixon, Robert Craven.

Highway Code, The *p.c.* Nat. Prog. for Min. of Transport and Pearl 980 *ft. reg.* 8.36 *d.* Charles Barnett *cr.* John Watt *f.* Leslie Hore-Belisha.

His Apologies *p.c.* Westanmor/ Famous 1785 *ft. reg.* 12.36 *p.d.* Widgey Newman *asst.* Roy Boulting *c.* John Miller *sc.* from story by Rudyard Kipling, "Thy Servant a Dog" *spoken by* Laidman Brown *f.* Roma Beaumont, Moore Marriott, Violet Hopson.

Historic Ceremonies in Westminster Abbey at the Coronation of Their Majesties King George VI and Queen Elizabeth, The 954 *ft.* 1937.

Historic Flights *p.c.* Vickers

Aviation 708 *ft.* 1932 *st.*
History of Electricity *p.c.* B.E.D.A.
1 *reel 16 mm. st.* about 1935 *p.*
Percy Nash.
Honeymoon in Devon *p.c.* Nat.
Prog. 1050 *ft. reg.* 1.33 *f.* Jack
Hobbs, Dodo Watts.
House of Windsor, The *p.c.* Pathé
3516 *ft. T.S.* 3.37 *d.* Freddie
Watts *cy.* Stephen King-Hall.
Housing Progress *p.* Matthew
Nathan for Housing Centre 20
mins. 16 mm. st. 1938.
How to Play Tennis *p.c.* Nat.
Talkies/Brit. Lion 5 *one-reelers reg.*
2.35 and 3.35 *play by* Fred Perry
and Dan Maskell *cr.* W. T. Tilden.
How to Take the Driving Test
p.c. Ace 911 *ft. reg.* 7.35.
How Woodbines Are Made *p.c.*
W.D. & H.O. Wills/W-E 1 *reel*
16 mm. 1933.
I Do Love To Be Beside the
Seaside *p.c.* Studio Film 1929 *d.*
Oswell Blakeston *m.* Edmund
Meisel.
Immortal Swan, The *p.c.* Immortal
Swan Prods. 4529 *ft. first T.S.*
1.36 and N.F.A. copy; 3414 *ft. reg.*
2.36; *sup.* Victor Dandré *d.sc.*
arranged Edward Nakhimoff *c.* Phil
Greenrod, Guy Green *asst.d.*
Richard Llewellyn *des.* Dennis
Wreford *ed. synch.* Julia Wolf *sd.*
A. G. Ambler *m.d.* Vladimir
Launitz *cr.* Aubrey Hitchens *f.*
Pavlova.
Inasmuch *p.c.* Brit. Nat./R.F.S. 2
reels 1934 *d.* Alec Saville *c.* Phil
Tannura *f.* Donald Wolfit.
In Defence of Madrid *p.c.* P.F.I./
Kino 45 *mins. 16 mm. st. Made* 1936
shown 1937 *p.* Ivor Montagu.
In Our Time *p.c.* David Mackane
Prod. 2180 *ft. reg.* 5.33 *alt.* **Religion**

in Our Time *d.sc.* Aveling Ginever
f. Ion Swinley etc.
In Search of the Gannet *distrib.*
L.M.B. 1500 *ft.* 1935.
Interviewing Wild Animals *p.*
Ratcliffe Holmes/Internat. 5816 *ft.*
reg. 6.30 *p.* F. W. Ratcliffe Holmes.
Island Nation, An See **Our Island**
Nation.
Jubilee *p.c.* North London Film
Soc. Cine Unit *half-reel 16 mm.*
1935 *c.ed.* Herbert A. Green, R.
Green.
Kamet Conquered *p.* F. S. Smythe
5000 *ft. reg. T.S.* 8.32 *d.sc.* F. S.
Smythe *m.d.* Noel Lee.
Kew Gardens *p.c.* Short/Fidelity
1675 *ft. reg.* 11.37 *p.* Harold
Lowenstein *sup.* Sir Arthur Hill *d.*
Philip Leacock *c.* B. Vivian Braun
m. Brian Easdale *cy.* Iolo Williams
crs. Bernard Miles, Cecil Winter.
King's Jubilee, The *p.c.* G.B.P.C./
G-BE 1789 *ft.* 1935 *comp.* Castleton
Knight *cr.* E. V. H. Emmett.
King's People, The *p.c.* John
McMillan/W.B. 5760 *ft. reg. T.S.*
3.37 *d.* John Stumar *sc.* John
Drinkwater.
King's Visit to Manchester, The
amateur, *16 mm.* 1934 *p.* Peter le
Neve Foster.
King With a Terrible Temper,
The *p.c.* Anson Dyer for Bush
Radios 386 *ft.* 16 *mm.* 1937 Tech.
cartoon d. Anson Dyer *sc.* Sutherland
Felce.
King With the Terrible Hiccups,
The *p.c.* Anson Dyer for Bush
Radios 169 *ft. 16 mm.* 1937 Tech.
cartoon d. Anson Dyer *sc.* Sutherland
Felce.
Land of Zinj *p.* M. A. Wetherell/
Internat. 6 *one-reelers T.S.* 12.33.
Lawrence of Arabia *p.c.* Ace about

4000 *ft. T.S.* 7.35 *p.* Ronald Haines with Imp. War Museum *cy.* Sir Ronald Storrs.

League of Nations anti-war film See **Lest We Forget.**

Lest We Forget *p.c.* Village Centres for Curative Treatment and Training Council 844 *ft. reg.* 10.37.

Lest We Forget *p.c.* L.N.U. 722 *ft.* 1926/7 *st.*

Let Dogs Delight *p.c.* Nat. Canine Defence League 1315 *ft. reg.* 10.35 *p.* Rowland Johns, Leonard E. Naylor.

Light Rhythms *p.c.* Pool Films *half-reel* 1930 *p.d.* Francis Bruguière *asst.* Oswell Blakeston *m.* Jack Ellit.

Lights o'London *p.c.* T.I.D.A. for Brit. Th-H 240 *ft. 16 mm.* 1938.

Lion and Albert, The *p.c.* Anglia/ Sd. City 692 *ft. reg.* 2.37 *colour cartoon d.* Anson Dyer.

Little Paper People *p.c.* Cyril Jenkins/A.B.F.D. 800 *ft. reg.* 5.36 *d.* Cyril Jenkins *marionettes* Margaret Hoyland.

Lobsters *p.c.* Bury/A.B.F.D. 1448 *ft. reg.* 10.38 *Made* 1936 *d.* John Mathias, László Moholy-Nagy *scientific sup.* Prof. Daniels *c.ed.* L. Moholy-Nagy *cr.* Alan Howland *m.d.* Muir Mathieson.

London River *p.c.* Brit. Films for T.I.D.A. 962 *ft.* 1939 *p.d.* Andrew Buchanan *c.* Henry Cooper, Horace Hughes *ed.* James Anderson.

Lone Scout, The *p.* J. H. Martin Cross 2500 *ft. reg.* 10.30 *st. d.sc.* J. H. Martin Cross *f.* Cyril Chant, Ursula Chant.

Loopytone News *p.c.* Internat. 583 *ft. reg.* 3.36.

Love on the Range *p.c.* George Pál for Horlicks Ltd/J.W.T. Prod. 1

reel 1937 Tech. *anim. puppets.* d. George Pál *m.* Debroy Somers and his Orchestra.

Low Water *p.c.* Turner-Robertson F./A.B.F.D. 1730 *ft. reg.* 4.36 *d.sc.ed.* E. Arnot Robertson *c.* H. E. Turner.

Lubrication by Shell for Shell-Mex B.P. 26 *mins. 16 mm. st.*

Lubrication Progress – The Clerosol Process *p.c.* Pritchard Wood and Partners for Vacuum Oil 2 *reels.*

Madrid Today *p.c.* P.F.I. 748 *ft.* 1937.

Magic *p.* N.F.L. 1 *reel 16 mm. st.* 1935 *p.ed.* Harry Price.

Making Fashions *p.c.* Dufay-Chromex/A.B.F.D. 1378 *ft. reg.* 5.38 *Made* 1937.

Mastership *p.c.* Gee Films/David Mackane Prod. 2150 *ft. reg. T.S.* 4.34 *alt.* **The Mastership of Christ** *d.sc.* Aveling Ginever *c.* Eric Cross *sc. based on material from* Rev. W. H. Lax and J. Arthur Rank *f.* Vi Caley, W. H. Lax.

Mastership of Christ, The See **Mastership.**

Medical Talk on a Serious Problem – A Doctor Talks, A *p.c.* C.C.H.E. 449 *ft. 16 mm.* 1939 *f.* Sir Drummond Shiels.

Meet Mr. Yorke! – A Speaking Likeness *p.c.* Brit. Pub. Talking F. with S. A. Benson for Rowntree's 584 *ft.* 1929 *d.* Bertram Philips *anim.* Joe Noble with apologies to Alfred Leet *c.* George Noble.

Memory Lane *p.c.* Nat. Talkies/F-N 4005 *ft. reg.* 7.36 *Made* 1934 *arranged* Vernon Clancey with Imp. War Museum *cr.* Hay Petrie.

Men Against Death *p.c.* C. H. Dand/A.B.F.D. 1395 *ft.* 10.33 *d.sc.*

C. H. Dand *c.* James Burger.
Men Against the Sea *p.c.* Frank Bowden and W. Haddock Farr 1800 *ft. reg.* 4.36 *d.* Vernon Sewell.
Men and Machines Theatrical version of **This Progress.**
Men Who Work *p.c.* T.I.D.A. with Austin Motor Co. 778 *ft.* early 1930s.
Message of the Drum *p.c.* Pub. F. for Cad. 1933 *d.* Walter Creighton.
Michael Faraday *p.c.* British Thompson-Houston/F.B.O. 800 *ft. reg.* 9.31.
Milestones *p.c.* A. Moncrieff Davidson/M-G-M 598 *ft. reg.* 4.36 *p.d.c.* A. Moncrieff Davidson.
Miracles Still Happen *p.c.* M.F.S. for Centenary Appeal of Royal Manchester Children's Hospital 20 *mins.* 11.35 *prod.man.* Peter le Neve Foster *d.sc.c.cy.* R. G. W. Ollerenshaw, *sd.* Harry Sheridan.
Missing Record, The for Nat. Hospital for Diseases of the Nervous System 1936.
Modern Miracle, A *p.c.* Brit. Ut./L.M.B. 1850 *ft. reg.* 2.35.
Monarchs of the Air 1933 or earlier, *st. d.c. lecture* Capt. C. W. R. Knight.
Mototo – Fire Baby *p.* Cherry Kearton/Pathé 3163 *ft. T.S.* 11.32 *d.c. dialogue* Cherry Kearton.
Mount Everest Film amateur *16 mm.* 1936 part-Koda. *c.* Frank Smythe.
My Fight for Prosperity 778 *ft.* about 1934 *f.* Lord Beaverbrook.
My Song Goes Forth *p.c.* Ambassador F. Prod./Gilbert Church 5011 *ft. reg.* 10.36 as **Africa Looks Up** *T.S.* 3.37 (later short version **Africa Sings**) *p.d.* Joseph

Best *f.* Paul Robeson.
Naval Occasion, A *p.c.* E.G.S. with Admiralty 15 *mins.* *16 mm.* 1937 *d.* Commdr. John Hunt.
New Architecture at the London Zoo amateur/Koda. 15 *mins.* *16 mm.* 1937 *st. p.* László Moholy-Nagy.
New London, A *p.c.* Under Forty Soc. 2 *reels* 1930 *d.* Michael Hankinson *c.* Jimmy Rogers.
News By Wire *p.c.* T.I.D.A. for B.E.D.A. 292 *ft.* 16 *mm.* 1939.
Night Patrol, The See **City of Shadows, The.**
Night Watchman's Story, The *p.c.* Pub. F. for Cad. 7 *reels* 1933 *d.* W. R. Creighton *c.* Jimmy Rogers *sd.* M. F. Cooper *f.* Donald Calthrop, Basil Gill, Brian Taylor, Mary Gaskell.
Nineteen-Thirty-One *p.c.* London Workers' F. Soc. 1932 *d.* Ralph Bond.
90° South *p.* Herbert George Ponting 6699 *ft. reg.* 6.33 *p.d.c.cy.* H. G. Ponting *f.* Vice-Admiral E. R. G. R. Evans *m.* Sir Walford Davies *m.d.* W. L. Trytel *alt.* **Story of Captain Scott, The.**
Non-Intervention *p.c.* P.F.I. 9 *mins.* 1938 *p.* Ivor Montagu.
Noona Be Nippy for J. Lyons and Co. 5 *reels* 16 *mm. st.*
Norfolk Bittern, The 1 *reel st. p.* Lord William Percy.
Northern Lights *p.c.* Stephen L. Courtauld/Albion F. Syndicate 3268 *ft. reg.* 5.32 *c.* Flt. Lt. H. I. Cozens *cr.* H. J. Farrar.
No: 62007 – A Study in Steel *p.c.* Topical Press Agency for L.M.S. 1595 *ft.* 1935 *alt.* **A Study in Steel.**
Once Upon a Time *p.c.* Short/ Techq. 1350 *ft. reg.* 9.38 Dufay *d.*

Harold Lowenstein.
One Hundred Years *p.c.* Nat.
Prog. with Min. of Health 1255 *ft.*
reg. 9.37 *d.* Charles Barnett *c.*
Geoffrey Faithfull *sd.* J. Ķ. Byers.
On Parade *p.c.* George Pál for
Horlicks Ltd. (J.W.T. Prod.) 661
ft. 1936 Gasp. *anim. puppets d.*
George Pál *m.* Debroy Somers
made in Holland.
On Safari *p.* F. W. Ratcliffe Holmes/
Equity Brit. 5770 *ft. T.S.* 1.32.
Our Farmer Prince *p.c.* Butch.
3621 *ft. reg.* 1.32 *d.* A. Stanley
Williamson *c.* D. P. Cooper *cy.*
Michael Joseph *cr.* R. E. Jeffrey.
Our Fighting Navy *p.c.* Butch.
5,620 *ft.* cut to 5250 *ft. reg. premier*
3.33 *d.* John Betts *c.* Frank Canham,
L. C. Rudkin, A. L. Fisher
Reissued 10.39 at 1917 *ft.*
Our Island Nation *p.c.* E.G.S. with
Admiralty/M-G-M 5505 *ft. reg.*
T.S. 9.37 *alt.* **An Island Nation**
p. J. D. Davidson *d.* Commdr.
J. L. F. Hunt *c.* Raymond Elton
f. Stanley Holloway, Elliott
Makeham, Amy Veness.
Out to Play *p.* Harold Lowenstein/
Den. 10 *mins.* 1936 *d.* Harold
Lowenstein *asst.* Philip Leacock *c.*
Edwin Catford *visual script* Kenneth
Martin *sd.* Edgar Vetter *m.* Molly
Berkley.
Oxford "High", The *p.c.* Oxford
U.F. Unit/Oxford F. Soc. 14 *mins.*
16 mm. st. 1938 *d.* Hyman Rudoff
(sic).
Pandamonium *p.c.* A.I.P.D./
A.B.F.D. 2509 *ft. reg. T.S.* 8.39 *p.*
Widgey Newman *f.* Ming, Hal
Walters.
Paper People Land *p.d.* Cyril
Jenkins/A.B.F.D. 1600 *ft. reg.* 11.39
anim. paper dolls made by Cyril

Jenkins, Margaret Hoyland, Peter
Barker-Mill *m.* M. G. Seiber
verses Wilfred Rolfe.
Peace and Plenty *p.c.* P.F.I. for
Communist Party of Great Britain
1200 *ft. 16 mm. shown* 5.39 *p.* Ivor
Montagu.
Peace on the Western Front *p.c.*
Internat. 3400 *ft. reg. T.S.* 12.30
d. F. W. Ratcliffe Holmes *f.* Moore
Marriott.
Peace or War *p.c.* B.M.N./W-E 2
reels *16 mm.* 1934 *f.* Lady Oxford,
Dr Maud Royden, Storm Jameson,
Madeleine Carroll.
Picture People 17 *mins.* 1938/Kinog.
d.c. John Behr.
Plane Sailing *p.* Bosworth Goldman/
Kinog. 1612 *ft. reg.* 3.37 *p.d.sc.*
Philip Wills and Bosworth
Goldman *cr.* Alan Howland.
Plantation People Pub. F. for Cad.
1682 *ft.* 1936 Tech. *d.* A. R.
Taylor *Tech. sup.* Ray Rennahan
sd. L. G. Page *m.d.* John Reynders.
Plenty of Time for Play London
Films for B.E.D.A./W-E 1935.
Point of View Spectator Short F/Den.
Should We Grow More Food?
1552 *ft. reg.* 6.39.
**State-Run Hospitals; Why
Make-Up? Why Not?** 1689 *ft.*
reg. 6.39.
**How Many Milkmen?; No Vote
– No Vote** 1559 *ft. reg.* 6.39.
Guns and Butter 1726 *ft. reg.*
11.39.
Seen in Bangkok 1475 *ft. reg.*
11.39.
Seen in Australia 1513 *ft. reg.*
11.39.
Pond Life amateur 1 *reel 16 mm.*
1934 *p.* G. H. Higginson.
Power *p.c.* Cambridge U. Cinema
Soc./Vis.Ed. 1 *reel* 1932 *d.sc.*

Gordon Taylor *sc.* Maurice Harvey.
Power Farming by Fordson *p.c.*
Pathé for Ford 1055 *ft.* 1937.
Prairie Winter *p.d.* Evelyn Spice
and Jenny Brown 1595 *ft.* 8.35 *c.*
John Gilbertson *Made in Canada.*
Prince of Peace *p.c.* G-BI/Excl.
2174 *ft. reg.* 3.39 *d.* Donald Carter
f. Pamela Kellino.
Prince of Wales, The *p.c.* G-B/
W & F 5754 *ft. reg.* 10.33.
Private Life of the Gannets, The
p.c. L.F.P./U.A. 1379 *ft.* 1934
p.d.cy. Julian Huxley *asst.* R.
Lockley *c.* Osmond Borrodaile *ed.*
Philip Charlot *m.d.* Muir
Mathieson.
**Production and Distribution of
Medical Gases** *p.c.* B.O.C. 680
ft. 16 mm. c. T. R. Thumwood.
Psychology Today *p.c.* Cambridge
U.F. Prod. Unit 1029 *ft. T.S.* 2.37
p. Raymund Hill *asst.* Geoffrey
Bell, A. S. C. Lawrence, Edward
Reynolds *d.sc.* Ronald Duncan *c.*
K. Asquith, K. O. King, Nigel
Spottiswoode *ed.* Stephen England
cr. Edward Reynolds *sd.* Ace
Studios.
Racing Matters *p.d.* John Betts/
P.D.C. 6 *one-reelers reg.* 2.30.
R.A.F. *p.c.* G.B.P.C./G-BD 3835
ft. reg. T.S. 6.35 *p.d.cy.* John Betts,
c. Horace Wheddon, Gordon
Singleton, *cr.* Sq. Leader W.
Helmore Band of the R.A.F.
Rat Menace, The for Min. of
Agriculture and Fisheries 2 *reels*
1935 *st.*
Real Abyssinia, The *p.c.* Ronald
Haines/Internat. 3500 *ft. T.S.*
10.35 *comp.* Ronald Haines.
Red Sails *p.d.* Ronald Haines 18
mins. 1936.
Reporter in Soho Techq. 1550 *ft.*

reg. 10.38.
Ripe Earth *p.c.* Charter F. Prod.
with Rev. Conrad Noel/A.B.P.C.
980 *ft. reg.* 9.38 *p.* John Boulting
d.ed. Roy Boulting *c.* Ken Perry *sc.*
Lionel Harrow *asst. ed.* Alfred S.
Kahn *cr.* Leo Genn *m.d.* Charles
Brill *musical research* Macdonald
Dodds, Charles Brill.
Road of Health, The *p.c.* B.S.H.C.
412 *ft. 16 mm.* 1938 *d.* Brian Salt.
Road to Hell, The *p.c.* S.F.C.
16 mm. 1933 *st. d.c.* Rudolph
Messel *f.* Naomi Mitchison,
Terence Greenidge, Raymond
Postgate, Ian Fox.
Romance of the Railway for
G.W.R. 40 *mins. 16 mm.* 1936.
Romance of the Swan amateur 1
reel 16 mm. st. p. E. C. Le Grice.
Rome Hunt *p.c.* U.A. 11 *mins.* 1938
Tech. *p.* F. W. Keller.
Rome Symphony *p.c.* U.A. 11
mins. 1938 Tech. *p.* F. W. Keller.
Round Africa with Cobham *p.c.*
G-B/G-BD 8 *one-reelers reg.* 1.29.
**Royal and Ancient City of
Canterbury, The** *p.c.* L. E.
Cousell/M-G-M 1781 *ft. reg.* 5.37.
Royal Duchy, The *p.c.* L.M.B. 1650
ft. reg. 11.35 *d.* Gerald Blake *c.*
D. P. Cooper.
Royal Tour, The *p.c.* G-BI/G.F.D.
2600 *ft. T.S.* 6.39 *cr.* E. V. H.
Emmett.
Royal Visit to Paris, The *p.c.*
Pathé 1000 *ft. T.S.* 7.38 Dufay.
**Rt. Hon. George Lansbury, P.C.,
M.P.** *p.c.* Peace Pledge Union
349 *ft.* 1937.
Rugged Island, The *p.* Jenny
Brown/Zeni 3920 *ft. reg.* 11.34 *d.c.*
Jenny Brown *f.* Enga Stout, John
Gilbertson.
Rule, Britannia *p.* Commdr. Hunt

for Director of Naval Recruiting 428 *ft. T.S.* 8.39 *ed.* J. L. F. Hunt *cr.* Tommy Woodroofe.

Rule, Britannia *p.* Frank Spickernell 6086 *ft. T.S.* 8.39 *d.* Bud Pollard.

Rural Electrification *p.c.* B.E.D.A. 4 *reels* 1936 *st.* See also **Country Currents.**

Rural Housing *p.* Matthew Nathan for Housing Centre 8 *mins.* 16 *mm.* 1938.

Russia Today Zeni 3433 *ft. T.S.* 2.34 *d.* Carveth Wells.

Safari *p.c.* M. A. Wetherell and Liberty F. 3728 *ft. T.S.* 9.37 *p.d.cy.* M. A. Wetherell *c.* B. Williams *sd.* H. Sheridan.

Sam and his Musket *p.c.* Anglia/ Reunion F. 850 *ft.* reg. 10.35 Dun. *anim. cartoon d.* Anson Dyer *anim.* Griffiths and Myller *f.* *voice of* Stanley Holloway.

Sam's Medal *p.c.* Anglia/A.P. & D. 835 *ft.* reg. 11.36 *colour cartoon d.* Anson Dyer.

Sea Food *p.c.* Pathé for Films of Scotland/A.B.P.C. 1090 *ft.* reg. 6.38.

Secrets of the Hand *p.* G. B. Savi/ Pioneer 6 *one-reelers* reg. 1.29, 2.29 and 3.29.

Secrets of the Stars *Comp.* A. Francis-Smith/Kinog. 16 *mins.* 1937.

See How They Won *p.c.* Rev. for Boots Drug Co. 7 *mins.* 1935 Brewstercolor *anim.* Ub Iwerks.

Service Brit. Nat. for R.F.S. 3 or 4 *reels* 1935 *d.* Aveling Ginever.

Seventeenth Lancers, The Requisite Prods./F-L 4583 *ft.* reg. 8.29 *st. p.sc.* John Betts.

Sewage *p.c.* M.F.S. 400 *ft.* 16 *mm.* 1935 *sd. on disc d.sc.c.* Peter le Neve Foster *m.* Evelyn Clayton

sup. William Porterhouse of Manchester Rivers Dept.

Sheep Dog *p.* Florinda Kingdon-Ward/B.S.S. 1380 *ft.* reg. 1.39 *d.sc.* John Alderson *c.* F. Searle *cr.* Neal Arden.

Shqypnia – Land of the Mountain Eagle *p.d.c.* Leslie Barbrook/Zeni 1750 *ft.* reg. 1.35 *cy.* E. Le Breton Martin.

Shrimp Fishers of Gravesend, The *p.* L. G. Jonas and J. G. Cunyngham Brown 793 *ft.* reg. 11.32 *d.c.* C. Gifford Brown (part of **Betwixt Land and Sea**).

Silt *p.c.* Pool Films 1 *reel* 1931 *d.c.* Dan Birt *sd.* Dallas Bower.

Silver Lining *p.c.* Brit. Ut. for H. & C.C. 1250 *ft.* 1935 *d.sc.* John Alderson *c.* James Burger *Theme* G. H. Green *ed.* C. A. Leeds *alt.* **Sunshine and Shadow.**

Sir Basil Gould in Lhasa, 1936 *p.* F. Spencer Chapman 705 *ft.* 16 *mm. st.* Koda.

Sky Pirates *p.* George Pál for Horlicks (J.W.T. Prods.) 720 *ft.* 1937 Tech. *puppets m.* Debroy Somers and his Orchestra.

Slate Quarrying in North Wales *p.* G. L. Hawkins 3 *reels* 1935 *st.*

Smith *p.c.* Embankment Fellowship Centre 1000 *ft. shown* 6.39 *d.* Michael Powell *f.* Ralph Richardson, Flora Robson, Allan Jeayes, Wally Patch.

Some Activities of the Bermondsey Borough Council *p.c.* Berm. B.C. Health Propaganda Dept. 1528 *ft.* 1931 *st. p.sc.* H. W. Bush *c.* C. F. Lumley.

So This Is London *p.c.* Nat. Talkies 3350 *ft.* reg. 10.38 *d.* Vernon J. Clancey.

Soul of a Nation, The *distributed by*

A.B.F.D. 5400 *ft. T.S.* 12.34 *d.* J. B. Williams *cr.* Felix Aylmer.

South Sea Sweetheart *p.* George Pál for Horlicks (J.W.T. Prods.) 1 *reel* 1938 Tech. *puppets m.* Debroy Somers and the Hawaiian Islanders.

Spanish A.B.C. *p.c.* P.F.I. 1697 *ft. reg.* 7.38 *p.* Ivor Montagu *d.ed.* Thorold Dickinson, Sidney Cole *c.* Arthur Graham, Alan Lawson *asst. ed.* Philip Leacock *cr.* G. C. T. Giles.

Sport in Scotland *p.c.* Sc.F.P. for Films of Scotland/A.B.P.C. 962 *ft. reg.* 11.38.

Spotting *p.c.* New Era 12 *split-reels reg.* 2.34 *d.* G. B. Samuelson.

Spring Comes to Town *p.d.* Matthew Nathan/Den. 1049 *ft. reg.* 2.38.

Springtime in the Holy Land *p.c.* Merton for Palestine Commission 511 *ft. 16 mm.* 1939 *d.* George Wynn.

Stampede *p.c.* B.I.F./Pro Patria 7494 *ft. reg.* 2.30 *st. d.sc.c.* Major C. Court Treatt, Stella Court Treatt and Errol Hinds *assoc. ed.* John Orton.

Stand Up and . . . Breathe! *p.c.* Brit. Ut. for Nat. Assoc. for the Prevention of Tuberculosis/L.M.B. 1700 *ft. shown* 10.35.

Stanley *p.d.* M. A. Wetherell/ M-G-M 3923 *ft. reg.* 11.33 *alt.* **With Stanley in Africa.**

Stark Nature *p.c.* B.I.F./Pro Patria 6256 *ft. reg.* 6.30 *d.* Arthur Woods *c.* Errol Hinds, Jack Parker *f.* Major and Mrs Court Treatt.

Steel Ace 2000 *ft.* 1936 *d.* Capelli *c.* John Silver.

Steve cartoons See **Come On Steve** cartoons.

St. Moritz *p.c.* Rayant Wonderfilms

17 *mins.* 1938 Dufay *d.* G. A. Gilkison.

Story of Captain Scott, The *p.c.* H.N./Internat. 5403 *ft. T.S.* 9.36 abridged version of **90° South** *p.c.cr.cy.* H. G. Ponting *introduction* Vice-Admiral Evans.

Story of Culross, The *p.c.* Sc.F.P./' Techq. 880 *ft. reg.* 5.39.

Story of Papworth, The *p.c.* Brit. Pictorial Prod./G.F.D. 1697 *ft. reg.* 5.36.

Study in Steel, A See **No: 62007 − A Study in Steel.**

Table Tennis Today *p.c.* Brunel and Montagu 1757 *ft. reg.* 1.29.

Tar (British Industries Series) *p.c.* Brit. F. 910 *ft. reg.* 4.32.

Television Comes to London *p.c.* B.B.C. T.V. 1754 *ft.* 1936 *p.* Dallas Bower, Gerald Cock *d.* Leslie Barbrook, James Carr *cy.* Cecil Lewis *cr.* Leslie Mitchell *m.d.* Hyam Greenbaum *f.* Adèle Dixon.

Tell Me If It Hurts *p.d.sc.ed.* Richard Massingham/Den. 1800 *ft. reg.* 1.38 *made* 1934 *shown* 1935 *c.* Karl Urbahn *m.* Harry Platts *m.d.* Joan Bickers and New London Orchestra *sd.* H. L. Sheridan *f.* Russell Waters, Patrick Ross, Freda Silcock, Peter Copley.

Tembi *p.d.* Cherry Kearton/W & F 7825 *ft. reg.* 7.29 *st. ed.* Brunel and Montagu.

Ten Little Dirty Boys *p.c.* H & C.C. for C.C.H.E. 1 *reel st. black and white cartoon.*

Territorial Cavalcade *p.c.* Oscar Deutsch/Odeon 1 *reel shown* 4.38 *p.sc.* Sir Michael Bruce.

There Is Sorrow on the Sea *p.c.* Shipwrecked Mariners' Society 4 *mins.* 1937 *comp.* Richard Q. McNaughton.

This Fishy Business *p.c.* Ace 1650 *ft. reg.* 5.35 *p.* R. W. Lotinga.

This Golf Game *p.c.* John Betts/ M-G-M 827 *ft. reg.* 12.33, and 1188 *ft. reg.* 1.34.

This Is Paris! That Was!! *p.c.* B.S.S./Wardour 935 *ft.* 1933 *cy.* Howard Gaye *cr.* Tommy Handley.

This Leg Theory *p.c.* Alba/L.M.B. 790 *ft. reg.* 5.34 *p.* S. C. Allen, R. Thorpe Bates *sup.* Lt.-Col. J. P. Jordon *cy.* Widgey Newman *cr.* R. E. Jeffrey *c.* Hal Young, D. P. Cooper.

This Motoring *distributed by* British Lion 20 *mins.* 1935.

This Motoring Ace 4014 *ft. T.S.* 3.36 *d.* Widgey Newman *f.* Sir Stenson Cooke.

This Oxford *p.c.* Merton Motion Picture Soc./Universal 2023 *ft. reg.* 1.31 *st.*

This Progress *p.c.* Gee for Austin 5 *reels* 1930 *d.* Aveling Ginever *alt.* **Men and Machines.**

Thoroughbred Ace 1640 *ft. reg.* 10.34.

Three Ha'pence a Foot *p.c.* Anglia/ Sd. City 840 *ft. reg.* 3.37 *colour cartoon d.* Anson Dyer.

Thunder in the Air *p.c.* Freenat/ Butch. 3006 *ft. T.S.* 1.35 *d.ed.* Hans Nieter *asst.* Tissie Symonds *p.m.* Fred A. Swann *c.* Bert Hopkins, Reg Wyer *cy.* Vernon Bartlett *m.* Horace Somerville *f.* Ralph Richardson, Hilary Eaves, David Wilton.

Tiger Hunt *16 mm.* 1938(?) *p.* Lt. Col. F. M. Bailey *ed.* Philip Godfrey *cr.* Norton King *sd.* H. L. Sheridan.

Timber *p.c.* Pritchard Wood for Timber Dev. Assoc. 1 *reel 16 mm. st.* 1937(?)

Tommy Handley in "Making a Christmas Pudding" *p.c.* Winads/M-G-M 1182 *ft. reg.* 3.33 *f.* Tommy Handley.

Top Dogs *p.* A. Moncrieff Davidson/ A.B.F.D. 1217 *ft. reg.* 6.37.

Town and Gown *p.* Peter Collin/ Kinog. 1588 *ft. reg.* 12.37.

Treasure of the Tropics for J. S. Fry and Sons Ltd. 3 *reels 16 mm.* 1937(?)

Triumph *p.c.* World Commonwealth Films *p.d.* Aveling Ginever, Michael Wayman.

Turning Her Round *p.c.* G. N. C. Brown & L. G. Jonas 1179 *ft. reg.* 1.33 *d.c.* C. Gifford (part of **Betwixt Land and Sea).**

Tusalava Film Society 589 *ft. shown* 12.29 *design* Len Lye *m.* Jack Ellit.

Twenty-five Years a King *p.c.* Pathé 4596 *ft. T.S.* 3.35 *d.* Aveling Ginever *p.m.* Freddie Watts *c.* C. Martin *comp.* with collaboration of John Drinkwater and Sir Austen Chamberlain.

Twitching Feet *p.d.* C. C. Ungley 650 *ft.* 1930 *st.*

Two Minutes *p.c.* G-BI/Excl. 3754 *ft. reg.* 3.39 *d.* Donald Carter *f.* Walter Hudd, Edana Romney.

Under the Eaves *p.c.* G. L. Hawkins 786 *ft. 16 mm.* 1935 *st. sup.* George Tickner, B. W. Tucker.

Up Country with the Settler *p.c.* B.I.F. 809 *ft.* 1930 *st.*

Vanishing Sails *p.c.* Steuart Films/ Kinog. 1525 *ft. reg.* 8.35 *p.d.c.* Ronald Steuart.

Varsity *p.* J. A. Combrinck Graaf/ Universal 3852 *ft. reg.* 6.30 *st. d.* Stuart Legg *f.* Geoffrey Beaumont, Rene Ray.

Virus Diseases of Plants – The

Formation of Intracellular Inclusion *p.c.* Rothamstead Experimental Station 1092 *ft.* 1930 *st. author* Dr F. M. L. Sheffield *c.* F. Percy Smith.

Vitamins *p.c.* Cambridge Film Productions 20 *mins.* 1937 *d.* Geoffrey Innes *c.* James Harris.

Voice of London, The *distributed by* Famous F. 3700 *ft. T.S.* 5.33 *d.* Charles Barnett.

Voyage of the "Ashanti", The *p.* Commander J. L. F. Hunt for Admiralty/A.B.P.C. 1005 *ft. reg.* 8.39 *c.* S. R. Elton *cy.* Howard Gaye *cr.* Geoffrey Sumner *m.* Arthur Dulay.

Wanderlust *p.c.* M. A. Wetherell and W. M. F. Cory/Internat. Prods. 3400 *ft. reg.* 4.33 *d.* M. A. Wetherell.

Warning, The *p.c.* Brit. Nat./ A.B.P.C. 3119 *ft. reg.* 3.39 *p.* Aubrey Baring *ed.* R. Q. McNaughton *m.* Ronnie Munro *appeal by* Sir John Anderson.

War Without End *p.c.* G-B Screen Services for King Ed. H.F.L./Excl. 1570 *ft. reg.* 7.39 *made* 1937/8 *d.* Francis Searle *sc.cy.* W. C. Stone.

Way of the Wild *p.* F. W. Ratcliffe Holmes/Pathé 3835 *ft. reg.* 4.35.

Wee Blue Blossom, The *p.c.* Pub.F. for Irish Linen Industry 12 *mins.* 1936 *d.* John Alderson *c.* Walter Blakeley.

Well I Never! *p.c.* London Films for B.E.D.A./W-E 2 *reels* 1935.

Western Highlands *p.c.* Alba "Our Island" Series 986 *ft. reg.* 11.33 *d.ed.* Duncan Robbins *c.* D. P. Cooper *cy.* Harry J. Clifford *m.d.* Alfred Filer *song by* Thorpe Bates.

Wharves and Strays *p.c.* L.F.P./ U.A. 16 *mins. shown* 4.35 *d.c.*

Bernard Browne *m.* Arthur Benjamin *m.d.* Muir Mathieson *f.* "Scruffy".

What Ho! She Bumps *p.* George Pál for Horlicks (J.W.T. Prods.) 720 *ft.* 1937 Tech. *puppets m.* Debroy Somers and his Orchestra.

What Men Live By *p.c.* G-BI for R.F.S./G-B and Excl. *T.S. 1*) 12.38 3798 *ft. T.S. 2*) 11.39 3803 *ft. d.* Donald Carter, Vernon Sewell *sc.* from story by Leo Tolstoy *f.* Esmond Knight.

What the Newsreel Does not Show *p.c.* S.F.C. 1933 *st.*

What the Stars Foretell *p.c.* Betta Films 12 *one-reelers T.S.* 3.33 *d.* Widgey Newman *based on series by* R. H. Naylor of the "Sunday Express".

When Scouting Won *p.d.sc.* J. H. Martin Cross for Boy Scouts' Assoc. 4815 *ft. reg.* 10.30 *st. f.* Cyril Chant.

Whither Germany? *p.* Mansfield Markham/B and N Films 3400 *ft. T.S.* 12.33 *sc.cy.* J. B. Williams.

Will Civilization Crash? *p.c.* Brit. M.N./W-E 1 *reel 16 mm.* 1934 *p.* Leslie Landau *ed.* Raymond Perrin *studio c.* Leslie Murray *sd.* Pat Sunderland *f.* Prof. C. E. M. Joad.

Wings Over Africa *p.* F. Roy Tuckett 3578 *ft. reg.* 5.33 *cr.* R. E. Jeffrey.

Wings Over Everest *p.c.* G.B.P.C./ G-BD 3769 *ft. reg.* 7.34 *d.* Geoffrey Barkas, Ivor Montagu *c.* S. R. Bonnett, A. L. Fisher, V. Veevers *sd.* R. L. Read, W. H. O. Sweeny.

Winter with the Lapps *p.c.ed.* Olive Murray Chapman 1782 *ft.* 1933 *st.*

With Cobham to Kivu *p.c.* Gaumont/G-B 6023 *ft. reg.* 9.32

236 Films of Comment and Persuasion of the 1930s

re-registered 10.32 as **Into the Great Unknown** 2335 *ft.*, **Monsters of the Swamp** 2165 *ft.*, & **Mountains of the Moon** 1977 *ft. c.* S. R. Bonnett *ed.* R. E. Dearing.

Wizard in the Wall *p.c.* London Films for B.E.D.A./W-E 1 *reel shown* 1.35 *d.* Alexander Esway.

Workaday *p.c.* Pub. F. for Cad. 4000 *ft.* 1936/7 *d.* Ralph Smart *c.* Jimmy Rogers.

World in Revolt, The *p.c.* Mentone/ A.B.P.C. 5038 *ft.* *T.S.* 9.37 *ed.* Arthur Dent, Howard Gaye *cr.* Grahame McNamee, Frederick Duprez, Alan Howland.

World Rolls On, The *p.c.* Merton for Dunlop Rubber Co. 8 *mins.* 16 *mm.* 1937 *d.* Ralph Smart *c.* Jimmy Rogers *sc.* H. V. Purcell *from story by* Sydney Box *cy.* H. V. Purcell.

World War and After, The *p.c.* Freenat for L.N.U. 4 *reels* 1926 and later editions, *st. d.* Hans Nieter.

World War and After, The (2) *p.c.* Ed. Com. of L.N.U. 2 *reels shown* 1935 35 *mm. sd. version with cr.* C. W. A. Scott.

Young Things *p.c.* Turner-Robertson F./Zeni 1700 *ft. reg.* 8.34 *d.c.* H. E. Turner *cy.* E. Arnot Robertson.

Youth at the Helm *p.c.* Navy League/M-G-M 1241 *ft. reg.* 4.39.

Youth Hails Adventure *p.c.* Y.H.A. 4 *reels* 16 *mm.* 1933 *st. p.* E. Selley *c.sc.* Morland Braithwaite.

Youth Marches On *p.c.* Eric Parfit for Oxford Group/Butch. 1920 *ft. reg.* 4.38 *d.* Eric Parfit, George Fraser.

Zetland Birds *p.c.* Bury/Techq. 1550 *ft. reg.* 3.39 *c.* Cyril Jenkins.

Index

Films of Comment and Persuasion of the 1930s

National Physical Laboratory 124
National Progress Films 160, 161
National Safety First Association 160
National Trust 60
Nation's Heritage, The 60
Naval Occasion, A 229
Naylor, R. H. 92
Nettleford, Archibald 139
Never Never Land 68
New Architecture at the London Zoo 119, 229
New Babylon, The 168, 169
New Clarion 174
New Era Films Ltd. 11, 80
New London, A 159, 169, 229
Newman, Widgey R. (1900-44) 91, 92, 93, 226, 230, 234, 235
News by Wire 143, 229
News from Spain 187
News of the World, The 93, 160
Newsreel Association of Great Britain and Ireland 15, 33
Nicholson, Harold 37
Nicholson, Irene 110, 223, 225
Nieter, Hans 62, 181, 182, 234, 236
Nightmail 5
Night Patrol, The *see* **City of Shadows, The**
Night Watchman's Story, The 133, 134, 229
1931 170, 229
90° South 80, 229
Noble, George (born 1902) 47, 122, 132, 228
Noel, Captain J. B. L. (born 1891) 80, 81, 82, 84, 89, 228
Noel, Rev. Conrad 111
Non-Intervention 190, 229
Noona be Nippy 137, 229
Norfolk Bittern, The 124, 229
Northern Lights 5, 76, 77, 229
North Sea 7
Norton, Lt. Col. E. F. 81
Noxon, G. F. 47, 132
No. 62007—A Study in Steel 134, 135, 229
Nuthall, Betty 21
Nyman, Ken 101, 102

Oasis 66, 72
Odeon Theatres Ltd. 14, 56, 58
Old English Taverns 61
Old Homesteads of England 61

Old Tom's Story 162
Oliver, P. R. 85
Olympic Kinematograph Laboratories Ltd. 48
Once Upon a Time 110, 229-30
One Family 4
One Hundred Years 161, 230
Onions, S. D. (born 1906) 117, 224
On Parade 135, 229
On Safari 68, 229
'Oppin 157
Optical Glass Manufacture 137
Orient Line 141
Orton, J. O. C. 69, 233
Ostrer, Isidore 57, 58
Ostrer, Maurice 51
Our Farmer Prince 29, 229
Our Fighting Navy 229
Our Friend the Horse 162
Our Island Nation 194, 229
Our Island Story 105
Our Royal Heritage 93
Out to Play 97, 110, 204, 229
Ovaltine 136
Owen, Frank 182
Oxford and Asquith, Countess of 176
Oxford Films 156
Oxford Group 149
Oxford "High", The 230

Pál, George (born 1908) 135, 228, 230, 232, 233, 235
Pandemonium 93, 230
Paper People Land 230
Paramount-British Productions Ltd. 12, 17, 30, 31, 34, 35, 36, 39, 43, 48, 202
Paramount Sound News 12
Parfitt, Eric 149, 236
Parker, Jack (born 1885) 70, 140, 233
Parkinson, Harry B. 5, 224
Passing of the Third Floor Back, The 149
Passing Show 48
Passport to Europe 192, 204
Pathé News 12, 28
Pathé Pictorial 91, 99
Pathé Pictures Ltd. 29, 30, 31, 32, 40, 132, 136, 146, 159, 205
Pathé Sound Magazine 12, 91
Pathé Super Gazette 16, 23, 24, 40, 41, 42
Pathétone Weekly 12

256   Films of Comment and Persuasion of the 1930s